AF335122

American Humor in France

American

TWO CENTURIES OF FRENCH CRITICISM

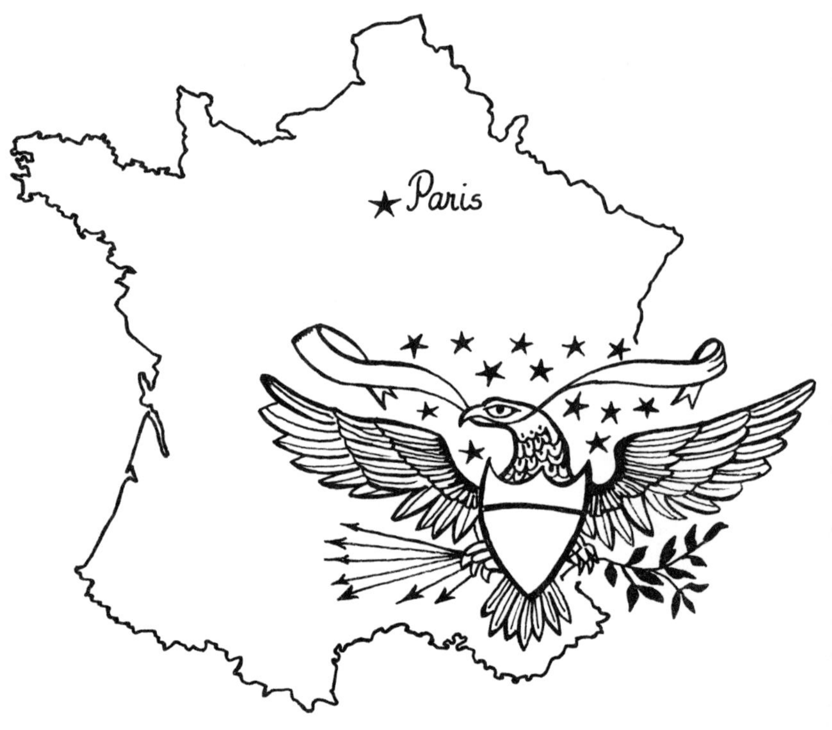

Humor in France

OF THE COMIC SPIRIT IN AMERICAN LITERATURE

James C. Austin WITH A
CONCLUDING CHAPTER BY *Daniel Royot*

Iowa State University Press / Ames

TO BRUCE
My Favorite Clown

JAMES C. AUSTIN is Professor of English, Southern Illinois University, Edwardsville. In addition to exchange professorships in the Philippines and England, he was a visiting professor of American studies at the Université de Provence, Aix-en-Provence, France, in 1972–1973. He has written five books on American literature, three of them on nineteenth-century American humorists. He is the author also of numerous journal articles on American literature.

DANIEL ROYOT is Doctor ès Lettres, Université de Clermont-Ferrand. He has visited England and the United States as student, researcher, and lecturer. His publications include articles on Yankee humor and Western American literature, and he is co-editor of an anthology of American literature for French university students.

Composed and printed by
The Iowa State University Press

First edition, 1978

Library of Congress Cataloging in Publication Data

Austin, James C
American humor in France.

Bibliography: p.
1. American wit and humor—History and criticism. 2. Criticism—France. I. Title.
PS433.A9 817′.009 78-771
ISBN 0-8138-1920-2

Contents

Preface

Let's imagine an international dialogue:

"Who reads an American book?"

"Who listens to a Frenchman?"

"France is the most intelligent nation in the world."

"America has longer rivers and more of them, and they are muddier and deeper, and run faster, and rise higher, and make more noise, and fall lower, and do more damage than anybody else's rivers. It has more lakes, and they are bigger and deeper, and clearer, and wetter than those of any other country. Our rail-cars are bigger, and run faster, and pitch off the track oftener, and kill more people than all other rail-cars in this and every other country. Our steamboats carry bigger loads, are longer and broader, burst their boilers oftener, and send up their passengers higher, and the captains swear harder than steamboat captains in any other country. Our men are bigger, and longer, and thicker, can fight harder and faster, drink more mean whiskey, chew more bad tobacco, and spit more, and spit further than in any other country. . . ."

I began to write this book because I wanted to find out why the country of *esprit* was so slow to appreciate the humor of the country of the tall tale. Why the people who produced Molière and Voltaire failed to notice Artemus Ward, recognized Mark Twain grudgingly, and were not very concerned about James Thurber. I was skeptical of the usual explanations: that humor is untranslatable, that regional dialect is an insuperable barrier, that comic writers operate on intimate cultural traits beyond the experience of outsiders, that humor is something unique to Anglo-Saxons, that, in sum, cultural differences cannot be surmounted.

During the eight or so years I was pondering this subject, I came to believe that my skepticism was justified, for so much American humor is floating around in France today that I wonder sometimes what happened to the old risqué pleasantry. I had the exhilarating experience of reading a few lines of one of Artemus Ward's lectures to French undergraduates in English—something I had not ventured to do even with American students because so much depends on timing and non sequiturs—and the response was happy. One French critic has gone so far as to say that American humor is no longer American but international.

While more than enough intercultural misapprehensions and misunderstandings still exist, and while many jokes do not deserve to survive transplantation either in space or time, still I feel a warm satisfaction that our friends understand us better. Until recently, the progress of this understanding was slow. The reasons for the slowness were social, political, economic, and philosophical, and in only one characteristic did they involve the essence of American humor itself—that is, in deliberate deception on the part of the humorist in the hoax, the tall tale, the shaggy dog story, the deadpan manner. Humorless American critics were also put off by this element. Not until the 1920s did American scholarship really come to terms with native American humor as part of American literature. Even today, it sometimes takes a French critic to show us the pervasive humor in Whitman, Poe, James, or Hawthorne.

In other words, the study of the reception of American humor in France can, I hope, show us something of ourselves and our literature—not only in what the French critics saw but in what they thought they saw and what they failed to see.

This book is a sampling of French criticism of American humor from the seventeenth century to the present. It is necessarily subjective in terms of the availability of material and the capabilities of the author. I have tried to be open-minded, and I think I have learned to be more so as I progressed with the research. Nevertheless, it cannot be denied that this is an individual twentieth-century American's view of two centuries of French views of American character.

For one thing, the survey reflects the opinions of only a select number of the French people—those who had enough interest in America to write about its literature, and mostly those who were proficient in the English language. This meant that they were of the cultural elite, and, as it happens, conservative in social, political, and literary views. The views of the rest of the people are only touched upon. In many cases, they probably had no views of American humor; in others, their views were reflections of those of the elite. The comparison of folklore and popular culture in France and America, especially in relation to humor, would make another study. Professor Royot's chapter at the end of this book suggests possibilities that I have not covered.

Another subject I have not attempted is the influence of American humor on French literature. I have occasionally mentioned such influence, and Professor Royot makes further suggestions; but I have left that subject for others more knowing in French literature than I am. Again, another book could be written.

Because this is a historical study, the proportion of space devoted to the earlier periods is much greater than the quantity of criticism would warrant. On the other hand, yet another book could be written on the post–World War II criticism and scholarship I have crammed into one chapter. Thus, the concluding paragraphs of Chapter 8 are not much more than a bibliographical survey—and one that is not exhaustive. I am sorry if I have omitted instances of current scholarship more important than some that I have included. But my object throughout has been to give the flavor of French opinions rather than every detail.

To get the flavor, I have quoted a good deal from the French critics. Their work, especially that of the earlier critics, is not easily available to American readers, and I have done my best to give them a fair showing. For the sake of the American reader I have translated the quotations into English (or, in a few instances, used others' translations), but I have preserved the original French in the notes, for comparison. Otherwise, the book would have seemed to me a most awkward macaronic, unnecessarily restrictive in its readership.

Because my topic is literary humor, I have included some background in the history of the reception of American literature in general in France. Until the 1920s, at least, the reception of American humor was dependent on the reception of our literature and can only be explained in those terms. I hope the reader will not feel that I have wandered too far from the subject on the one hand, or, on the other, that I have been too sketchy in dealing with French views that are not strictly on humor.

Many of the critics and scholars whose work I am considering are not well known even to French readers. I have included a few biographical details, including birth and death dates, whenever I could. My sources were a number of biographical dictionaries whose authority and up-to-dateness vary. Sometimes I have had to forgo such information altogether; other times I have had to use a question mark to indicate my failure to find a date. I have not even tried to follow through with biographical information on the present generation of scholars. But I hope the details I include will help the reader to place the critics in their historical context and maybe will even inspire further investigation of these often interesting personalities.

I conclude with a bibliography of all the works I have consulted that directly relate to the reception of American humor in France. I have not included works of American writers that the critics discuss or those peripheral references that may be in the footnotes.

I am very grateful for the final chapter, "American Humor and the French Psyche," by Professor Daniel Royot, Université de Clermont-Ferrand. In his chapter, the reader can find a further perspective—a contemporary French point of view—as well as a reminder of the things that would otherwise be beyond the scope of this book. Furthermore, Professor Royot has looked over most of the manuscript and helped me out of several blunders.

My acquaintance—through their work, their correspondence, and their personal friendship—with several French scholars of American studies has been a source not only of information, encouragement, and inspiration, but also of deep satisfaction. To all my colleagues in the Département d'Américain, Université de Provence, Aix-en-Provence, 1972-1973, and to the members of the Association Française d'Etudes

Américaines who attended the meeting in Pont-à-Mousson in 1973 and the meeting in Seignosse-le-Penon in 1977, I am especially grateful. To list all who helped me—often without even knowing it—is impossible. But I wish to state here that an international community of scholars still exists and can exist. I cannot conclude without mentioning two professors who were especially helpful in encouragement: Roger Asselineau of the Université de Paris IV (Danton-Sorbonne) and Pierre Deflaux of the Université de Provence in Aix.

My debt to those noble and unsung heroes, the librarians of the world, cannot be sufficiently expressed. I thank them all, from the woman in the reading room of the Bibliothèque Nationale in 1966 whose name I don't know but who patiently listened to and answered my requests in spite of my abominable French, to the students and the civil servants who made photocopies, tracked down details, and negotiated interlibrary loans. Special thanks are due to my colleagues in the Lovejoy Library of Southern Illinois University: John Dustin, Humanities Librarian; John Abbott, Director of the Library; Virginia Bradburry, in charge of interlibrary loans; and Marjorie Blixen, chief clerk.

I owe a great deal to the work of several student assistants, who not only typed manuscripts but took care of desk work to free me for research and did various jobs of collecting materials.

Special thanks are due to Nicholas Joost, Professor of English at Southern Illinois University, and, until recently, editor of *Papers on Language and Literature,* who encouraged my research and who published my preliminary study, "American Humor in France," in his Summer Supplement, 1969. Most of that study is incorporated here and there in this book, with the permission of the Board of Trustees of Southern Illinois University, publisher of *PLL.*

Thanks to Southern Illinois University, Edwardsville, I have had the time, cooperation, and funds to carry out my research. Special thanks go to John A. Rodman, Coordinator of Research in the Graduate Office, and to the various committees that allocate research expenses; to Gerald Runkle, Dean of the School of Humanities; to John I. Ades, Chairman of the Department of English Language and Literature; and to Andrew Kochman, Vice President and Provost.

And, of course, I include the many others—students, friends, colleagues—who cannot be listed but who, believe me, helped.

American Humor in France

1

The Point of View

To know a country one must know its humor. To translate American humor is to translate America. Until recently, the French have failed to translate American humor, either in the literal sense of putting it into the French language or in the more figurative sense that gets into the whole tough problem of intercultural understanding.

To face that problem we must look at its various sides. And we quickly become aware that there are more than two sides. René Rémond, in the beginning of his fine study of French opinions of America between 1815 and 1852, said that in the dialogue between France and the United States there were actually six interlocutors: the real France and the real United States, the image that each country has of itself, and the image that each country has of the other.[1] It is the French image of the United States that concerns us first, but that image can only be understood in the context of the other five partners of the dialogue. There is a further complication, due to the element of time. We can never see the point of view of someone in the past without screening it through our own contemporary point of view. We like to think that the passage of time brings objectivity to our views. But does it? We cannot avoid registering our present-day amusement, irritation, skepticism, admiration of the views that people once held. So this adds a seventh interlocutor to the dialogue—our "sophisticated" present-day reader and writer—you and me.

Obviously, there are now further complications. You are not me; and the French reader of today is not the American reader of today, in spite of the advances that we hope we have made in international understanding and that this study hopes in its little way to further. Nor, for that matter, is the American reader or the French reader a single person. Each brings to his reading his own wisdom and his own blindness. And the same applies to the French critics, scholars, and popularizers that we shall be discussing here. There is no single-minded French view or image of the United States; rather there are a great many views, some of which are contradictory and some of which are in agreement. It is the area of general agreement that we think of as the French image of our country.

The American writer Henry James was acutely aware of the significance of what he called "point of view," especially in terms of intercultural understanding. In a story entitled "The Point of View" (1882), he contrasted comically the views of American civilization expressed by a British Member of Parliament, a French academician, and several Americans. The Frenchman, Monsieur Gustave Lejaune of the French Academy, represented the typical attitude of the French aristocrat. He is shocked at everything he sees in America:

> We have seen few interiors (no one speaks French); but if the newspapers give an idea of the domestic *moeurs,* the *moeurs* must be curious. The passport is abolished, but they have printed my *signalement* in these sheets—perhaps for the young ladies who look for the husband. We went one night to the theater; the piece was French (they are the only ones), but the acting was American—too American; we came out in the middle. The want of taste is incredible. An Englishman whom I met tells me that even the language corrupts itself from day to day; an Englishman ceases to understand. It encourages me to find that I am not the only one. There are things every day that one can't describe.

And particularly of American writing he says:

> I have opened some of the books; *mais ils ne se laissent pas lire.* No form, no matter, no style, no general ideas; they seem to be written for children and young ladies. The most successful (those that they praise most) are the facetious; they sell in thousands of editions. I have looked into some of the most *vantés*; but you need to be forewarned, to know that they are amusing; *des plaisanteries de croque-mort.*

James was, of course, mocking the French aristocratic stereotype of democratic America. But his vision went much deeper than that. At the same time that he was ridiculing Monsieur Lejaune, he was making fun of American newspapers, theater, language, books, and, especially, humor; for we know that his own attitudes were remarkably similar to Monsieur Lejaune's. Yet James had the saving grace of the American humorist, the ability to make fun of himself. In the very next lines he had Monsieur Lejaune say: "They have a novelist with pretensions to literature, who writes about the chase for the husband and the adventures of the rich Americans in our corrupt old Europe, where their primeval candor puts the Europeans to shame. *C'est proprement écrit;* but it's terribly pale." In fact, every character in James's story was ridiculed, and the author's view was never explicitly stated. The point of the story was "the point of view." Perhaps it was because of the plain but skillful balance of contrasting views that the story was taken up by the distinguished French critic Th. Bentzon (pen name of Marie-Thérèse de Solms, Mme. Blanc, 1840–1907), who reviewed and translated it in the prestigious *Revue des deux mondes* in 1883.

The delicate balance between points of view was not apparent in the work of Mark Twain. His reception into French literary criticism was originally friendly but progressively abrasive. It was the same critic, Mme. Bentzon, who introduced Twain to the French reading public in an essay "Les Humoristes américaines" in the *Revue des deux mondes* in 1872. (See Chapter 6.) Like many other people, Twain believed that American humor could not be translated, and he "proved" it in his "Private History of the 'Jumping Frog' Story" (1894). The "history" is as follows: In Mme. Bentzon's essay she translated into French "The Celebrated Jumping Frog of Calaveras County," one of Twain's best known stories. Twain related:

> The result was not what should have been expected, for the *Revue* struggled along and pulled through, and is alive yet. I think the fault must have been in the translation. I ought to have translated it myself. I think so because I examined into the matter and finally retranslated the sketch from the French back into English, to see what the trouble was; that is, to see just what sort of a focus the French people got upon it. Then the mystery was explained. In French the story is too confused, and chaotic, and unreposeful, and ungrammatical, and insane; consequently it could only cause grief and sickness—it could not kill.

To illustrate Twain's point, let us look at a few lines of the original "Jumping Frog," then Mme. Bentzon's translation, and then Twain's retranslation.

> *ORIGINAL:* Well, thish-yer Smiley had rat-tarriers, and chicken cocks, and tom-cats, and all them kind of things, till

you couldn't rest, and you couldn't fetch nothing for him to bet on but he'd match you. He ketched a frog one day, and took him home, and said he cal-lated to educate him; and so he never done nothing for three months but set in his back yard and learn that frog to jump. And you bet he *did* learn him, too. He'd give him a little punch behind, and the next minute you'd see that frog whirling in the air like a doughnut—see him turn one summerset, or maybe a couple if he got a good start, and come down flat-footed and all right, like a cat.

TRANSLATION: Eh bien! ce Smiley nourrissait des terriers à rats, et des coqs de combat, et des chats, et toute sorte de choses, au point qu'il était toujours en mesure de vous tenir tête, et qu'avec sa rage de paris on n'avait plus de repos. Il attrapa un jour une grenouille et l'emporta chez lui, disant qu'il prétendait faire son éducation; vous me croirez si vous voulez, mais pendant trois mois il n'a rien fait que lui apprendre à sauter dans une cour retirée de sa maison. Et je vous réponds qu'il avait réussi. Il lui donnait un petit coup par derrière, et l'instant d'après vous voyiez la grenouille tourner en l'air comme un beignet au-dessus de la poêle, faire une culbute, quelquefois deux, lorsqu'elle était bien partie, et retomber sur ses pattes comme un chat.

RETRANSLATION: Eh bien! this Smiley nourished some terriers à rats, and some cocks of combat, and some cats, and all sort of things; and with his rage of betting one no had more of repose. He trapped one day a frog and him imported with him *(et l'emporta chez lui)* saying that he pretended to make his education. You me believe if you will, but during three months he not has nothing done but to him apprehend to jump *(apprendre à sauter)* in a court retired of her mansion *(de sa maison).* And I you respond that he have succeeded. He him gives a small blow by behind, and the instant after you shall see the frog turn in the air like a grease-biscuit, make one summersault, sometimes two, when she was well started, and re-fall upon his feet like a cat.

Twain concluded his retranslation with the remark: "It may be that there are people who can translate better than I can, but I am not acquainted with them." Besides the disarming self-mockery of the words, he probably meant to point out, not any incompetence of the translator, Mme. Bentzon, but the futility of attempting to translate his dialect and humor at all.

Nevertheless Mme. Bentzon was offended, as the sequel to

the "Private History" reveals. One can see how she might be offended; and it is unfortunate, since she had honestly introduced native American humor to a French reading public almost totally unaware of its existence. Furthermore, she had explained in the same article that it was impossible to capture the true flavor of the original.

Shortly after the publication of the "Private History," she told her friend Grace King, also a friend of Twain, that she thought an apology was in order. Twain probably never wrote to Mme. Bentzon, but his reply to Miss King showed how he felt about French character apropos of humor. He had not meant to offend Mme. B., he had not offended her, and he could not pretend to be sorry. "You see, the whole trouble lies in the French character. It hasn't a shred of humor in it, consequently there is no depth to it; its compass, regulator, balance-wheel, is lacking."[2]

Twain was wrong. The sale of his own work in France since the 1890s shows that the French were at least capable of learning to appreciate some of his humor. The number of translations of his work shows that the translation of humor is not impossible. Furthermore, the amount of French criticism and scholarship devoted to Twain has probably equaled that devoted to any other American writer. Today in France Twain is one of the half dozen best known American authors.

Both James and Twain were contending with a French attitude toward America that already had a history of more than a hundred years. It was a complex and self-contradictory attitude, and it had its basis in French social, cultural, political, and economic relations with the New World. In one way, it was singularly lacking in an appreciation of American humor. The term *humour* itself was imported into France from England in the eighteenth century and was the subject of considerable confusion, inquiry, and definition. On the other hand, French critics often picked up elements of humor in American writers—such as Poe, Hawthorne, James—that serious American critics missed. The French image of the American has had a gradual metamorphosis from a doctrinaire approach in the eighteenth century to a condescending one in the nineteenth to a bedazzlement in the middle twentieth century.

The idea of an American did not take shape in the French mind until the middle eighteenth century. Before that, America was known through the accounts of explorers, traders, missionaries, and finally soldiers. It was a land of wonder, of exoticism, of adventure. The English settlers were presumed to have all the stereotyped traits of their fellow citizens in England. It was not until the eve of the Revolutionary War that Americans began to think of themselves as a people, nor did the French think of them as such.

But by the 1750s, the French philosophes had begun to think of America in terms of their doctrines. America was the land of the noble savage and the hardy immigrant, who, growing close to nature, became free and virtuous. Or, on the contrary, it was a country of degenerate flora and fauna where men degenerated, physically, mentally, and morally. America was made to illustrate primitivism, agrarianism, and perfectibility. Or it was held up as an example of a fearful retrogression to barbarism.

Benjamin Franklin, quite cannily, let himself be taken as the representative American by those who saw the New World in a favorable way. Already known for his scientific achievements, he made himself deliberately conspicuous as minister to France during the Revolutionary War. In his beaver hat and simple dress, he was the practical philosopher, the man of science, the statesman, the farmer, the man of letters, the rationalist. Of course, he had a few detractors, whose picture of him was different, but they did not count in the popular image.[3] Franklin was the ideal American.

After Franklin's departure and the vicissitudes of the French Revolution, the French picture fluctuated between the dreams of the optimists and the nightmares of the pessimists, according to the political orientation of the observer. America was the ideal of the friends of democracy and industrialization, and the bugbear of their enemies. To both it was the land of the future—a future of political equality, of material prosperity, of social perfectibility, or, on the contrary, of the tyranny of the majority, of dollar-worship, and of the leveling of culture to the lowest common denominator—a future toward which France itself was inevitably drawn, for better or for worse. Most of the critics were elitist and antidemocratic. Hence, they were quick to note the vulgarization of American popular literature, or they ignored the popular, including the journalistic humorists, and pointed out what they deemed a reaction against American society in the writers they happened to like, such as Edgar Allan Poe.

American visitors to France and French visitors to the

United States made inestimable impressions on the image. Most notable, on the one hand, were Franklin and James Fenimore Cooper; on the other hand were the Marquis de Lafayette and Alexis de Tocqueville. But many more French visitors published their impressions of America or transmitted them orally when they returned to France. And the number of American diplomats, tourists, and students in France increased through the nineteenth century and made their inevitable impressions.

By the middle of the nineteenth century a veritable stereotype of the American was taking shape. It was not a reflection of Franklin or of Washington or, least of all, of Andrew Jackson. There was not yet a nickname—such as Jonathan, or Yankee, or Sam—to designate the American, but the reports of travelers to America, both French and British, were beginning to form a picture and it was not pretty. Most often the American was characterized as generally impassive but proud of his nationality—that is, insensitive and chauvinistic. More specifically, he was rude in his manners, laconic in conversation, and single-mindedly mercenary. He was pictured with his hands always moving, whittling on a stick of wood, his body stretched out, his hat on the back of his head, his feet in the air, and constantly chewing and spitting tobacco even in the presence of ladies.[4]

In 1868, the great historian of English literature Hippolyte Taine described the typical Yankee—the term was now recognized—as a man "who eats at the table d'hôte, his hat on his head, and tells you dogmatically, while blowing cigar smoke at you through his nose: 'A miserable old world, your Europe! A bunch of lackeys and rotters. But free America will sweep away all that vermin.' "[5] By this time the picture had solidified. The traits most persistently recorded were vulgarity, chauvinism, dollar-worship, and violence. The last of these, violence, was associated with the frontier, but then all of America was considered a frontier.

Now, these were also the traits adopted by the American crackerbox humorists—Jack Downing, Sut Lovingood, Artemus Ward, Mark Twain, and the rest. All of them posed as lowbrow provincial Americans, proudly American, smart traders, and continually involved in slapstick violence. When that great practical joker P. T. Barnum published his *Autobiography* in 1854 he was soon taken up by French observers as the personification of American traits, replacing to some degree the images of

Franklin and Washington. And it was the same P. T. Barnum who inspired Charles Farrar Browne's popular American comic hero Artemus Ward in 1858. Barnum flaunted most of the traits that the French were disposed to expect in Americans, and Browne, of course, caricatured them:

> To the Editor of the ________
>
> Sir—I'm movin along—slowly along—down tords your place. I want you should rite me a letter, sayin how is the show bizniss in your place. My show at present consists of three moral Bares, a Kangaroo (a amoozin little Raskal—t'would make you larf yerself to deth to see the little cuss jump up and squeal) wax figgers of G. Washington Gen. Tayler John Bunyan Capt. Kidd and Dr. Webster in the act of killin Dr. Parkman, besides several miscellanyus moral wax statoots of celebrated piruts & murderers, &c., ekalled by few & exceld by none. Now Mr. Editor, scratch orf a few lines sayin how is the show bizniss down to your place. I shall hav my hanbills dun at your offiss. Depend upon it. I want you should git my hanbills up in flamin stile. Also git up a tremenjus excitemunt in yr. paper 'bowt my onparaleld Show. We must fetch the public sumhow. We must wurk on their feelins. Cum the moral on 'em strong. If it's a temprance community tell 'em I sined the pledge fifteen minits arter Ise born, but on the contery ef your peple take their tods, say Mister Ward is as Jenial a feller as we ever met, full of conwiviality, & the life an sole of the Soshul Bored. Take, don't you? If you say anythin abowt my show say my snaiks is as harmliss as the new born Babe. What a interestin study it is to see a zewological animil like a snaik under perfeck subjecshun! My kangaroo is the most larfable little cuss I ever saw. All for 15 cents. I am anxyus to skewer your infloounce. I repeet in regard to them hanbills that I shall git 'em struck orf up to your printin office. My perlitercal sentiments agree with yourn exackly. I know thay do, becawz I never saw a man whoos didn't.
>
> Respectively yures,
> A. Ward.
>
> P. S.—You scratch my back & Ile scratch your back.[6]

The more favorable critics of America could not overlook those characteristics that seemed so flagrantly obvious, but they attributed them to the childishness of the new nation. Rudeness, egotism, materialism, and violence were natural to a people who had only recently become a nation, who were still subduing the wilderness, whom a benevolent Nature had destined to free the world. Furthermore, childishness denoted a natural innocence, uncorrupted by Old World civilization. America, with all its youthful excesses, was a new start, a throwing off of the chains of the past, a rebirth for mankind.

Every element was there to make the French image the same as that which many Americans held of themselves. Every element but one: humor. One might almost say that the French—though certainly not the French alone—were the victims of the greatest hoax since the Trojan horse. Native American humor, if it has any distinguishing characteristic, relies on the hoax, the practical joke, the innocent pose. Americans took the French image and gave it back, just as they had taken the sarcastic jingle "Yankee Doodle" from their British enemies in the Revolutionary War and made of it a national folk anthem. Not that the French had invented the image. It had much in common with that held by the English. It was seriously shared by many Americans. It had, in fact, a basis in truth, for there were many Americans like P. T. Barnum. The humorists simply took that image and played with it, often to the discomfort of the Frenchman, or the Englishman, or the dude from Boston. The "natural innocence" of Huckleberry Finn had a good deal of craft behind it. It was not mere youthful mischief, although that had a lot to do with it and should not be overlooked. American mischief—American humor—was at the heart of the Americans' own search for a national character. If they were to be treated as children by the great powers of the world, they would play the part to their own advantage. They would even exaggerate the part, ridiculing their own shortcomings, so as to bring down, under the guise of innocence, the pretensions of their detractors, both inside and outside the United States. Would it be going too far to say that American humor was the key to American character?

At any rate, the French as a whole missed that crucial element. Though our study will show that individual critics detected humor in American literature, they did not usually include it in their composite picture of the American. In fact, they were as often as not put off by it; and that is not surprising for it was sometimes so intended. There almost seems to have been a tacit agreement between France and America to misunderstand each other. If England was the mother country, France was the mother-in-law, and the love-hate relationship was more outspoken if less profound than that with Mother England. While the English thought they understood Americans, and often did, the French agreed not to. Americans were the wayward children of Mother England, and France looked on with amusement, disdain, shock, or repulsion—as the situation might suggest.

A further consideration of the French point of view toward the American character involves the publishing business. Most French readers and French critics were able to see only that part of American culture, American literature, and American humor that were brought somehow to their attention. France was never a very significant market for American publishers—because of the smallness of the French reading public, the lack of international copyright protection, the difficulties of transportation and of distribution in France, and the risk of poor translation. Consequently, American books were brought to the attention of French readers, publishers, and critics through chance personal contacts, the reviews in the foremost American magazines that happened to be read by a French reviewer, and, most importantly, the approval of British reviewers and the British publication of American books. In other words, there was an intensive, though unpremeditated, screening of American works before they were heard of in France; and the screening nearly always eliminated all but the most respectable and marketable.

By the 1850s there was a literary establishment in the United States, consisting of Ticknor and Fields in Boston, the Harpers in New York, Carey and Lea in Philadelphia, and a few others on the east coast. These companies published almost all of the highbrow literature, and they maintained relationships with British publishers, such as Longman's and John Murray, to benefit American authors abroad as well as English authors in the United States. The British publishers had much closer contacts with France simply because of the ease of transportation and communication. The hundreds of other American publishers were not concerned about promoting American literature abroad. Among these were the publishers of American crackerbox humor, who sold in cheap editions of tens of thousands in the United States while their elite competitors sold in editions of mere thousands. Thus, the more popular works had less chance of reaching France. The economics of publication and distribution has played a vital part in the reception of American literature abroad from the eighteenth century to the present day.[7]

While the publication of polite literature in the United States was concentrated in the hands of a half dozen publishers on the east coast, the publication of literature in France was in the hands of dozens and dozens of publishers concentrated in Paris. Almost every Parisian bookseller was his own publisher. The history of this phenomenon goes back, of course, to the Renaissance, but it has continued to the present day. Each French publisher-bookseller publishes the books that he sees fit to publish, with his branches in the cities outside Paris necessarily following suit. The successful publishers usually develop specialties—mathematics, science, medicine, encyclopedias, illustrated editions, classics, recent literature, etc.[8]

Some have tried to develop an interest in American literature, but the history of this development is yet to be written. A few names might be mentioned. The houses of Baudry, of A. and W. Galignani, and of A. Mame published dozens of editions of Washington Irving between the 1820s and the 1880s, and other publishers carried on into the twentieth century. H. Gautier published Bret Harte and Oliver Wendell Holmes, as well as Irving, in the 1880s. Harte and Irving were published by Hachette in the late nineteenth century, and that great publishing house continues to take some interest in American authors. More recently, the house of Stock, purchased in 1921 by Maurice Delamain and Jacques Boutelleau, was successful with Sinclair Lewis as well as with Louis Bromfield and Pearl Buck. R. Julliard has published, among other American writers, the humorists Robert Benchley, James Thurber, and Art Buchwald. But this listing is not even a fair representation of the several publishers, such as Gallimard, Seghers, Charlot, Denoël, and Seuil, who have ventured occasional translations or English-language editions of American writers. Mention should also be made of the twentieth-century English-language presses in France, such as Gertrude Stein's Plain Edition and Contact Editions, Three Mountains Press.

The twentieth century has brought many changes in the French image of America and the American. First of all, the mere presence of American strength and material progress demanded attention. The two world wars proved this, and the presence of the doughboys and the GIs on French soil was bound to make an impression, good or bad, on segments of the French population that were previously unaffected by American culture. Probably even more important than the soldiers, however, were the new communication media—the movies, radio, comic strips and cartoons, the phonograph, and then television. Far from replacing literature, these media increased the appetite for American books. Better transportation made for improved distribution of American literature abroad, and also offered more opportunities for travel in both directions. The French educational system gradually became more and more cognizant of American studies, so that now there is a solid scholarly tradition in the subject.

But the nineteenth-century image has not disappeared; it has simply been overlaid with new impressions, often semiconscious, half-assimilated, contradictory. The juke boxes play French folktunes to American rock rhythms. French students wear faded blue jeans and University of Kentucky sweat shirts. The comic strips, when they are not imported from America with French words, are full of cowboys and talking animals; and the work of French cartoonists often reminds us of James Thurber or Saul Steinberg. On the other hand, the same people who watch Mickey Mouse in the movies and "Bonanza" on television may be vociferous about Yankee imperialism. Scholarly dissertations are written on the spirit of revolt in Sinclair Lewis or Mark Twain, while books on the "menace of America" still appear. But, after all, American culture is contradictory and ambiguous, and contemporary French views simply reveal a more sophisticated awareness of its complexity. While French culture seems to be assimilating vast quantities of American culture, there perhaps cannot be a clear stereotype of the American.

But one conclusion can be made. American culture can be translated. And with it American humor. In 1947, for example, Maurice Coindreau published his translation of Erskine Caldwell's *Tobacco Road.* His problems were the same as those of Th. Bentzon in translating "The Celebrated Jumping Frog of Calaveras County" in 1872. The book was loaded with lowbrow American humor; the dialogue was almost entirely in dialect; the vulgarity and the violence were extreme. Yet Coindreau, with others, made Caldwell both popular and respected in France—more respected than in the United States.

The following passage will illustrate the translator's art. First is Caldwell's original, then the translation:

> *ORIGINAL:* "Me and Dude is going to get married," she said. "The Lord told me to do it. I asked Him about it, and He said, 'Sister Bessie, Dude Lester is the man I want you to mate. Get up early in the morning and go up to the Lester place and

marry Dude the first thing.' That's what He said to me last night, the very words I heard with my own ears while I was praying about it in bed. So when the sun came up, I got out of bed and ran up here as fast as I could, because the Lord don't like to be kept waiting for His plans to be carried out. He wants me to marry Dude right now."

Dude looked around nervously as if he was thinking of trying to run off to the woods and hide. He had forgotten how anxious he had been to go home with Bessie the evening before when she first mentioned marriage.

"You hear that, Dude?" Jeeter said. "What you think about doing it with Sister Bessie?"

"Shucks," he said. "I couldn't do that."

"Why can't you do that?" Jeeter demanded. "What's ailing you? Ain't you man enough yet?"

"Maybe I is, and maybe I ain't. I'd be scared to do that with her."

TRANSLATION: —Dude et moi, on va se marier, dit-elle. Le Seigneur m'a dit de le faire. Je Lui ai demandé Son avis et Il m'a dit: "Soeur Bessie, Dude Lester est l'homme que Je veux te voir épouser. Lève-toi de bonne heure, va chez les Lester et épouse Dude sans perdre une minute." Voilà ce qu'Il m'a dit, hier soir, Ses paroles mêmes que j'ai entendues de mes propres oreilles pendant que je priais dans mon lit. Alors, dès que j'ai vu le soleil, je me suis levée et je suis accourue au plus vite, parce que le Seigneur n'aime pas qu'on retarde l'exécution de Ses desseins. Il veut que j'épouse Dude immédiatement.

Dude regardait tout autour de lui d'un air inquiet, comme s'il avait envie de courir se cacher dans les bois. Il avait oublié combien, la veille au soir, il avait eu envie de s'en aller avec Bessie quand elle avait parlé pour la première fois de mariage.

—T'entends, Dude? dit Jeeter. Ça te dirait de faire ça avec soeur Bessie?

—Bah, dit-il, j'pourais pas.

—Pourquoi ça? demanda Jeeter. Qu'est-ce que t'as donc? C'est-il que t'es pas assez homme?

—Peut-être ben que oui, peut-être ben que non. J'aurais peur de faire ça avec elle.[9]

Neither Caldwell nor the present writer has attempted to translate the passage back into English as Twain did the "Jumping Frog." Coindreau made no attempt to give the dialogue a distinctly regional character, nor did Caldwell himself use many, if any, expressions that could be identified as strictly Georgian.

Although it was impossible to translate "ain't" and "we is," the low-class and rustic tone was accomplished with other expressions, such as "on va se marier," "j'pourais pas," and "ben" for "bien." Perhaps a better translation than "bah" for "shucks" could have been found, but there was no way around the quite different connotations (Catholic and celibate) of "Soeur Bessie" and "Sister Bessie," except to let the context explain itself. Coindreau was unable to translate the physical implications of the verb "mate" without excessive crudity, but he made up for it by the quite clear "de faire ça" for Caldwell's subtly ambiguous "doing it." Throughout the translation, the clear distinction between the language of the characters and that of the author was maintained without destroying the simple purity of Caldwell's narrative style.[10]

According to André Maurois, "Caldwell is particularly difficult to translate because he is a bold writer, who achieves a sad comedy by uniting an impassive style with Rabelaisian license. To retain in French the violence of expression without falling into obscenity was not easy. Maurice Coindreau succeeded because he transposed more than translated."[11]

Caldwell may not be a great American writer, but he is certainly an authentic humorist and a very skillful stylist. Coindreau did not succeed by improving on the original—as has been said of the translators of James Fenimore Cooper and Edgar Allan Poe—but by "transposing" a slice of American culture into French culture. It can be done.

2

L'Humour

Humour: Forme d'esprit qui consiste à présenter ou à déformer la réalité de manière à en dégager les aspects plaisants et insolites. —Robert Paul, *Dictionnaire alphabétique et analogique de la langue française,* 1966.

Humour: Mot anglais qui signifie gaieté d'imagination, veine comique. —Emile Littré, *Dictionnaire de la langue française,* 1967.

The term *humour* is a French borrowing from English that means in general a kind of comic writing or speaking that is characteristically English, as distinguished from that of France. The distinction is understood to deeply involve national character.

While the American word *humor* is often used today in the broadest sense of comedy—as it is in the present volume unless otherwise indicated—the French always distinguish *l'humour* from other categories of *le comique.* It is neither *l'esprit*—brilliance, poignancy, ingeniousness, wit—nor *bouffonnerie*—clowning, foolery. It is not necessarily *satire* nor is it *farce.* These terms and others constantly turn up in French attempts to classify *l'humour.*

Perhaps these efforts to define and classify are futile. Perhaps they illustrate the Platonic superstition that words have real, ideal meanings—that a word has an absolute essence which is corrupted in its usage but which is more or less discoverable. But whether or not the "true meaning" can be found, it is not a waste of time to pursue the French discussion of the term: first, because the fact that the French distinguish *humour* from other things indicates that a distinction, however vague and variable, exists in their minds; and second, because French discussions of *humour* can tell us something about French attitudes toward American humor and even American character. Evidently something in the British and American characters, or at least in the Frenchman's image of them, has created a need for the term.

The English term (spelled "humour" in England) is well known to have derived from the medical term "humour," which in turn came from Old French and which, at least until the sixteenth century, referred to a bodily fluid—generally blood, phlegm, choler, or melancholy—that affected the emotional and mental state of a person. The French language retains the word *humeur,* meaning bodily fluids or the human dispositions or temperaments arising from them. At the end of the sixteenth century, the English word took on a different meaning. As illustrated and perpetuated in the plays of Ben Jonson it meant the individual temperament produced by the fluids, the eccentricity that characterized an individual or type; and its connotation was generally comic. In the eighteenth century, with the advent of sentimentalism, attention shifted from the humorous character to the "humorist," someone with a sense of humor, that is, the ability to see the comedy in human eccentricities. The history of the English and American word "humor" since then has shown a continuous broadening of meaning, so that today it sometimes means anything that is funny or comic.

Until the eighteenth century, the French usually translated the English "humour" as *humeur,* though to have *de l'humeur* generally connoted unpleasantness or sullenness. Voltaire, who resented the borrowing of the English word, claimed that Corneille had used the French *humeur* in the sense of *humour* in the seventeenth century, but his citation hardly proved his point.[1] With the reception of the English writers Joseph Addison, Jonathan Swift, and Henry Fielding came an awareness of the inadequacy of the French language to express the new meaning. Montesquieu wrote: "English humor is something separate from *l'esprit* and distinguished from it. . . . This humor is distinguished from *la plaisanterie* and is not *la plaisanterie;* it is rather *le plaisant* of *la plaisanterie.*"[2] That is, humor is the comic quality conveyed by the amusing saying.

One of the best and earliest definitions in the eighteenth century was that of l'Abbé Le Blanc in *Lettres d'un Français* (1745): "From our word *humeur,* the English have made 'humour'; but they have given it an altogether different signification from that of the French word. The word *humeur,* generally speaking in our language, conveys an idea of sadness and disaffection. *Avoir de l'humeur* is to be vexed. 'Humour,' on the other hand, expresses the idea of a singular joy that is perhaps a little mad. 'Humour,' says one of their authors, 'is a ridiculous extravagance of conversation by which one man differs from all others.' It is some habit, passion, or strange state of mind which is peculiar to an individual. But this is not the only sense that this word, which is very familiar to them, has in their language; it applies just as well to the subject of a work of wit as to the subject of the character of a person, and always signifies in both cases a certain amusing turn of phrase which is not quite the natural tone and yet not totally opposed to it."[3] The Abbé recognized both the Jonsonian meaning of the English word—eccentricity—and the modern meaning.

He also touched upon the one distinguishing feature of *l'humour* that has been almost universally pointed out by the later French critics. That characteristic is the technique of pose; the humorist, says the French interpretation, always pretends to be somebody he isn't. He masks his sanity with a pose of eccentricity, or his sadness or anger with a pose of gaiety.

During the first part of the nineteenth century, the word *humour* became fairly common in French criticism. It was used nearly always in reference to British literature, though sometimes to German, and occasionally to American. The meaning, however, was far from fixed, each critic seeming to have his own conception, which might have nothing in common with that of the next critic. Often the reader is at a loss to know what the critic meant by the word, although occasionally the personality of the critic makes a reasonable guess possible.

Perhaps the equivocality of the term restrained the poet Charles Baudelaire (1821–1867) from using it in his "De l'essence du rire et généralement du comique dans les arts plastiques" (1855). Nevertheless, his essay represents French insights into the subject. The source of comedy, he said, is pride: "The essence of the comic is a seeming unawareness and the development in the spectator, or in the reader, of a delighted consciousness of his own superiority and of the superiority of Man to Nature." Note Baudelaire's reference to the comic pose, in the words "a seeming unawareness." He continued:

> Artists create the comic. Having studied and marshalled all its elements, they know that this or that man is comic, but only on the condition of being ignorant that he is so. Similarly, by virtue of an inverse law, the artist is an artist only on condition that he has a double personality, and is fully aware of all that results from that condition.[4]

Baudelaire characterized the comic spirit in England as tending toward what he called "the absolutely comic" or the grotesque or the comic for its own sake, combined with ferocity. "If we seek the ferocious, the wildly ferocious, comic we must cross the Channel and visit those foggy climes where *spleen* is king." In contrast, French comedy, he said, was generally "the significantly comic"—that is, humor aimed at a moral or philosophical purpose—and was inclined to be rational and moderate. Baudelaire considered English comedy—what others would call *l'humour*—esthetically the more valuable.

In 1862, Léon Dumont (1837–1877), a young lawyer and philosopher, published a serious volume on the comic, *Des causes du rire,* in which he devoted six pages to defining *l'humour,* a term "that French criticism has long accepted but of which the import is far from being clearly determined." Strictly employed, he said, the term has two meanings. First, it is "the state of a soul who has the habit of abandoning himself entirely to his humor, or rather to the different humors or to the natural dispositions that succeed one another in him. . . . One calls a 'humorist,' in this sense, a writer who lets his imagination ramble on subjects widely different, going from the low to the sublime, from the sad to the gay, and who consequently brings together the most remote things." Secondly, *l'humour* is "a sad humor or melancholy [that] is realized in its most elevated and striking form, that is, (1) when it exists in a continuous manner in an individual and forms the basis of his character; (2) when it is caused by a consciousness of human faculties, of imperfections of society, and of the miseries of life; and (3) when it expresses itself in the form that most commands the attention, that is to say with pleasantry." Thus *l'humour* is "the melancholy of a superior soul who speaks comically," and the comic aspect is a manifestation or result of *l'humour,* not its essence. Comedy is merely a form or device for presenting something forcefully. It is good or poor only in regard to whether its subject is good or poor. It "has value only in the mouths of serious men."[5] Dumont placed a high value on *l'humour,* but he disapproved the German use of the term to refer to everything comical, and he deplored the tendency of every witless funnyman to call himself a humorist.

The dark side of *l'humour,* found in different ways in both Baudelaire and Dumont, was again expressed by the historian of English literature Hippolyte Taine (1828–1893) in *Notes sur Angleterre* in 1872:

> [The English] have a wit which is all their own; true, it is not very pleasant, but it is altogether original, its savour powerful,

> keen and even somewhat bitter, like their national drinks. They call it "humour": it is, as a rule, the joking of a man who, while joking, keeps a straight face. . . . It results on the one hand in clownish caricature, or on the other hand in sustained, deliberate sarcasm. It shakes the nerves or it sinks deep into the memory. It is a work of either comic imagination or concentrated anger. Its spirit rejoices in violent contrasts and unexpected travesties. It dresses folly in the garments of reason, and reason in the cloak of folly. . . . The man who uses it is rarely benevolent and never happy: he feels deeply and fiercely denounces life's discords. He is not really amused by them; at bottom they make him suffer, and anger him.[6]

Besides emphasizing the basic seriousness, even moroseness, of the English humorist, Taine's remarks reflected other facets of French critical views. He noted the difference between the humorist and the humorous pose. He contrasted *l'humour* with French *esprit,* which Taine elsewhere defined as "the talent, *faire des mots,* the taste for the short, lively phrase, unexpected, ingenious, and spiced with gaiety or malice. Foreigners greatly admire this gift; and they say that it is accompanied by taste, and that both qualities are universal and precocious among us."[7] The contrast between national characters is rather profound: the English are typically sad, misanthropic, angry; the French gay, outgoing, though sometimes malicious. Often English gloom is associated with puritan asceticism, and English seriousness with puritan morality. English humor also carries the suggestion of vulgarity, which presumably is never to be found in France. The extravagance and violence that Taine points out were even more strikingly noted in American humor, as was the presumed vulgarity.

One pictures the bewildered French visitor trying to fathom the intentions of the straight-faced and slow-spoken Englishman. Yet we should not overlook the dismay of the English squire in the presence of a first-rate display of the fireworks of French wit. These are stereotypes, of course, but they can tell a good deal about intercultural relations. Indeed, these pictures recall the stock confrontation in American humor between the slow-spoken frontiersman and the supercilious Easterner (or Englishman, or Frenchman).

In 1893, Auguste Angellier (1848–1911), a leading professor and critic of English literature, published his dissertation *Robert Burns,* which set the stage for a controversy that dominated the theorizing on *l'humour* and *le comique* through the first half of the twentieth century. Basically, the argument was between the affective theory, which held that humor involved the emotions of both the humorist and the audience, and the cold-blooded theory, which held that humor required an aloof impassiveness. Angellier represented the affectivists.

He defined humor as a combination of raillery or mockery with realism: "If we should have to define *l'humour,* we should say that it is raillery in direct and concrete observation or representation of life—or by means of them." Raillery can appear as both wit and humor, but wit generalizes while humor particularizes. Insistence on concrete particularity is what distinguishes *l'humour* from other forms of *le comique.* Angellier produced a good deal of scholarly support for this definition and developed it in detail:

> It may be that the proposed definition appears vague at first glance. One will perhaps change this judgment and recognize that it fairly comprises the constituent elements of *l'humour,* if he will pay attention to the following remark. It is necessary only to detail each of the two terms of which it is composed, to particularize them by means of adjectives, according to the ordinary process of defining, in order to grasp each of the varieties of humor and even to mark the individual formula of each humorist. If we put a bitter, a somber, even a hateful raillery with a sense of observation pitilessly stark, have we not defined the humor of Swift? If we join a compassionate raillery to a minute, indeed microscopic, observation, have we not that of Sterne? A joyful, overflowing, torrential laughter, happily drunk with its own noise, combined with a swelling observation that exaggerates the dimensions of objects and madly twists them around, is this not Rabelais? Gaiety and buffoonery in laughter together with sadness and tears in observation, is this not the strange contrast of Dickens? Raillery full of good nature and smiling observation, is this not Goldsmith? A simple, sly laughter with a coarse and self-interested observation of life, is this not Sancho Panza?[8]

Thus, while emphasizing concrete detail as part of the essence of *l'humour,* Angellier brought in the temperament of the humorist in such a way as to lead subsequent critics to place him in the vanguard of the affectivists. The manner of the humorist depended on his individual use of raillery and observation, which, in turn, depended on his emotional attitude.

By the end of the nineteenth century, *l'humour* began to have its enthusiastic partisans in France. René Doumic (1860–1937) in an article "Nos humorists" in the *Revue des deux mondes* (1899) bewailed the lack of humorists in France and the poorness of their humor.[9] The critic and translator Gabriel de Lautrec (1867–1938), in the preface to his 1900 translation of stories of Mark Twain, violently asserted that the French had no humor and had never had it. Rabelais was powerfully obscene, Molière was mere bawdiness, Voltaire lacked imagination; the great humorists were Shakespeare, Swift, Addison, Dickens, and Twain. Though he entitled his introduction "Definition de l'humour," it is difficult to summarize his notion of humor because of his passionate style.

> It is a turn of mind toward all kinds of impressions. It is an equal and unexpected disposition toward sadness as well as joy; but the joy is often melancholy and the sadness breaks out in cheerful and comical gestures. Some of its subtle pursuits of thought almost fatigue the reader. Some of its profound naivetés disarm him. The same writer rigorously condemns the banal cruelties of existence, and then indulges freely in the easy pleasures of every day, without looking back. Indeed, it is not easy to note the essential qualities that make an author a humorist, for this diverse disposition is for one person cruel, for another sad, farcical here, correct and discreet there. To bring them together, one must find a tendency that is the same for all, in spite of the contrasting forms it takes. It seems that one can find it in an extreme sensitiveness, taking this word in its broadest sense. This sensibility lets no impression, however light, go unperceived. An observer with vibrant nerves, with a curiosity ever awake, will feel strongly. To satisfy himself, if he writes, he will have to find a form equally intense. Thus, he will be led, whether intentionally or not, to a concrete and fitting style, which will follow faithfully the movement of his thoughts, with its searchings, its unforeseen turns, and its exaggerations.[10]

Lautrec's views illustrate the general ferment concerning the subjects of *l'humour* and *le comique* at the turn of the century. The quoted passage places him firmly in the camp of the affective theory of humor.

The philosopher Henri Bergson (1859–1941) was the father of the cold-blooded theory, though he certainly had his predecessors. The eighteenth-century philosopher or philosophe Denis Diderot, for example, had asserted that all artists, but especially the great actors, had to have no feelings of their own so they could represent a variety of feelings. His "Paradoxe sur le comédien" (written 1773, published 1830) was a somewhat impassioned argument that the actor must lack passion but be able to counterfeit it voluntarily.[11] He was attacking the notion, particularly prevalent among the English sentimentalists, that the actor or artist must be a person of "sensibility"—that is, of sensitive emotion. Other writers—notably the English novelist George Meredith—had insisted on the intellectual basis of comedy. The comic writer viewed the evils of the world cold-bloodedly—"scientifically," to use Bergson's term.

In his essay *Le Rire* (1900), Bergson spoke only briefly of *l'humour* as distinguished from other forms of the comic; his emphasis was on the realism of it:

> The most common of [comic] contrasts is that between the real and the ideal, between what is and what ought to be. Here again the transposition may take place in either direction. Sometimes we state what ought to be done; then we have *irony*. Sometimes, on the contrary, we describe with scrupulous minuteness what is being done, and pretend to believe that this is just what ought to be done; such is often the method of *humour*. Humour, thus defined, is the counterpart of irony. Both are forms of satire, but irony is oratorical in its nature, whilst humour partakes of the scientific. Irony is emphasized the higher we allow ourselves to be uplifted by the idea of the good that ought to be: thus irony may grow so hot within us that it becomes a kind of high-pressure eloquence. On the other hand, humour is the more emphasized the deeper we go down into an evil that actually is, in order to set down its details in the most cold-blooded indifference. Several authors, Jean Paul amongst them, have noticed that humour delights in concrete terms, technical details, definite facts. If our analysis is correct, this is not an accidental trait of humour, it is its very essence. A humorist is a moralist disguised as a scientist, something like an anatomist who practices dissection with the sole object of filling us with disgust; so that humour, in the restricted sense in which we are here regarding the word, is really a transposition from the moral to the scientific.[12]

Bergson's notion of "transposition" was essential to his definition of the comic: "Any arrangement of acts and events is comic which gives us, in a single combination, the illusion of life and the distinct impression of a mechanical arrangement." The combination may be that of the real world and the ideal, the literal and the figurative, the absurd and the commonplace, a high style and a low style, but it always involves a transposition from one world to another, or from one frame of reference to another. It often gives the impression of a topsy-turvy universe (an idea taken up later by Louis Cazamian)—of "the prisoner at the bar lecturing the magistrate [or] a child presuming to teach its parents." Or it may be the imposition of the world of dream or fantasy upon the world of actuality (an idea later borrowed by Robert Escarpit): "The reasonings at which we laugh are those we know to be false, but which we might accept as true were we to hear them in a dream."[13] The assertion is well illustrated by the turning of realism into extravagance in the American tall tale. Further, Bergson's insistence on the basic human element in comedy, as opposed to the mechanical, relates comedy to the humor of eccentricity and even to the sentimental school of Addison, Lamb, and Dickens. But to relate all the implications of Bergson's essay and their effects on theorists of the twentieth century is out of the question. Whether one accepts his theories or refutes them, *Le Rire* has been the most influential study of the comic upon the French mind.

The impact of Sigmund Freud's work on the comic, *Der Witz und seine Beziehung zum Unbewussten* (1905), was possibly in the long run as great as that of Bergson's work. For Freud humor was a defense—a means of displacing such feelings as anger, pity, and disgust, with something else. "Humour is a means of obtaining pleasure in spite of the distressing affects that interfere with it; it acts as a substitute for the generation of these affects, it puts itself in their place."[14] But humor is often only a partial substitute, and hence it is often accompanied by some of the feelings it serves to displace. Although Freud considered humor to be the highest form of the comic, most observers emphasize the somewhat negative aspects of his theory—its defensive origin and its association with undesirable emotions. Freud's influence is so pervasive throughout twentieth-century thought that to try to trace its ramifications is useless. Furthermore, his psychology in general may have had more influence on French theorizing about the comic than his own theorizing did.

In 1907, Fernand Baldensperger (1871–1958), author of numerous books on French, English, and German literature, published a forty-seven page essay "Les Définitions de l'humour" in his *Etudes d'histoire littéraire.* It was, and still is, an excellent summary of the history of the word "humor" and its cognates in Italy, France, England, Germany, and the United States, from the Renaissance to the twentieth century. Though the medical term "humour" was extant in the languages of all these countries in the Middle Ages, Italy, said Baldensperger, first introduced the term in a sense related to character and wit. He then traced its development in Elizabethan and seventeenth-century England, noted the adoption of the English term in eighteenth-century France, Germany, and Italy, and followed the changes in meaning to the present time. He was sharply cognizant of the divergent interpretations of the adopted term in different countries—interpretations that could tell us as much about the adopting country as about the nature of humor. Of particular interest is the influence of German humor, especially that of Jean Paul Richter and August Heinrich Hoffmann, on the French interpretation of the term. Frequently the French marked *l'humour* as characteristic of the Northern or Germanic temperament. Other writers had noted from time to time that humor was not exclusively English, that it existed in the work of Cervantes and Rabelais, to mention two striking examples.

Baldensperger concluded his long list of definitions by declining to produce his own. "There is no *humour,*" he said; "there are only humorists."[15] And he suggested that psychology might be able to tell us something about the individual humorist that esthetic deductions had been incapable of revealing.

Michel Epuy (1876–?), an editor and translator of Mark Twain, also refused to attempt a formal definition in the Preface to his *Anthologie des humoristes anglais et américaines* (1910). Subtitling his essay "Some Reflections on Humor," he suggested that *l'humour* was not a literary genre but "an aptitude of the Anglo-Saxon mind" reflected in English literature. From this beginning he proceeded to analyze the Anglo-Saxon mind, finding it grave, moral, and impassive. He praised English morality. Though sometimes hypocritical, the English were so only in regard to respectability, not to virtue. English and American humor were noteworthy for being often vulgar but never immoral, while French humor was never in poor taste but often basically immoral. British gravity he related to the Protestant conscience, then suggested that conscience itself was developed by the difficulty of the northern climate. The British even took their humor seriously, and therefore it nearly always had a moral meaning. *L'humour* was "a sort of lay sermon, or anti-sermon, but still a sermon even in its essay form—in the novel and in the story." Impassivity, caused by the gravity of existence and reflecting self-control, was the basis of the humorist's solemn pose.

> *L'humour* is more a particular disposition of *l'esprit* than a literary genre susceptible of complete definition. It could be the disposition of a man who received an austere education, who had an unpleasant childhood and hard and sad youth. He perceives that after all there are some pleasant things in the world. He ventures at first to smile with a little constraint at the rough mishaps that he sees; then he dares to laugh at them, and this laugh, which is not familiar to him, is strong, sonorous, loud, boisterous. After this, he learns to discern and relish finer comedy, that which causes only a smile and which, especially in the beginning, is closer to tears than laughter. But all the while this man never forgets his past and could not neglect the voice of his conscience, and even when he arrives at the perception of the tranquil sweetness of the enjoyment of *esprit,* he avoids *evil.* Often, from then on, a reserve, a constraint, a difficulty in speaking of anything gracefully, but, on the other hand, a great loyalty, great frankness and sincerity. And finally, as one must suffer in order really to sympathize with afflictions, there is in this disposition a warm, a burning, compassion for the unfortunate, a compassion which refuses to complain, but which, in its strength and pride, turns aside to punish the guilty.[16]

That is the humorist, according to Epuy. That, also, is the Anglo-Saxon; one could call almost all Anglo-Saxon authors humorists. Humor, said Epuy, "is a sort of spice that one finds a particular taste for, *sui generis,* in *all* Anglo-Saxon works. It can be there imperceptibly but it is there."[17]

By the late 1920s a second generation of affectivists and intellectualists had grown up. The chief representative of the former was Floris Delattre (1880–1950). He had been a student of Angellier in his youth, although he was later to publish several studies of Bergson, perhaps partly because of the debates on the nature of humor. He was also influenced by Jean Jules Jusserand (1855–1932), whose *Histoire littéraire du peuple anglais* (1894, 1904) supported the affectivist view. Borrowing heavily from that work, Delattre summarized the view of both himself and Jusserand in "La Naissance de l'humour dans la vieille

Angleterre" (1927). English humor, he maintained, was a result of the mixture, sometime after the Norman Conquest, of English saturninity and French mirth. "One evening, amid the motley throngs of old England, Laughter met Kindliness. They did not know each other. They were very different the one from the other. They loved each other. From their kiss was born a son. He was called Humor."[18]

On the intellectualist or cold-blooded side of the controversy was Louis Cazamian (1877–1966), professor of English literature at the Sorbonne. Cazamian's *The Development of English Humor* (1930, 1952) is the classic history of humor and made its author the foremost scholar on the subject, regardless of nationality.

While accepting the historical thesis of Delattre and Jusserand, Cazamian pointed out that it was an oversimplification. Humor, or at least laughter, had existed in England before the Conquest, though it seldom reached the solemn pages of monkish manuscripts. The French romances brought a lighter note to English literature as French aristocratic society brought a pleasure-loving reading public. Chaucer represented the first full flowering of English humor.

Cazamian thus introduced a note that may be discerned again and again as an overtone in French criticism of English and American humor. The English comic sense, he more than implied, was almost exclusively lower class until it was freed by the liberality of French society. But while it adopted, in literature, the sophistication of the French *plaisanterie,* it sustained not only something of the gloom of the English but also something of the vulgarity of the common people. It was this comparatively democratic vulgarity as well as the paradoxical combination of mirth and gloom that made the new combination incomprehensible to many French readers and critics.

Cazamian refused to define humor formally, but his informal working definition indicated the central position he gave to the comic pose. "We make a thing humorous," he said, "by expressing it with a certain twist, a queer reserve, an inappropriateness, and as it were an unconsciousness of what we all the time feel it to be." And he was quite aware of humorists in France as well as in England and America:

> A tentative list of markedly humorous French writers from the Renaissance to the end of the nineteenth century would include Rabelais, Molière, La Fontaine, La Bruyère, Lesage,

> Montesquieu, Voltaire, Beaumarchais, Balzac, Mérimée, Flaubert, Claude Tillier, Daudet, Taine, Jules Renard. Many more names could be added; and it is only in a quite relative sense that one may speak of a deficiency of humor in modern French literature.[19]

Finally, Cazamian recognized that the elements of kindliness and sympathy that were sometimes attributed to English humor, especially by eighteenth-century and nineteenth-century English writers, were not essential ingredients. Rather they were products of the sentimentalism of Addison, Sterne, and Lamb, but were not necessarily a part of the humor of Swift or Byron. Humor, he had written in 1929, must be distinguished from goodwill *(bienveillance)*. Although they have a natural affinity for each other, especially in England, humor may go equally well with hatred.[20]

In 1931, Delattre reviewed the first part of Cazamian's book. Although largely complimentary, he took issue with Cazamian's emphasis on the intellectual method of humor as opposed to what Delattre considered the emotional content. The reviewer summarized Cazamian's view of the nature of humor as follows: "Humor, that mental attitude which has become one of the dominant traits of the British genius, is a manifestation of a special constraint, an arrest by the humorist of the normal flood of his sentiments and ideas—a conscious reserve in the articulation of the instinctive reactions of the individual."[21] The definition implied, according to Delattre, an underlying essence of sentiment or emotion.

> The classification of humor, as here delimited, is it not a little too near to that of paradox, wit, and especially irony, those other varieties of the comic, of which a deliberate effort seems to be the principal characteristic, according to our new definition of humor? On the other hand, can't we suppose that the voluntarily transposed presentation of our ideas and sentiments constitutes not the matter of humor but its form, its procedure alone, and that its positive reality resides in "the direct presentation that can be discovered at the basis of the indirect expression"? Thus is it not, as M. Cazamian wrote not long ago "the lesson of tenderness, of bitterness, of pity, of anger, of highest duty, of noble sadness, or of optimism"; is it not, in other words, "the emotional resonance," "the moral and philosophical suggestions" emanating from humor which seem to constitute rather "the essential aroma"?[22]

An attempt to reconcile the views of Cazamian and Delattre was undertaken in a published dissertation on William Makepeace Thackeray, *Thackeray, l'homme, le penseur, le romancier* (1932), in which Raymond Las Vergnas (1902–) examined sentimental humor on the basis of the English writer's often quoted remark: "Humour is wit and love." The cold-blooded theory, he said, held that the humorist must remain emotionally uninvolved in order to achieve comic effect. The affective theory maintained, like Thackeray, that humor was *l'esprit* plus *bienveillance.* Las Vergnas used Cazamian's distinction between the matter and manner of the humorist to show that sentiment was a part of Thackeray's matter—part of the personality of the humorist that was conveyed through his writing—rather than an essential part of the humoristic manner, which, according to Cazamian, was the only concern of the analyst of humor per se. Las Vergnas's conclusion, then, was not in conflict with Cazamian's; that is, that sentiment or kindness or *bienveillance* may well be a part of the message of the humorist, but is not a definitive element of humor in general. Thackeray's definition applies to Thackeray but not necessarily to another humorist.

In 1961, Tony Mayer (1902–) approached the subject of *humour* somewhat lightly, for once, in the preface to his anthology *L'Humour anglais.* The greater part of his essay concerned the subject matter of humor, and he cited numerous examples. He found a common element in all English humor: blackness. "However brilliant, however lucid it may be, English humor always rises from a distinctly somber basis, like fireworks embroidered on the cloak of night."[23] The term "black humor" was not new to Mayer; it was used, for example, by André Breton (1896–1966), one of the founders of surrealism, in his *Anthologie de l'humour noir* in 1940; and the 1966 *Petit Larousse* dictionary defined it as "humor which underlines the absurdity of the world with cruelty, bitterness, and sometimes despair." Like many of his predecessors, Mayer did not finally attempt a formal definition of *l'humour.* "For me," he said, "humor is a mask."[24] And it was the variety of masks, or poses, that he undertook to illustrate.

In 1962, one of the leading apologists of American literature in France, André Maurois (1885–1967), defined *l'humour* briefly and neatly in his preface to Michel Chrestien and Jacques Sternberg's anthology *Un Siècle d'humour anglo-américain.* He made what is apparently the same distinction that Bergson set forth, but his terms were different. In distinguishing humor from satire, he used the term *satire* in the sense of a literary genre that directly attacks vice by contrasting it with virtue.

> There are two manners of fighting [one's] fears. One is openly to attack the objects of fear by satires, lampoons; the other is to annihilate them by ridicule. *Humour* employs the second method. It does not irritate; it does not condemn. It imitates, but it imitates with enough exaggeration that the dictator ceases to be a true dictator and becomes a comic personage.[25]

Maurois developed in greater detail than Bergson the realistic aspect of *l'humour.* The humorist, he said, mimics the evils of the actual world either by narrating them solemnly as they actually exist—as in Dickens or James Thurber—or by creating a fantasy world where they become glaringly absurd—as in Swift or Lewis Carroll. But in either instance the use of exact detail is necessary: "without it the mind of the reader detaches itself from a story that is too obviously false."[26] In either case, also, the pose of impassiveness, of naiveté, is essential. The humorist appears to be simply relating the facts without understanding their implications.

A more ambitious definition was *L'Humour* (1963) by Robert Escarpit (1918–), professor at the University of Bordeaux and writer of paragraphs for *Le Monde.* It was preceded, in 1959, by a public discussion with Professor Jean Dulck, at which the latter read a paper supporting Cazamian's theory of *l'humour* as a purely mechanical or intellectual process.

> M. DULCK [to Escarpit]: You conceive *l'humour* to be essentially committed, that is, taking sides on a moral, sociological, or metaphysical point.
> M. ESCARPIT: In effect, I don't believe that *l'humour* could be purely mechanical.
> M. DULCK: On the contrary, I define *l'humour* as a mechanical procedure. Otherwise, you ought to admit with Delattre the existence of a humor of charity.
> M. ESCARPIT: Indeed, I do.[27]

Escarpit's 1963 volume was partly an attempt to reply to the inconclusive discussion of 1959. He began by distinguishing between the word *humour* and the thing. Part I, of two parts, took up the history of the word, relying largely on Cazamian and repeating much of the same material that Baldensperger originally set forth, but bringing them up to date. The sense of humor, said Escarpit, is an essential part of the British character:

> It is this consciousness, natural and intuitive but lucid and deliberately smiling, of one's individual character in the midst of other characters.
>
> Now, this sense of humor, which is one of the most precious gifts transmitted by English education since the Renaissance, appears as the fundamental attitude of compromise, on which all English national life rests. It is ambiguity par excellence, the no man's land of values where eccentricity plays hide-and-seek with moral equilibrium, conformity with revolt, smiles with bitterness, seriousness with skepticism.
>
> Thus, the word proposed by Ben Jonson for his heroes of comedy has framed for flesh and blood Englishmen a social attitude, a national reflex.[28]

Humor may be found in other countries than England, said the writer, but only there, until recently, was there a general consciousness of it—an awareness of a tradition. "Since the sixteenth century the word *humour* has constantly accompanied the phenomenon [in England], giving it a coherence, if not rational at least empirical, and binding it to a phenomenon equally empirical, of a kind both psychological and social."[29]

English humor, Escarpit felt, reached its peak in the eighteenth century and gradually declined in the nineteenth because of the decorum imposed by the Victorian temperament. Humor sprang up, however, in America, especially in Mark Twain.

> We can see how much separates Mark Twain from the mechanics of laughter that are the most renowned humorists of England, brothers of Jerome K. Jerome and P. G. Wodehouse. The fellow-prankster of Tom Sawyer, the printer, the pilot on the Mississippi, the gold miner, the journalist cares little for the intellectual comfort of his readers. But none of the lessons of the great masters of the eighteenth century is forgotten. There is something of Sterne, of Smollett, and of Fielding in this sentimental journey of American eccentrics in Europe, *Innocents Abroad*. There is also in Mark Twain much of the somber Swiftian metaphysic.[30]

With twentieth-century mass communication and rapid transportation, American humor has spread—to England, to France, and to the world. *The New Yorker* was especially credited, by Escarpit, with revitalizing humor in the contemporary world. Humor is now no longer a national characteristic of the English, but is universal. The term *humour*—finally admitted into the dictionary of the French Academy in 1932—has brought to consciousness the empiric thing itself in virtually all the nations of the world.

In Part II of *L'Humour,* Escarpit undertook a philosophical analysis of the phenomenon *humour.* Like Las Vergnas, he recognized the conflict between the intellectualist and affectivist theories and attempted to reconcile them. Each theory he said is partly right. There are two movements *(temps)* in the "dialectic" of humor; the first primarily intellectual, the second affective. Each movement is composed of three aspects:

> 1. The ironic paradox, which is the first movement of *l'humour,* is obtained by placing in sudden contact the daily world with a world deliberately reduced to the absurd.
>
> 2. The reduction to absurdity is obtained by the voluntary suspension of accepted beliefs accompanied by a mental comportment otherwise perfectly normal and above all perfectly logical.
>
> 3. The suspended belief is that of a given social group and the humoristic paradox exists only for the members of the social group accepting the belief—which explains, by the way, why the *humour* of a given country is often inaccessible to the inhabitants of another country.

So far, the process requires a deliberate detachment that is purely intellectual. However, the second movement involves the emotions.

> 1. The situation created by the reduction to absurdity, obtained by means of the humoristic paradox, is intolerable and calls a second time for humor, which would cause affirmation to follow negation.
>
> 2. This second time, which especially involves the feelings, comprises essentially an attitude of faith, confidence, or at least affective solidarity toward the humorist and, through him, toward the world order that his irony is intended to unsettle and that he alone has the power to reestablish.

> 3. The humorist invites his reader to this "rebound" from the absurd by some more or less subtle indications, which are sometimes implicit, but, while creating a complicity between man and man, are intelligible only in a given social group—thus, there is imposed on humor a second level of human localization.[31]

In the "second movement of the dialectic of humor" the emphasis is then on the humorist and his relation to the reader. There must be a mutual understanding, a complicity between them. Or perhaps it could be phrased thus: the humorist must pose as a detached narrator but the reader must understand that the pose is a pose and that he and the humorist share something, more or less secretly, in common. The humorist's complicity is revealed by his individual manner. What is hidden behind the pose is the character of the humorist, his attitude toward life. In conclusion, Escarpit declared, humor is an art of existing.

> It seems . . . that at the end of this study it may be possible to make out a general form, a movement, an intention—what the English language would call a *pattern* (a word for which, to the displeasure of the purists, there is no translation). It is a will and at the same time a means of breaking the circle of automatisms which—fatally maternal—social life and life itself crystalize about us as a protection and a shroud. A man without humor lives the life of a larva, under its envelope of silk, sure of a future without permanence, half-conscious, unchangeable. Humor bursts the cocoon into life, progress, the risks of existing. Most often it brings forth only an uninteresting and vulgar mite; but sometimes the multicolored butterfly of a laugh like that of the gods springs forth, or indeed one may divine in the shadow of the mysterious unfolding of wings a moth the color of night.[32]

So ended Escarpit's *L'Humour*. Rhetoric aside, he brought together the affective and intellectual views of humor as well as the historical interpretation of the word and the actual phenomenon itself. Humor is a completely conscious act on the part of the humorist, contrasting the real world with a world of absurdity, but relying on the character of the humorist to bring the reader back from the world of nonsense to a changed view of the world of reality. Humor is a revolt against stultifying conventions; nothing should be immune from it; it opens the door to new understanding.

An even more recent work on humor is Albert Laffay's *Anatomie de l'humour et du nonsense* (1970). Again, it was the relationship of rationality and of feeling to humor that was at the center of the author's thinking. "The humorist," he said, "reproduces reality, not without deforming it more or less, but always pretending with a certain complaisance to be perfectly objective." His objectivity, however, is merely feigned. Actually he identifies himself with the apparent object of his ridicule.

> He puts himself *on the side of* [his] pretended victim, who finally is not a victim. He caricatures him in his main features, or so finely that one can hardly doubt his veracity: in all cases the humorist assimilates himself to his "victim." When he attacks, it is from the interior, as one might attack oneself. The impassive style hides a profound sympathy. . . . His *he* appears as a *you* and finally as an *I*. . . . The imperturbable expression of the humorist shows that the passion of vengeance with him, at least in appearance, is better than dissimulated: it is dominated. Humor *recognizes* existence, in the same sense that one *recognizes* someone that he has seen before; in the manner also that we say that a patrol has *reconnoitered* a little woods; and finally as one says of a father that he *knows* his child. The known is refound, explored, and finally accepted.

Humor is not logical; in fact, the humorist accepts with a certain relish the illogicality of life.

> Humor brings out, to the accompaniment of a certain inward satisfaction, the incoherence of men and events. It is not rational in principle; it takes pleasure, rather, in the profound absurdity of things. . . . To say the *absurdity* of the world is perhaps to speak badly of it. As for existence, it will be more exact to retain the word *irrational,* regretting meanwhile that there is no word *a-rational,* which would express better the insufficiency of all reasonable explanation.[33]

Laffay's definition of humor, then, was "a manner, deliberately impassive and with a quasi-scientific attention to minutiae, of describing the bizarre, the unusual, or the ridiculous, with the ulterior motive of making us accept its particularity under the effect of a mutual tolerance."

The French critics defined *l'humour* analytically and impressionistically—historically, esthetically, and psychologically. About the only thing that they agreed on was that the term refers to a phenomenon characteristically Anglo-Saxon, though it may occasionally be found outside the British Empire and the United States. The sum of their impressions, however, though often contradictory, can reveal a great deal about the French perspective of English and hence American humor. Indeed contradiction itself was often considered to be an element of humor. Historically, *l'humour* was held to be a combination of English "puritanism" and French mirth, with a special interest in human character deriving from comic stage types. It is thus a solemn or straight-faced rendering of absurdities, or, on the other hand, a joking manner with serious import. It is moral to the point of gloominess. Its content is often, perhaps always, moral or social; frequently it is criticism of society on moral grounds. It was often said to present a contrast between the real world and the ideal; for example, everyday meanness presented as if the humorist thought it were ideal behavior. Hence, it involves a split in the humorist's character, a pretense that he is unaware of the incongruity that he is expressing, a pose, a mask, a complicity. The person behind the mask may be compassionate, bitter, angry, good-humored, but we can only infer this from his manner.

The contrast between the real and the ideal leads to an emphasis on the former in order to point up its faults and absurdities. In fact, realistic detail was often held to be essential to *l'humour.* In its attention to everyday detail it was thought to be vulgar (though never immoral) and democratic. It was further believed by some to be a manifestation of liberty, in its freedom to criticize.

On the other hand, some critics stressed the unreality of *l'humour;* that is, its extravagance and fantasy. They maintained its relation to pure nonsense, which they attributed to a childishness or immaturity in British character. This charge was even more frequent in regard to American humor.

In the twentieth century, the Bergsonian theory of the comic, including humor, dominated French criticism in spite of the unresolved conflict between the intellectualists and the affectivists. Louis Cazamian followed Bergson in insisting on the purely intellectual or mechanical nature of the humorist's activity. And even his chief challengers, Floris Delattre and Robert Escarpit, tried to reconcile their belief in the emotional involvement of the humorist with other implications of Bergson's position. Most critics agreed, particularly, on transposition as the essence of humor. The humorist must act in two worlds at once, must adroitly juggle two frames of reference. In *l'humour,* these were the real world and an ideal or fantastic world.

Although discussion of the nature of *l'humour* will no doubt continue, French criticism of it reached a very high degree of sophistication in the twentieth century. It was now time to concentrate this wisdom on the mainstream of contemporary *humour,* which was to be found in the United States. But French critics were slow to define American humor as distinct from humor in general. They felt that American humor stemmed from the British and was therefore essentially British. At the turn of the century, Lautrec noted this and asserted that the chief distinction was in the subject matter, which, in turn, influenced the imagery and turns of phrase.[34] Others, such as Maurois, believed that American humor relied on overstatement whereas British humor used understatement: America "has discovered that one can free himself from reality, not only by belittling it in a tone of indifference but on the contrary by painting it larger than nature."[35]

In an essay on the humor of New York in 1929, Cazamian saw humor as a significant aspect of American character and American strength:

> New York has a sense of humor. It allows the foreigner who mocks and passes on to have his say. It even asks for it. Is not tolerance the virtue of the strong? Does not America hold the present and the future?[36]

John Charpentier (1880–?), however, was not so pleased with American humor. As late as 1935 he wrote that French *esprit* was sociable, English humor was individualistic, Irish humor carried individualism to the point of revolution, while American humor went even further: it was purely destructive. Using Mark Twain as representative, he said: "This is Homais, dressed in the feathers of the redskin and dancing the scalp dance around the body of Pallas Athena, after having completed his devotions before the altar of the Machine-God." And again: "I see in him [Twain] the incarnation of an art in which muscle participates as much as intelligence."[37] Grudgingly, however, he recognized American humor as a powerful force and as illustrative of the coming age.

In the anthology of *l'humour* by Jacques Sternberg, Jacques Bergier, and Alex Grall, *Les Chefs d'oeuvre du sourire* (1964), the preface was by Sternberg (1923–), one of the most effective contemporary promoters of American humor. Sternberg did not attempt to add much to the discussion of the essence of humor, but he did emphasize a point that occasionally turns up in the explications of black humor, a point that calls to mind the humor of Poe and the interpretations of Baudelaire.

> There is a singular correlation between humor and terror. . . . Most of the great humorists were equally tempted by the fantastic and the nightmarish, and . . . finally the common ground of all humorists is simply lucidity, a terrible lucidity of the first degree to which is naturally added aggressiveness. Humor, then, should be less a literature than a way of seeing things, a vision deformed and deforming, and the ability to translate this vision not with lyrical howling but with a smile, preferably frozen, sometimes contemptuous. But polite. A little condescending.[38]

Perhaps more than a hint of Freudian theory is in those lines.

Sternberg readily pointed out that the majority of the humorists selected in the anthology were Americans (the rest were chiefly French and English): "This is neither an accident nor a need for exoticism: it is proof that the humorists of the United States have taken a certain lead over our old Europe, which is still under the yoke of analyzing the humane God, and, even optimistically, we must admit that we have little chance of catching up for several years, certainly not in a single volume."[39] Perhaps Sternberg overstated the case, but his view seems to be rather generally held in France today: that is, American humor has taken over the heritage of English humor and is now leading the rest of the world to both an understanding and an adoption of *l'humour*.

3

The Age of Franklin

French criticism of American humor from the eighteenth century to World War I may be divided into four periods. The age of Franklin—to 1820—was a period of sanguine anticipation. America promised a paradise where men would be close to nature (primistivistic and agrarian) and governed by reason (rationalism, constitutionalism, liberty, equality, fraternity). American literature was confidently expected to reflect those ideals in a way that would be gloriously new to the world. From 1820 to 1835—the age of Cooper and Irving—the promise was in part fulfilled, at least by Cooper; but already there was disappointment that he and Irving were not original enough, were imitative of the English. From 1835 to 1870—the mid-century—disillusionment set in. Because of the leveling tendency of democracy, it was felt, good literature could not be expected. America (and expecially American humor) was antiaristocratic, anti-Catholic, and materialistic, and French critics could not imagine literature without aristocracy, authoritative religion, and spirituality. From 1870 to 1914—the age of Twain—the same preconceptions held. Any such writer as James, who did not fit the theory, was simply a lucky aberration. Twain had to be recognized, but he more often than not symbolized the vulgarizing effects of democracy. After World War I a great change took place. Partly because of America's new role in the world, partly because of the presence of so many Americans on French soil, partly because of increased distribution, partly because of the international and intersocial spread of the new mass media, partly because the study of American literature came of age in America—for these and other reasons French scholarship in American literature has become knowing and valuable.

From the eighteenth century, America was of interest to the French more for political and social reasons than for literary. American democracy was an object lesson from which the French could learn either to adopt its virtues or to avoid its faults. From the restoration of the Bourbons after the defeat of Napoleon in 1815 to the establishment of the Third Republic in 1870–1871, France was ruled by the authoritative hand of king or emperor. Furthermore, the majority of the National Assembly, which set up the Third Republic, were monarchists. Although there were grumblings among the middle and lower classes, French literature and criticism favored the establishment. Hence, the critics were predisposed to look down on American literature as the fruit of democracy and especially to disdain lowbrow American humor as vulgar, plebeian, dangerous. A modern French critic, Jean-Jacques Mayoux, has put the French attitude in a word that is perhaps the best brief explanation of the poor reception of American humor in France: "The people, in France, are full of humor," he said. "But our literature has been, since the seventeenth century, aristocratic."[1]

Folk humor was plentiful in France but it seldom received the notice of the critics. For example, several French critics were horrified by Mark Twain's story "Cannibalism in the Cars" but seemed unaware of the widely known French folksong "Il etait un petit navire" on the same theme. Furthermore, the theme was repeated in cartoons in the January 8, 1973, issue of the satirical weekly *Charlie Hebdo,* and the result, based on an actual occurrence, was far more revolting—deliberately so—than Twain's version. But we know little about the connections, if any, between American humor and the French people before World War I. We know that Benjamin Franklin was loved and that sayings by and about him were popular for some time after his death. We know that Washington Irving was read in the French schools. We know, of course, that there are themes and motifs in folklore that have widespread international variations. But that is about as far as the present study can go. It should be recalled that the mainstream of American humor was not accepted by serious American literary scholars until after Mark Twain's success. Native American humor was lowbrow and popular, or at best it was folklore.

Popular interest in writings from and about America began with the accounts of voyages of discovery in the New World. They appealed to a natural interest in the exotic and also to national rivalry for imperialistic exploitation. Accounts and descriptions by Spanish, English, and French travelers were eagerly absorbed. The *Jesuit Relations* of the French missionaries in Canada and the Mississippi Valley were well known.

And of course the French were keenly aware of the successful English colonies, both as a threat to French possessions in the New World and as an asylum for the Huguenots. Aside from popular and political interest, French writers drew upon the wonders of new lands for exotic material, and the philosophes found opportunity for the weaving of social theory from comparison of the primitive and colonial societies with the over-civilized Old World. By the middle of the eighteenth century, the French image of America was forming, contradictory and inconsistent as it was. The late Léonie Villard (1878–1970), one of the pioneer professors of American studies in France, wrote:

> Up to the moment when our Revolution began, America had not ceased, for more than two centuries, to nourish the spirit of adventure of our voyagers, to awaken or stimulate the attention of the cultivated public, the cupidity or naïveté of speculators, and the reflection of philosophes, at the same time that its exoticism offered themes and rich colors to the imagination of fiction writers and dramatic authors. We had then, in the domain of spirit and aside from all influence due to political vicissitudes, a long tradition which also was a long habit of interest and love in regard to America. For various reasons, this tradition had derived, even from its variety, a persistence that exterior events tended to weaken but not to eliminate.[2]

This was the tradition that greeted Benjamin Franklin when he visited France in 1767 and 1769 and again in 1776–1785, and that he knew so well how to exploit. It was based much more on imagination and speculation than on fact. It represented America as the land of the noble savage and the honest farmer, where liberty and prosperity flourished and Nature ruled. Of course, there was an obverse side of the image; there were those who saw the New World as degenerate in its flora and fauna and hence in its effects on inhabitants, and there were those who saw it as a threat to the civilization of the Old World. But the dominant view from the middle eighteenth century until the 1790s was rosy.[3]

It was, however, very serious, and left little room for an appreciation of American humor. French newspapers often reprinted American political and scientific news, but they did not reprint American humor, wit, or satire—with the exception of Franklin's. Nor was there, through the first third of the nineteenth century, any awareness of the comic and satirical strain which played an important part in American magazine and newspaper journalism from its beginnings.[4] America was a case study for serious political philosophy; its humor was irrelevant. Even Franklin, our first ambassador of American humor, was not entirely successful in creating an appreciation of it, though he succeeded brilliantly in adapting his own wit to French tastes.

Franklin's *Experiments* were published in France in 1752, and by the time he arrived as representative of the rebelling colonies in 1776 many of his writings had been published there, including a two-volume edition of his works, translated by the medical doctor and pamphleteer Jacques Barbeu Dubourg (1709–1779) in 1773. His literary reputation in France was based chiefly on his autobiography and "The Way to Wealth." Neither of those works was especially comic, and what humor there was was lost on the French. "The Way to Wealth," that compilation of prudential maxims from *Poor Richard's Almanac,* was regarded as "sublime philosophy," and went through more than thirty editions in France before 1830. The praise of the mathematician and social philosopher Antoine Caritat de Condorcet was no more extravagant than that of many others: "Nothing in the thoughts nor in the style is above the least developed intelligence, but the philosophical mind easily discovers noble aims and profound intentions."[5] No one caught the self-deprecating smile in Franklin's lines: "I own that to encourage the practice of remembering and repeating those wise sentences, I have sometimes quoted myself with great gravity." Nor were the French at all aware of the many bawdy and cynical sayings to be found in other parts of *Poor Richard's Almanac.*

Meanwhile Franklin's political writings had been taken up by the journal of the Economistes, the *Ephémérides du citoyen,* edited by the Abbé Nicolas Baudeau (1730–1792) and the Marquis de Mirabeau (1715–1789) from its beginnings to 1767 and by Pierre-Samuel Du Pont de Nemours (1739–1817) from 1767 to 1772, when it was suppressed by the government. The first piece by Franklin to be published in the *Ephémérides* (1767) was his letter "On the Price of Corn, and Management of the Poor," signed "Arator" and translated from the London *Chronicle.* It is likely that the editors did not know who wrote it, but they found, in its ironic advocacy of free trade, support for their physiocratic doctrines concerning the primacy of agriculture as against manufacture and finance. In the years following 1767, several of

Franklin's minor pieces were published in the *Ephémérides,* largely through the sponsorship of Franklin's friend Dubourg.[6]

The extent of Franklin's impact on French thought is yet to be measured. Although it is easy to trace the popularity of "The Way to Wealth" and the *Autobiography,* Franklin's influence cannot be attributed to those works alone. "We should like to suggest," said Gilbert Chinard (1881–1972), the foremost twentieth-century French student of Franklin, "that the influence of Franklin and Franklin's writing did not stop at the end of the eighteenth century and was not limited to the prosaic precepts of *Poor Richard's Almanac.* Further investigation extending through the nineteenth century may lead to the discovery of unsuspected repercussions of his philosophical thinking."[7]

Probably the first clear example of American humor to be published in France was Franklin's "An Account of the Captivity of William Henry," which in translation in the *Ephémérides* for 1769 was entitled "Mithologie et morale iroquoises." Its reception proved to be typical; it was misunderstood. Franklin's "Account" was a hoax, designed to burlesque the philosophical Indian in literature. For example, one of the myths it reported was of the great Manitta's daughter, who descended naked to earth and sat down on a hill, where she met some Oneida warriors and advised them to return to the same spot a year hence. The account read: "They came accordingly after twelve moons, and found growing where she had pressed the ground with her right hand, corn, where with her left hand, beans; and where her back parts had pressed it, there grew tobacco." Along with the piece was the French editor's comment that it "does not seem too absurd, although it is perhaps no more so, actually, than those [mythologies] of the Egyptians, the Phoenicians, the Greeks and the Romans, which comprise some very sage and true principles, under an appearance of extreme folly."

> The Iroquois mythology is simpler, and, we might say, more savage than that of those learned peoples. But also it is more closely bound to morality; and it is surprising enough to see that savages on the banks of the Ohio could, on this last point as well as on the true principles of politics that derive from it, give lessons to most of the nations of Europe.[8]

The hoax was accepted as true because it flattered the primitivistic and deistic preconceptions of the journal and its editor. The acceptance of American tall tales as fact was apparently not unusual. As late as 1813, two others of Franklin's hoaxes, "The Sale of the Hessians" and "The Boston Independent Chronicle," were published as history by "the Chevalier de Langeac," who was intent on proving the vileness of the mixed monarchy of England.[9]

On the other hand, Franklin seemed to have no trouble adapting to French *esprit,* as his bagatelles so well illustrate. The great literary historian and critic Charles Augustin Sainte-Beuve (1804-1869), many years later, called him a "prince de l'esprit." In 1790, one M. Grouvelle (probably Philippe-Antoine Grouvelle, 1757-1806, writer and statesman) extolled the brilliance of Franklin's bagatelles: "It is the naïveté and finesse of La Fontaine, it is the profundity and elevation of the Holy Scriptures and the oriental moralists, it is the concealed irony of Socrates without the prolix subtlety of Plato. Finally, it is the superior and indulgent spirit of a sage, who has judged man both in the rural frankness of the pioneer and in the artificial refinements of French politeness."[10] Extreme as that praise is, there can be no doubt of the success of Franklin's bagatelles, in all their diversity, with the society at which they were aimed. From the subtle flattery of "The Ephemera" to the innuendo of "To Madame Helvétius" to the moral simplicity of "The Whistle," Franklin knew how to appeal to the taste of the French aristocracy.

Furthermore, Franklin's sayings—and sayings attributed to him—were very much in vogue during and after his nine-year residence in France. He was quoted and misquoted, burlesqued and imitated in journals and memoirs. For example, it was reported in the *Correspondance littéraire* (August 1783) that when people questioned the value of the earliest balloon ascensions, asking "What good is this discovery that they make so much noise about?" Franklin replied, "What good is a new-born baby?" Or again, in the same journal (July 1778), was the story of Franklin's reply to the supercilious Frenchman who, during the period when Franklin was negotiating for French aid to the American rebels, attempted to start a conversation with: "One must admit, monsieur, that it is a great and superb spectacle which America offers us today." The terse reply was, "Yes, but the spectators do not pay." One of the coarsest anecdotes, but also one of the most popular, was recorded by Charles Pougens in his *Lettres philosphiques . . . sur divers sujets de morale et de littérature* in 1826. When the British Parliament was considering the repeal of the Stamp Act, someone suggested that the colonists should at least pay for the printing of the stamps. Franklin responded with the story of the French ironworker who offered to thrust a red-hot iron rod into the rump of a passerby. When the offer was refused, he demanded: "At least pay me for my coals."[11]

But as far as humor is concerned, Franklin's success was entirely personal. Above all, it was his personality that created the greatest sensation in France. According to a recent study, "Virtually every French memoir or collection of letters of the period had something to say about Franklin." He was portrayed in the fiction, drama, poetry, and oratory of the age. It seemed that with his skill at pleasing, he was everything to everybody. "His acquaintances called him Excellence, his friends called him Docteur, his intimates, men and women, called him Papa."[12] He was admired by Voltaire, who pictured him as the Good Quaker. To the physiocrats, he was a champion of agrarianism. To followers of Rousseau, he was the primitive backwoods philosopher. Thus the myth began, a myth that powerfully influenced French views of America and American literature for at least a century. Frenchmen expected to look at America, as they had looked at Franklin, and see the reflection of their own ideals.

Yet even Franklin had his detractors—often inspired by British propagandists and implemented by confirmed French royalists. Louis XVI, whose politics were not in agreement with Franklin's though he consented to aiding the American Revolution, presented as a gift to the Comtesse Diane de Polignac a chamber pot with Franklin's portrait painted inside. Nor did the appreciation of Franklin's wit carry over to an appreciation of American humor in general, at least not among the literate classes. Contact with American humor was virtually nonexistent in France, but the reaction to American theater of one of the French emigrés to America in the 1790s, Moreau de Saint Méry, foreshadowed later criticisms of American humor whenever the intellectuals deigned to look at it: "The performances of the interludes are boisterous and even indecent. It is by no means rare to hear such words as 'God damn,' 'b____', 'rascal' and 'son-of-a-bitch.' The women turn their backs to the stage during these interludes. . . . The plays, English or in the English style, are extremely coarse and of a humor repugnant to good taste."[13] There is no particular reason to doubt the justice of Saint Méry's criticism, but his views, and those of numerous contemporaries, were to set the pattern for the stereotype of the vulgarity of American humor for decades to come. The age of Franklin—because of Franklin—was the period of the greatest success of American humor in France until after World War II; but already in the 1790s a reaction had set in. Despite Franklin's personal achievement, the French literati were prepared to look at American humor, if at all, as a crude excrescence of democratic libertarianism.

4

The Age of Cooper and Irving

Very little critical notice was accorded American literature in France until the 1820s. Scholars and commentators continued to be interested in American society, American science, and American scenery, but they relegated the literature of the New World to a place of insignificance. With the crumbling of the dream of the social and political perfectibility of America, it became fashionable to be disappointed in American accomplishments. Especially in literature was the dream unfulfilled. In place of the wished-for magical emergence of a full-blown original literature, completely independent of Old World influences and representative of the natural grace and liberty of the new Eden, only weak imitations of British models appeared, without originality and unworthy of critical analysis. The developing American society, French observers deduced, was inimical to the spirituality and imaginativeness necessary to the arts. The view of Félix de Beaujour (1765–1836), Napoleon's consul-general in the United States, was not altogether unreasonable when we consider the state of American literature in 1814 when these words were published, but it was a view that was to be repeated by others for decades to come.

> We may presume Americans will never have, or will have after only many years, a national literature, for they have no national language, and English literature, so rich in every genre, will for a long time supply their lack. Moreover a nation, no matter how enlightened, can scarcely hope to have a literature until it has a distinctive character, of which the literature is a faithful expression. Americans still do not have any such character, and they still form less a people than an amalgam of several peoples.[1]

Behind much of the ill feeling reflected in French criticism of America lay the diverging politics of the two nations. As France succumbed to another long period of monarchical rule, the United States moved toward Jacksonian democracy. Most of the French critics, reacting against the excesses of the French Revolution and its aftermath, viewed American society with suspicion and American literature with what was almost contempt.

A more favorable impression of American literature was reflected in a brief, anonymous comment reprinted in an American periodical in 1824 (here reproduced in full). The French writer's views were restrained. But by this time, he could not fail to notice the achievements of Washington Irving and James Fenimore Cooper, and he looked forward to the greater exploitation of native American subject matter.

> Within a few years, America has produced several distinguished authors. Washington Irving was the first to start in the career of romance, and he has been followed by several of his countrymen. Mr Cooper in "The Spy," and in "The Pioneers," has signalized himself as the pupil of a great master, Sir Walter Scott; but he reminds us too often, in his best scenes, that he is only an imitator. Still, we must congratulate America upon these achievements in the regions of imagination. Although not rich in ancient tradition, she presents to her historians, subjects full of interest—the energetic character of a people which has founded its own liberty, industry, and commerce—the animated and glorious scenes of a recent war, undertaken in a noble cause—the struggles of the savage aborigines with the civilization which threatened to overwhelm them; and the mixture of the English and American manners and customs.[2]

While the critics ignored or condescended, however, American literature was beginning to find an audience in France. The works of Franklin continued to be published and read. Joel Barlow, who was given honorary French citizenship in the 1790s, was well known. Charles Brockden Browne's *Wieland* was probably the first American novel to be translated into French (1808).[3] Catherine Maria Sedgwick's romantic and moral novels were known at least by the 1830s. James Kirke Paulding was recognized as one of the authors of *Salmagundi,* which was printed in English in Paris in 1824; and between 1829 and 1833 several of his works were published in translation. But by far the most popular American writers, from the 1820s to the 1840s, were Cooper and Irving, both of whom were abundantly translated into French.

Aside from Franklin, Irving, and Paulding, none of these writers contributed appreciably to American humor. Barlow's polemical satire could rarely be called funny, and he was best known for his idealistic *Columbiad*. Cooper's attempts at humor generally bored the French, though a reviewer in the *Revue de Paris* in 1835 admired the satire in his *The Monikins*—"both an entertaining romance and a philosophical satire of actual society."[4] Popular as Cooper was, and popular as he has remained in France, he can hardly be said to have transmitted any appreciation of American humor abroad.

Quite the opposite is true of Washington Irving. Though not quite as popular as Cooper, he was introduced to French readers by a notice in the *Mercure étranger* in 1814, and after 1820 most of his books were republished in French within a year after their original publication: *Voyage d'un Américain à Londres* (*The Sketch Book,* 1819-20) in 1821, *Le Château de Bracebridge* (*Bracebridge Hall,* 1822) in 1823, *Contes d'un voyageur* (*Tales of a Traveller,* 1824) in 1825, *Histoire de New York* (*History of New York,* 1809) in 1827, *Salmagondis* (*Salmagundi,* 1807-1808) in 1833, and *Contes de l'Alhambra* (*The Alhambra,* 1832) in 1833. This list does not begin to illustrate his success. His stories were translated individually in magazines—"The Wife," from *The Sketch Book,* even before 1820—and his biographical and historical works were translated. Furthermore, there were new translations of his fiction through the nineteenth century and in the twentieth. And works of Irving were recommended in the list of English authors to be studied in the French schools in the nineteenth century.[5] Probably Irving has been the most popular American humorist in France, rivaled only by Franklin and Mark Twain.

Critical notice both led and followed popular acclaim. Before the founding of the *Revue des deux mondes* in 1829, its leadership was both casual and infrequent. Besides the *Mercure étranger* (1813-1814) brief notices and occasional translations appeared in the *Revue encyclopédique,* published between 1819 and 1832 by Marc-Antoine Jullien; in *Le Globe* in the 1820s; and in the two journals, the *Messenger* and the *Literary Gazette,* published by John Anthony Galignani and William Galignani, publishers of English and American books in Paris.[6] Irving received the intermittent attention of these and a few other magazines, but it was not until the 1830s that his work came under the careful scrutiny of important French critics, namely Antoine Fontaney (1803–1837), the romantic poet and essayist, and Philarète-Euphemon Chasles (1798–1873), the leading critic of American literature in the mid-century—both in the *Revue des deux mondes.*

The recurrent criticism of Irving—as also of Cooper—was that he lacked originality. As early as 1827, one E. D. in *Le Globe* found that Irving seemed to write "under the eyes of England and not under those of his mother country." Adélaïde Montgolfier in the *Revue encyclopédique* (1831) praised him for making the most of "a small talent and a small wit." And Fontaney in the *Revue des deux mondes* (1832) concluded: "This, the author of *The Alhambra,* is a very witty and elegant writer; but the more carefully one studies him, the better one perceives that he fails completely in originality. He can marvelously employ four or five manners, but they are all assumed; he has not a manner of his own."[7]

Fontaney's remark, however unsympathetic, may be the first French recognition of the comic mask that was an important part of American humor. Irving's Diedrich Knickerbocker was almost as pedantic as James Russell Lowell's Homer Wilbur (in *The Bigelow Papers*) and as straight-faced as Samuel Clemens's Huckleberry Finn; and the humor of his *History of New York* derived largely from the contrast between matter and manner. And Irving could also pose as Jonathan Oldstyle, Launcelot Langstaff, or Geoffrey Crayon. Irving's "manners" were contrived for comic effect. In fact, the comic pose is a major technique in the whole tradition of American humor, from Franklin's Silence Dogood to Sinclair Lewis's Lowell Schmaltz—and beyond. The hoax, the tall tale, and the burlesque—all elements in native American humor—are dependent on a comic mask. It was not until the French began to penetrate that mask that they began to understand American humor.

On the other hand, there is something to be said for Fontaney's charge of imitativeness. Irving did cater to British tastes in his struggle to achieve recognition in England. Fontaney, who perhaps discovered Irving's work in England, where he resided for a while, recognized the influence of English literature on Irving—an influence that was reiterated by other French critics.

> Take the first *Sketch Book,* the *Tales of a Traveller, Bracebridge Hall.* What do you find? Often the harmonious grace of Addison, sometimes the verve of Swift, sometimes the caprice and whimsies of Sterne, also the amiable sweetness and sentimental nonchalance of Mackenzie. Where is Washington Irving?

Also frequently cited by French critics was Oliver Goldsmith, who certainly influenced the American writer, and Charles Lamb, who was a contemporary if not an influence. It is true that Irving's work belongs to the tradition of sentimental humor, yet where else was he to begin if not within the traditions of English literature? He could hardly create his own traditions, as the French apparently expected him to do.

Furthermore, though Irving deliberately set out to please his English readers, he might never have been heard of in France if he had not. For the French relied on British judgments of American works before accepting them themselves. Fontaney tacitly admitted as much. Cooper and Irving were the only American writers, he said,

> whose reputation, crossing the sea from the United States and arriving in England, the mother country, has spread from there and solidly established itself in the rest of Europe. What certifies their vogue and success with us is the promptness with which our publishers have released reprints and translations of their books and the eagerness with which they are sought by the public.[8]

An anonymous reviewer in the *Revue encyclopédique* (1828) was even franker in his dependence on English reviewers and publishers: "Before judging [a work], one would do well to consult our neighbors overseas. . . . If the English give [it] an eager reception, our translators can set to work, but if the public of London neglects the new American production, the Parisians will receive it still more coldly."[9] Thus, American writers were caught in a crossfire of French prejudices. If they were not accepted in England, they were not read in France. If they were accepted in England, they were unoriginal.

Chasles summed up in 1844 what by then had become the established judgment of Irving:

> The charming style of Washington Irving is composed of an elegant imitation of Addison and of a felicitous study of the old

> poets. It is difficult to carry agreeableness and ingenious sweetness further than M. Irving; he is neither forceful nor profound. His scenery is sweet and velvety, his illumination pure and well disposed, his characters are happily grouped like those of Wouwerman; like the painter he is exempt from neither monotony nor mannerism.[10]

That Irving was an imitator was by now taken for granted. The French were also quick to note his lack of vigor and depth—faults, if they are faults, that must be admitted. On the other hand, like most of his English and American critics, the French generally praised the charm and perfection of his style.

Such praise would seem to indicate an appreciation of Irving's humor, as would the regular classification of the American writer with the English sentimental humorists. And such was the case, whether or not the French readers caught all the comic nuances of Irving's prose. As might be expected because of its local subject matter, the Knickerbocker *History of New York* was the least popular of Irving's fiction in France, although it was the most replete with native American humor. Yet one important critic, Fontaney, ranked it as the author's best. There was no real analysis of Irving's humor among the French reviews and criticisms; still, the critics continually described his fiction as *spirituel, charmant, piquant, satirique, amusant,* and *heureuse.* The reviewer in *Le Globe* in 1827 felt that *Bracebridge Hall* was "sometimes amusing, sometimes tiresome," but he was more enthusiastic about *The Sketch Book:* "One may say that nothing more piquant and original has appeared since the days of Sterne."[11] An anonymous reviewer in the *Revue encyclopédique* in 1828 found "passages full of charms" in Irving's work.[12] And Fontaney noted "the grace and elegance of his style, the *esprit* and agreeableness of its details."

"His satirical history of New York," he added, "is still unquestionably the wittiest and most piquant of his works. *Bracebridge Hall,* with its exaggerated humorists and its forced descriptions of old English customs, does not compare with the precious sketches and the curious content of *Salmagundi.*"[13]

As Fontaney's criticism illustrates, the French critics generally found Irving at his best in his descriptions of American scenes and manners. The natural phenomena and the social conditions of the United States were what they were most interested in. Consequently, they admired the native content in the work of both Irving and Cooper, often to the neglect or the disparagement of their other attributes.

Furthermore, one can detect a feeling of resentment toward Irving's love of England. The English were still the traditional foes of France; and in spite of their reliance on English publishers, French critics could still disapprove of English manners and customs. The reviewer in *Le Globe*—twelve years after the Battle of Waterloo—found Irving's descriptions of private life in England too flattering. Fontaney concluded his essay with the observation that Irving's work would not survive: "We would wish that, in the interest of the perpetuation of his name, Washington Irving had applied his craft and talent more often to subjects that he could treat uniquely and without rivals, to fantasies purely transatlantic, such as the *History of New York* and *Salmagundi*."[14]

But Irving's work did survive, in France as well as in the United States. In the 1960s at least two editions of works by Irving, one in French and one in English, were published in Paris; and the Bibliothèque Nationale acquired five of his books in modern American and English editions. By all indications, he continues to be read and is, in fact, one of the best known American authors in France.

5
The Mid-Century

Literary criticism in the period I have called the mid-century was even more politically and socially oriented than before. During this period France was ruled by Louis Philippe's July Monarchy from 1830 to 1848, and by Louis Napoleon, first as President of the Second Republic, 1848–1852, and then as Emperor Napoleon III, 1852–1870. The prevailing temper of the government, despite the Revolution of 1848, was conservative and monarchistic. Democracy was to be shunned as contrary to the interests of those in power and to the ideals of civilization and culture. The United States was accepted now as more than an experiment; in fact, it was frequently seen, along with Russia, as the great power of the future; but in the French ruling class it excited more fear than envy. It was observed assiduously and often keenly, but largely as an object lesson of what France should avoid. It was portrayed as a land of violence (but compare the riots, rebellions, and successful and unsuccessful coups d'état in France during the period). Its institutions were felt to be suppressive to art, idealism, and culture. Materialism was rampant and the dollar was god. And all things were leveled to the desires and abilities of the average man.

That was the view of the establishment, but it was not necessarily the view of the majority. French liberals continued to look on America as the symbol and expression of freedom, democracy, and republicanism. They pointed with partisan glee at its material wealth, its physical growth, its opportunities for the individual, and its religious tolerance. In the 1860s, Abraham Lincoln joined Franklin and Jefferson as heroes of the cause of liberty, and the French were virtually unanimous in expressing sympathy at the time of his death.[1]

French critics, however, were as reactionary as the government. Sainte-Beuve, for example, though not especially interested in American literature, changed from ardent democrat to a believer in limited monarchy, and held government positions under both Louis Philippe and Napoleon. Nineteenth-century literary critics valued American literature chiefly for what it told them about American society; or rather—too often—they valued it according to how well it fit their preconception of American society. Disillusioned with democracy in France, they were bound to find fault with "democratic" literature.

Still, the mid-century was the period of the first extensive criticism of American literature. According to one twentieth-century scholar: "Before 1835 American literature can hardly be said to have had a real critic in France."[2] The new interest was expressed mainly in one magazine, the *Revue des deux mondes,* and by one man, Philarète Chasles.

After an unsuccessful beginning in 1829, the *Revue des deux mondes* was purchased in 1831 by François Buloz, a shepherd boy who, with the help of a benefactor, had made good. In fact, with the *Revue des deux mondes* and later the *Revue de Paris,* he became a wealthy man. Under Buloz's hand, the *Revue des deux mondes* became an important instrument of French thought, publishing some of the most important French writers as well as reviews and translations of English and American writers. Its editorial policy was conservative, both politically and literarily; it favored the romantic and idealistic writing of the earlier part of the century and disapproved the realism of the 1840s. It had a strong influence on French criticism and especially on criticism of American literature through the rest of the century.[3]

Chasles began writing for the *Revue* in 1835. Son of a member of the Revolutionary Convention who voted for the execution of Louis XVI, he nevertheless represented the dominant aristocracy in his criticism of America. He was associated with the *Revue britannique* at its founding in 1825 and for many years after. He was one of the major literary critics of the nineteenth century, and he brought to the attention of the French reading public the literatures of England, Germany, Scandinavia, Spain, Italy, and the Orient, as well as that of the United States.

His approach to American literature was conditioned by his attitude toward America: "a horrible example of the effects on a people of the mercantile and industrial spirit that Europe is beginning to adopt."[4] His disillusionment with the great experiment was complete. True literature could not exist under the ascendancy of the money grabbers and the tyranny of the majority. Nor could there be any national literature without a national religion, which "one could embrace without effort and with which he could mingle his own individuality."[5]

The job of the critic, according to Chasles, was to observe and interpret the trends of modern culture: "True criticism, perpetually vigilant, has better things to do than weigh syllables and analyze styles; it should show what directions human activity is incessantly taking."[6] For him, America represented above all the trend of the present and future—a trend that was leading civilization into another Dark Ages.

> Did the Greek period not have its epilogue and its long train of twilight? Did the vast domination of Roman intelligence not give way for three centuries before the emergence of the modern spirit? To consider the European and Christian people as but the aggregate of modern civilization, to see feudal and monarchical institutions only in their totality—is not this vast organism falling into fragments that are dissolving here, are rotting away there, and are elsewhere held up by tottering props, which are but fragile themselves? Finally, is not the definitive and complete expression of this ruin of the monarchies the society of North America? And is not one of the evident proofs of this ruin the irresistible return to the savage life that we have previously noted in the facts and in the books of this country?
>
> Everything shows itself under a new face; the spark of life is hidden under cinders. The elements of force abound, and among these elements, which play and will long play their role of destruction and abasement before reaching their phase of creation and organic wholeness, must be placed in the front line this materialization of the intelligence, this domination of industrial procedures, this vulgarization of ideas and facts, and this general assimilation of weak doctrines.[7]

In spite of the gloominess of Chasles's picture, he offered a glimmer of hope for the future when the new culture should reach its "phase of creation and organic wholeness." Chasles did not predict what that phase would bring, but he indicated a preference for that future over the future foreshadowed by the other world power he saw emerging. "Of the two new and menacing societies which are evolving, the one under the law of the Czar, the other under the invocation of Washington, the most interesting in its energy, its traditions, its Teutonic heritage, and its free form is North America."[8]

Chasles's views had much in common with those of the foremost French observer of America, Alexis de Tocqueville (1805–1859), and it is likely that the two writers influenced each other. The first part of Tocqueville's *De la démocratie en Amérique* was published some months after Chasles's 1835 review, "De la littérature dans l'Amérique du nord," in the *Revue des deux mondes,* and the second part, which contained Tocqueville's reflections on American literature, did not appear until five years later. On the other hand, Tocqueville's work—based as it was on his sojourn in the United States in 1831 and 1832—seems to have influenced all subsequent French criticism of America.

Tocqueville's observations on American literature were few and general. "The inhabitants of the United States have then, at present, properly speaking, no literature," he wrote in 1840. "I am convinced that they will ultimately have one; but its character will be different from that which marks the American literary productions of our time, and that character will peculiarly be its own."[9] And he went on to predict the character of the literature of the future:

> Taken as a whole, literature in democratic ages can never present, as it does in the periods of aristocracy, an aspect of order, regularity, science, and art; its form will, on the contrary, ordinarily be slighted, sometimes despised. Style will frequently be fantastic, incorrect, overburdened and loose,—almost always vehement and bold. Authors will aim at rapidity of execution, more than at perfection of detail. Small productions will be more common than bulky books: there will be more wit than erudition, more imagination than profundity; and literary performances will bear marks of an untutored and rude vigor of thought,—frequently of great variety and singular fecundity. The object of authors will be to astonish rather than to please, and to stir the passions more than to charm the taste.[10]

French criticisms of American literature—and especially of American humor—throughout the rest of the century seem to be simply illustrations and specific evidences of the presumptive truth of Tocqueville's predictions. No matter how precise and craftsmanlike the American writer, the critic was on the alert for signs of the vulgarizing effects of majority rule and industrialization. It only remained for Chasles to add in 1844: "I readily believe that the first man of genius to whom this people will give birth will be some great satirist."[11] And so we see before us Mark Twain—not only the real Twain but the mythical one that the French were prepared to find, displaying in full scope all the qualities that Tocqueville—and Chasles too—predicted.

Tocqueville's prediction was accurate for at least one important segment of American literature—that which grew out of journalism and popular literature. The revolution in journalism brought on by the penny newspaper — a revolution that made the newspaper into something like the mass medium that it is today — had barely begun when Tocqueville made his visit to the United States. His perceptions, therefore, were brilliant. "The only authors whom I acknowledge as American," he said, "are the journalists. They, indeed, are not great writers, but they speak the language of their countrymen, and make themselves heard by them."[12] Since the tradition of American crackerbox humor developed largely in the newspapers, Tocqueville's remarks are pertinent.

Chasles, too, was concerned with American popular literature, though not specifically with the newspapers. Like Tocqueville he saw in it the signs of the future, and he was even less pleased. In an article entitled "Littérature pseudo-populaire en Angleterre et en Amérique" (1847), he noted the growth of "vulgar novels" and sensational autobiographies. These works were pseudopopular because, according to his use of the term, they did not really speak for the people but were foisted upon them by the merchandisers.

> Within the last few years, the United States and England have thrown on the market — the commercial expression is here the proper term — more than twenty works attributed to men of the people, fabricated by speculators in literary merchandise, and simulating the joys and sorrows of the poor, the complaints of the workers, the remorse of habitual criminals. These are some of the recent products that seem to me to serve as indices of a new literature with popular pretensions, incomplete and mendacious, full of desires and aspirations, and so far quite sterile in results.
>
> The newcomer in the course of civilizations, North America, is bold in this genre; it affects an aristocratic familiarity; it does not hide its anti-idealistic tendencies and its love of materialistic and violent portrayals. It outrages and openly attacks the spiritual end of art.[13]

The books that Chasles was reviewing in that article merited his scorn. In an earlier review, "Des tendances littéraires en Angleterre et en Amérique" (1844), he was somewhat less scathing. Here, among a number of other books, he considered the *Career of Puffer Hopkins* by Cornelius Mathews (New York, 1842) and *The Adventures of Tom Stapleton* by John M. Moore

(New York, 1843)—"novels, highly popular, published in quarto in a periodical entitled *Brother Jonathan* ('Jonathan' is the national type, the American John Bull), with horrible woodcuts, and giving for twelve and a half cents (about eleven sous) the value of three volumes in octavo of three hundred pages each, a little more than three sous and a half per volume."[14] Chasles's description of the "mammoth weekly" *Brother Jonathan* was accurate. It was perhaps the most important of several such periodicals of the 1840s that specialized in cheap fiction, especially some they pirated from England but including such native material as the novels of Moore and Mathews.[15] Though deploring the materialistic morality of these novels, Chasles saw in them a typical American irony "still in a raw state; it develops rudely, but it will refine itself; today its essence is singularly bitter and coarse."

Chasles's remarks are among the earliest recognitions in France of a native American humor. Although both Mathews's and Moore's novels were highly derivative of Charles Dickens in style and method, they were American in language, setting, character types, the use of hyperbole, and a broad satirical irony. As usual Chasles had a sociological explanation: "Those nations, young and old at the same time, inheritors of an ancient civilization, seeing before them an unknown world of industry and politics to conquer and organize, find themselves surrounded by such ridiculous contrasts that they are naturally inclined toward irony." The critic did not here use the word "humor," but he was referring to what we today would call humor—he certainly was not speaking of tragic irony. "It is especially in outward caricature," he said, "that Americans of the Union are talented."[16] And he was right in finding that the only merit of the two books in question, aside from their sociological value as symptoms, was their humor.

Chasles reserved the word *humour* for very special cases, and he did not define it. "Today, in France as in America and England, superior men who pretend to great honors are afraid to show themselves humorists," he wrote elsewhere in the same article. "There are hardly two or three so reckless as to dare to dream, to meditate, and not to dogmatize eternally. . . . All America possesses not one humorist; England can count only Carlyle."[17] In view of his high praise of Carlyle—of his iconoclasm, his individualism, and his bold eccentricity—it is clear that Chasles valued highly what he considered true humor.

His failure to do more than suggest the already strong surge of native American humor was probably due to his not having discovered it. Like most of his compatriots, he was dependent on the British for announcements of American books. He was aware of one crackerbox humorist however: Thomas Chandler Haliburton, creator of Sam Slick. Haliburton was a Nova Scotian, and his books (with one minor exception) were first published in England, where they were very popular.[18] *The Clockmaker; or the Sayings and Doings of Samuel Slick,* First and Second Series, were published in London in 1837 and 1838, and in Paris, both by the Galignanis and by Baudry, in 1839. The Third Series (London, 1840) was published by Baudry in 1841. Of Haliburton's other books, *The Letter-Bag of the Great Western* was published by the Galignanis in 1840, the same year it appeared in London; *The Attaché,* First and Second Series (London, 1843–1844), was published by the Galignanis and by Baudry in 1843–1845; and *The Old Judge* was published by Baudry in 1849, the same year as the London edition. These works comprised the main body of Haliburton's humorous writings. Though his works apparently were never translated into French—except for excerpts in Chasles's and Emile Montégut's articles—there was obviously a market for them in France.

It is unfortunate that one of the poorer representatives of crackerbox humor should be virtually the only one known in France before Mark Twain. Haliburton was not only comparatively inaccurate in his representation of the speech and manners of the United States; he was also generally unsympathetic toward American politics and society. Of course, Chasles could not be expected to catch the inaccuracies, and the attacks on New World culture were fuel for his fire.

The title of Chasles's review of *The Clockmaker* in the *Revue des deux mondes* (1841) was "Scènes de la vie privée dans l'Amérique du Nord," and his focus, as usual, was on the social implications of the work. Yet, his enthusiasms and his prejudices considered, his essay is one of the best that has been written on Sam Slick.

> Do not look for a novel, a history, a drama, a philosophical treatise, a travel narrative, an account, or a declamation; this dialect book, written by a colonial of Halifax—a book full of adages à la Sancho Panza and of stories worthy of Bonaventure Desperiers—is certainly the best and

> the most curious work that English literature, today so poor, has produced in the last five years. All at the same time it explains the sketchy and vital civilization of the United States, the pale and twisted civilization of Canada, and the profound torpor of the neighboring British possessions. It enters into the secret details of private manners and clarifies all that the English travelers leave in shadow.[19]

And of the characterization of Sam Slick, he said:

> Since the characters of Walter Scott, no one has invented anything better than Samuel Slick. This clock salesman of Connecticut is an excellent and spirited creation, not with *esprit* in our manner—that wit already old, a hundred times told, a little rancid, a little shabby, faded by its transmigrations, having passed through the schools, through Greece, through Rome, through Egypt, and through some thirty centuries of descendants—but a good naïve and native wit, which springs from experience as a spark from a flint: lively, brief, penetrating, not troubling with words, something like Sancho Panza turned politician, Sancho a republican. Here is the sole sensible observer of American manners.[20]

Chasles appreciated the Yankee dialect of Sam Slick, claiming that he was able to master all its niceties in less than a week. His translations of numerous passages were free and not always strictly accurate (he explained in a footnote that "Yankees" were "Americans of the south of the United States"), but his intention was to convey the spirit rather than the letter, and as one of the earliest attempts to translate American dialect into French his results are commendable. He recommended the study of the dialect to the philologists "in place of operating on the etymological cadavers" of Greek, Hebrew, and Sanskrit. "Here," he said, "are no hypotheses but realities, not conjectures invented and superimposed but incontestable facts."[21]

Chasles was not the only French critic to give Haliburton serious and admiring attention. In 1850 the young Emile Montégut (1825-1895), destined to become one of the major critics of comparative literature, reviewed *The Attaché, The Letter-Bag,* and *The Old Judge* in "Un Humoriste anglo-américain" in the *Revue des deux mondes.* His reaction was similar to Chasles's, although he felt that the Sam Slick of the later books was "more gross and more curt" than the Sam Slick of *The Clockmaker.* "This modest painter of manners," he said, "is a philosopher also, all the more so in that he does not theorize, that he has no system; but he is the most faithful mirror of a whole portion of humanity, and he could tell the destiny of America better than Mr. [Henry] Clay himself."[22]

Montégut saw Haliburton as perhaps the first original American writer, unlike Irving and Cooper and the other writers of the United States. Like them, Haliburton began with the English literary tradition but he went beyond. "Thus Halliburton [*sic*] has all the English qualities, the firmness, the force, and also all the English faults, the minuteness and the prolixity; but he has especially the fundamental quality of the British genius, humor, and that power of expression and phrasing which engraves as solidly as on steel the impressions that reality makes on the spirit and imagination. . . . Halliburton is one of the modern English writers who excel at making caricatures, the exaggeration of character; he does it as well perhaps as Dickens, and better, we think, than Thackeray." About the character of Sam Slick, Montégut was even more enthusiastic than Chasles: "Spirited, judicious, profound Sam Slick!"[23]

In a later essay, Montégut reviewed Haliburton's *The English in America,* a historical argument against the government and society of the United States. Most of the essay was a development of Montégut's theory of history as a product of the "genius of the races," and especially an application of his theory to the present and future of America. His observations of America were much like Chasles's; he noted the commercialism, the materialism, and the brutality that were supposed to be conspicuous in American life, but he was more sympathetic with the energy, the social equality, and the great future that he saw. And he condemned Haliburton for the prejudice and inconsistency of his attitudes. "Mr. Halliburton," he said, still misspelling the name, "has accustomed us to writings both more amusing and more serious beneath their light form."[24]

Like Chasles and Tocqueville before him, Montégut was concerned with the popular literature of America as symptomatic of the ideals and morals of the masses. In "Le Roman populaire et le rôle du romanesque en Amérique" in the *Revue des deux mondes* (1856) he distinguished between serious literature, "that which survives its time and the country of its birth," and popular literature, "that which is condemned to die with the generations which it nourishes, and which is never exhumed from its grave but by the curiosity of researchers and the needs of historical science." The latter, he said, "can alone help us judge, in perfect knowledge of the cause, that which one could call the *moral situation* of such and such an epoch."[25] It is interesting that in a list of popular American writers, Montégut mentioned only one humorist, Cornelius Mathews. He too seemed to be unaware of Davy Crockett, Augustus Baldwin Longstreet, or Seba Smith's Jack Downing.

However, French critics did appreciate a very different kind of American humorist, Oliver Wendell Holmes. In 1860, another major critic, Eugène-D. Forgues, considered Holmes along with G. W. Curtis and Fanny Fern (Mrs. Sara P. Parton) in "La Fantaisie aux Etats-Unis," again in the *Revue des deux mondes.* Holmes's sophisticated wit, not too far removed from French *esprit,* was difficult for Forgues to reconcile with the notion that America was inhospitable to intellect. Concerning *The Autocrat of the Breakfast-Table,* Forgues admitted Holmes's originality, his erudition, his cleverness, his literary skill, and his popularity in the United States. His criticism was eminently just; he placed Holmes somewhat below Hawthorne, Poe, and Emerson, among American writers, and in the tradition of Robert Burton and Laurence Sterne.

> He has indeed the slow, discursive allure of the old *essayists.* He knows as they did how to imitate the vagabondage of a dream or a casual conversation—grafting one idea on another, mixing one subject with another subject. He also knows how, after he has led you into the sublime regions of transcendental philosophy, to bring you down brusquely by a cunningly arranged buffoonery. These are, however, only the signs of the humorist, not humor itself.

Though he hesitated to afford him the high title of *humoriste,* Forgues could not deny the excellence of Holmes's fantasy and taste. His only explanation of the phenomenon was that "a people specially aspires toward success in those things for which nature did not intend them. . . . The Americans are known to dispute the qualities, acquired or innate, that constitute elegant literature, which the vulgar cannot comprehend and the dilettantes adore, and they have seized the first reasonable pretext to protest against this humiliating decree.—*Ed anch' io son pittore.* 'We, too, have our humorists.' "[26]

Holmes's reputation in France was good if not great. In

1862, Forgues translated his *Elsie Venner* (Boston, 1861); in 1887 appeared a good unrhymed translation of "The Last Leaf"; and *The Autocrat of the Breakfast-Table* and *The Poet at the Breakfast-Table* were translated in 1889 by Olivier de Gourcuff. He was extravagantly praised by another critic, Auguste Laugel, in the *Revue des deux mondes* in 1879:

> He has made himself a place apart in American literature, a place in the frontier; he touches on everything: science, the novel, philosophy, physiology, medicine. Add to this extensive technical knowledge an extraordinary dose of imagination, with an exquisite delicacy of heart, a very pronounced native flavor and an American kind of realism; then mix the ideality of poetry with the neatness and trenchancy of science, and you will have the principal elements of the personal genius of the author of so many popular books in the United States, . . .[27]

And according to his biographer, he was given a long, appreciative notice in *L'Echo de la semaine* at the time of his death, and another French periodical praised him as an example of the commendable achievement of New England, "that strait cradle of American civilization and genius, that little point on the coast of the Atlantic which is like the soul of the nation."[28] Despite his timely allusions and his "Yankeeism"—to quote Forgues—Holmes was comparatively well received in France.

The most important and original achievement of nineteenth-century French criticism of American humor was the discovery of the comic elements in the more serious American writers. Again, Chasles held a position of leadership. Of Herman Melville Chasles wrote:

> Here is a curious novelty, an American Rabelais. Imagine what the prodigious Pantagruel would be if our curate of Meudon had thrown on his canvas with his vigorous irony some elegiac tints, transparent and pearly, and had enhanced the invention of his arabesques with a pantheistic metaphysics. Imagine Daphnis and Chloë or Paul and Virginie dancing I know not what fantastic gavotte in the bosom of the clouds, with Aristotle and Spinoza escorted by Gargantua and Garganelle. An outrageous work, worthy of a Rabelais without gaiety, a Cervantes without grace, a Voltaire without taste—*Mardi or the Voyage Thither* [*sic*] is nevertheless one of the most singular books to have appeared in a long time on the face of the globe. One could accumulate for the purpose all the epithets that

> Mme. de Sévigné affected: a book extraordinary and vulgar, original and incoherent, sensible and senseless, badly written and mixed with dazzling pages, stuffed with interesting facts and drivel, with profound instruction and mediocre epigrams. You could call it the dream of a ship's boy who has not mastered his studies, who is drunk with hashish, and whom the wind balances on the top of a mast during a warm night in the tropics.[29]

Chasles had high praise for Melville's *Typee* and *Omoo,* especially the former: "There is a sound idea at the bottom of these amusing recitals which seem humoristic and fanciful; the germ of civilization, that is to be found in the most barbarous customs and that Mr. Melville brings out with a mixture of irony and picturesque sentiment, makes the charm of his book."[30] But *Mardi* admittedly confused him, as it has many American critics. It is interesting to note that the comparison with Rabelais was made by Evert Duyckinck in *The Literary World* (New York) in April 1849, the month before Chasles's review was published, and that Chasles's review was translated in *The Literary World* the following August. But whether or not the idea was original with him, Chasles developed it soundly, pointing out the Rabelaisian satire and allegory in *Mardi,* as well as the exaggeration and exuberance. He also recognized the hoax-like structure of the book, beginning—like Daniel Defoe, Chasles noted—with meticulous realism, and ending with extravagant fantasy. The structure was, after all, that of the American tall tale, as Melville was probably aware.

The comic element was also discovered in Nathaniel Hawthorne. In the *Revue des deux mondes* for April 15, 1852, E.-D. Forgues said: "In his prefaces it is clear—his books also confirm it—that Hawthorne belongs to the class of humorists, of humorists like Sterne and Lamb."[31] In a succeeding issue of the *Revue des deux mondes,* Emile Montégut took issue with that statement and asserted that Hawthorne had wit and fancy but no humor. The darkness of some of Hawthorne's best known work has led many critics, French and American, to overlook both his humor and his wit. Although Forgues perhaps overstated the case in classifying the American writer as a humorist, he deserves credit for recognizing the prevailing tone of good-natured indulgence of human follies and foibles in much of Hawthorne's work.

We have here a nice example of the ambiguity of the word

humour in nineteenth-century France. Forgues found Hawthorne a humorist; Montégut did not. Montégut, on the other hand, cited Haliburton as a humorist; and Chasles did not. Chasles found Carlyle to be the only contemporary example of the humorist in the English language. Forgues, in his criticism of both Hawthorne and Holmes, related the term to the English tradition of sentimental essayists—Addison, Steele, Goldsmith, Sterne, Lamb. Their humor consisted of an indulgent warmth and an individualistic style. For Montégut the true humorist was of the school of Dickens and Thackeray, and their outstanding trait was their skill at caricature. Chasles seemed to be using the term *humorist* as it was used in the middle eighteenth century in England, referring to an eccentric person—such as Carlyle showed himself to be in his writing and as Melville aspired to show himself.[32] All three critics used the term in very narrow senses and reserved it for what they considered some of the best English prose writers.

The high respect they had for the term contrasted with the way it was sometimes used in America. The puritan element in American society looked on the humorist with suspicion, if not with stolid disapproval. Even the humorists themselves often aspired to a place in "serious" literature. Mark Twain, looking back on the native American humorists of the nineteenth century, wrote: "Humorists of the 'mere' sort cannot survive. Humor is only a fragrance, a decoration."[33]

While the erudite critics of the *Revue des deux mondes* were analyzing both the popular literature of America and the serious literature of New York and Boston, other critics were examining the surprising works of Edgar Allan Poe. In 1846 E.-D. Forgues wrote in the *Revue* the first French study of him. Unacknowledged adaptations of some of Poe's stories had appeared earlier, and Isabelle Meunier translated four stories in 1847. Numerous translations followed, by Charles Baudelaire and others, but Baudelaire's "Edgar Allan Poe, sa vie et ses ouvrages" in the *Revue de Paris,* March-April 1852, is generally credited with initiating the remarkable popularity of Poe among French writers and critics. A recent American scholar has called Baudelaire's essay "the most widely-known study of an American author," though he has also pointed out that it was largely cribbed from two American critics in the *Southern Literary Messenger*—"a hoax, if you will, but a hoax that Baudelaire's master, Poe, would have appreciated to the fullest."[34]

The 1852 essay was reprinted with some revision as the preface to the first volume of Baudelaire's translations of Poe's stories, *Les Histoires extraordinaires* (1856), and as such it may be taken as representing Baudelaire's mature opinion, whether or not it was original. Only one reference to the comic appeared in that essay: Poe's stories, Baudelaire said, "contain violent buffoonery, the pure grotesque, passionate aspirations toward the infinite, and a great interest in magnetism."[35]

In further criticism, however, Baudelaire showed himself to be aware of the comic element in Poe's stories. "Poe was always great," he wrote, "not only in his noble conceptions, but also as a prankster." Baudelaire appreciated the vein of the hoax, not only in the obvious cases such as "Hans Pfaal" but in much of Poe's apparently serious work. It was an expression, according to Baudelaire, of Poe's "scorn and disgust for democracy, progress and *civilization.*" The United States was "the noble country of Franklin, the inventor of a counting-house morality," and Poe, reacting against such a society, frequently employed the hoax, exaggeration, burlesque, and a certain impertinence. Even in "The Philosophy of Composition," Poe spoke with tongue in cheek.

> I said that this article seemed marred by a slight impertinence. Confirmed advocates of inspiration would be sure to find in it blasphemy and profanation; but I believe that it is for them especially that the article has been written. Just as certain writers feign carelessness . . . so Edgar Poe, —one of the most inspired men I know, —has made a pretense of hiding spontaneity, of simulating coolness and deliberation.[36]

Although American critics have frequently found Poe humorless, the French have continuously recognized his comic aspect. For example, Baudelaire's contemporary, the novelist and irascible critic Jules Barbey d'Aurevilly (1808-1889), felt that Poe's tendency to play the jongleur in all his works prevented his achieving any higher rank than "king of the Bohemians."[37] One Brunet (probably the bibliographer Jacques-Charles Brunet, 1780-1867) in Joseph François Michaud's *Biographie universelle* (1854) recognized that Poe "amused himself by creating *canards* (if it is permissible to employ that vulgar word) to which his subtle art gave a striking verisimilitude."[38] In the twentieth century Léon Lemonnier noted Poe's infatuation with the perverse in human nature, his utilization of the canard, and his mathematical wit.[39] Marie Bonaparte, in her monumental diagnosis of Poe, *Edgar Poe, étude psychanalytique* (1933), exposed the Freudian implications of Poe's burlesque "Loss of Breath" and pointed out the "buffoonish tone" of "King Pest," the "liveliness" of "Hop-Frog," and the "tragi-comic" effect of "Never Bet the Devil Your Head."[40] And one of the most recent editors of Poe's stories, Roger Asselineau, devoted several pages of introduction to Poe the humorist. Following Marie Bonaparte, Asselineau ascribed Poe's humor to his need to reconcile the two sides of his split personality—his love of the ideal and his recognition of the real.[41]

The great tradition of Poe criticism in France can contribute an understanding of an important aspect of Poe that has often been neglected in American criticism. There truly is a comic spirit in much of Poe's prose, black as it may be. There is also a comic spirit in the writings of Melville and Hawthorne, but it has too often been overlooked by busy and overserious critics.[42] Furthermore, we are more and more recognizing what Tocqueville and Chasles foresaw in the middle nineteenth century: that popular literature was to play an important role in American culture, American literature, and American humor. Although the critics in France were often uninformed and prejudiced by their theories, they were no more so than their American counterparts. And the more closely we look at their observations and interpretations, the more we can learn from the sidelights they throw on our own observations and interpretations.

6

The Age of Twain

Aside from articles on Sam Slick in 1841 and 1850, the first substantial notice of "native American humorists" or "cracker-box philosophers" was a series of two articles in the *Revue des deux mondes* for July 15 and August 15, 1872, by Marie-Thérèse de Solms, Mme. Blanc (Th. Bentzon, 1840–1907). It was the most important recognition of the comic predecessors of Mark Twain published before the 1950s, although journalistic humor was occasionally mentioned with disdain as a part of popular literature.

Madame Bentzon dominated French criticism of American literature in the last three decades of the nineteenth century. She introduced Mark Twain, Henry James, and Walt Whitman to the French public, "but," said the *Dictionnaire de biographie française,* "it is a question whether, in introducing these foreign writers to us, she understood them very well herself." The *Dictionnaire* was too harsh. Her criticisms, though not profound, compared favorably with American criticisms of the period, and her misunderstandings were not unique. If she furthered the antidemocratic and anti-Protestant biases of her predecessors, she nevertheless recognized the vigor of the humorists and the skill of Henry James.

The humorists she discussed in her 1872 article were Artemus Ward (Charles Farrar Browne), Josh Billings (Henry Wheeler Shaw), Hans Breitmann (Charles Godfrey Leland), and Mark Twain (Samuel Langhorne Clemens). She explained:

> When M. [Jean Jacques] Ampère, returning from his *Promenade en Amérique* [1855], declared that the literature of the United States was, properly speaking, neither American nor democratic, he left out of account the humorists. His eyes fixed on the writers of the first rank, Prescott and Bryant, Emerson and Longfellow, Hawthorne and Washington Irving, whose diverse talents surely proceeded from European literature, and whom English literature particularly could claim, although

> they were inspired by the history and manners of their own country, the eminent traveler declined to rank as writers those who worked to amuse the masses. Meanwhile, from this disdained group arose poets and prose writers who were absolutely American and whom he sought elsewhere without success.[1]

She recognized the difficulty of overcoming a cultural barrier in order to understand American humor. "It must be said," Mme. Bentzon admitted, "that certain pages of *Eye-openers, Screamers,* etc.—the great reputation of which astonishes us—have all their point only for those who basically understand the corruptions that they attack."[2] She attempted, in all humility, to supply some of the necessary background, but she was not very successful. She characterized Artemus Ward, for example, as a Western folk humorist—confusing the author with the character, the Artemus Ward letters with the Artemus Ward lectures, and the occasional Midwestern and Western matter with the Down-East manner of the humorist.[3] She included in her article copious examples of the humorists' work in her own translations, although she realized the impossibility of complete accuracy in translating the misspellings, dialect, and puns.

Her final opinion of Ward, Billings, and Breitmann was not unjust, except that she preferred Leland's Hans Breitmann above the others. "An agreeable mixture," she said, "of good sense, honest mirth, fair and fine raillery, heightened by a deliberate dose of Yankee salt—such is the entire talent of Josh Billings, and this talent is not to be disdained. Above him, above Artemus Ward, we must place Hans Breitmann, or, to give him his true name, M. Charles Leland." Her peculiarly French reason for preferring Leland was that he ridiculed the Germans: "When we consider the incalculable number of Germans that emigration has thrown into the United States, when we imagine that in most of the towns and villages there is hardly a bakery, a grocery, a confectionery, or a restaurant that does not belong to one of them, we are no longer surprised at the Germanisms that continue to slip into the English language as it is spoken in America. These foreign hordes have thus begun a conquest that grows unceasingly under a peaceful appearance."[4] But it must be noted that these words were written less than two years after France's defeat and the occupation of Paris by the Prussians.

Like the earlier critics, Mme. Bentzon decried the vulgarity of democracy, of which Artemus Ward's writing especially was symptomatic. "There is in the American spirit," she wrote, an inclination to gross mirth, to pranks, which reveals that in certain respects this great people is still a childish people. To gain its favor, in the West especially, one must be willing to sacrifice to buffoonery; political orators, even preachers have to take this dominant taste into account. . . . If we present—to readers more critical than the oracles of Pfaff's Club (a literary club of New York)—if we present some debauches of wit that one would hardly dare call literary, it is rather to offer a measure of the popular taste of a people who think themselves very superior to the Old Europeans than to expose the sad spectacle of a man of talent who squanders brilliant faculties on foolishness.[5]

Artemus Ward received some recognition from a highly perceptive and sympathetic critic, Henry Gauthier-Villars (1859–1931), in a lecture on Mark Twain published later in 1884. The author, a humorist in his own right who wrote under the pen name Willy, acknowledged Th. Bentzon as the chief source of his remarks, and it is questionable whether he had read any of Artemus's work other than that in Bentzon's translation. Comparing Twain with James Russell Lowell, Charles Godfrey Leland, and Artemus Ward, the critic reserved the highest honors for Twain, although he pointed out that some critics accorded the first rank to Artemus. "As to the finesse of Artemus Ward, it is difficult to seize; his style, splashed with violent colors and streaked with unheard-of metaphors, is otherwise as preposterous as that of Mark Twain. . . . Mark Twain is solemn beside Artemus."[6]

One other article on American crackerbox humor is worthy of note. This is Charles de Varigny's (1829–1899) "La Littérature comique aux Etats-Unis" in the *Revue bleue,* April 16, 1887. A writer of novels and books on travel and geography, Varigny was also a diplomat, and, as French Consul to Hawaii in the 1860s, he could have met Mark Twain at the beginning of the latter's fame. Like Mme. Bentzon, Varigny used most of his allotted space in translating selections from the humorists, and, in fact, he acknowledged her leadership in bringing American humorists before the French public. His critical comments were limited almost entirely to generalizations about American life and especially to the mixture of nationalities that made up the population of the United States. He attributed to the melting-pot idea the emergence of a new American literature, and he was one of the first French critics to receive that new American literature with something like cordiality. "From this mixture of nationalities and disparate elements, modified through contact, through climate, and through social organization and political institutions, is born a particular literature, a kind of spirit that is neither English *humour,* French *esprit,* nor German *Gemüth,* that does not depend on Dickens and Thackeray any more than on Heinrich Heine, About, or Dumas, that is essentially American."

Varigny was the first French critic to note the difference between Yankee humor and Southwestern humor, and the first to recognize the latter. "In those humorists who come from the Southern states," he said, "we do not find . . . that bitterness, that savagery which Th. Bentzon has so well noted. Their mirth is more naïve as well as more free; their laughter is more contagious; under the warm sun of Georgia and Virginia, the plant has brought forth flowers and fruits different from those of the harsh climates of Maine or the Rocky Mountains."[7] Varigny did not explain what he meant by "bitterness" and "savagery." Although he acknowledged the humor of Sut Lovingood (George Washington Harris), Bill Arp (Charles Henry Smith), Major Jones (William Tappan Thompson), Mozis Addums (George William Bagby), and Mark Twain, he seems to have based his criticism entirely on Henry Watterson's somewhat mild collection, *Oddities of Southern Life and Character* (1882). The sadism of Sut Lovingood did not seem to have reached him.

Mark Twain excepted, no other crackerbox humorists seem to have been known in France, unless we include Joel Chandler Harris and Bret Harte. Two unauthorized translations of Harris's Uncle Remus stories were published in France, but he apparently was not honored by critical notice.[8] Harte was far more popular. Th. Bentzon translated ten of his stories in the *Revue des deux mondes* between 1872 and 1876, and she and others translated several books of his stories.

Mme. Bentzon's praise of the California romancer was extreme. "We can readily agree," she said, "with the opinion of Charles Dickens, who, a few months before he died, saluted with noble emotion the advent of a rival. . . . For moderation, the rare talent to condense into a small number of pages a lively interest in the action and a profound analysis of the characters, Bret Harte comes closer to another exquisite model, Mérimée." The irony of Dickens and the exoticism of Mérimée—these were truly what made Harte popular in France. He pictured the far West as Europeans would like to dream of it, and in a slick, modern tone that made it seem adult. His tone, like Dickens's, was chiefly one of comic irony. In a later essay on Harte, Mme. Bentzon spoke more dispassionately and more accurately: "His principal merit consists in an astonishing vigor of conception, in a mixture [she loved her *mélanges*] of roughness, irony, and sensibility, to which nothing compares finally in the gripping strangeness of subjects evidently seen and lived through." And she conceded: "He was unable to develop a moral thesis, to carry on a dialogue, or to portray the details of ordinary life with any precision."[9]

Although Harte was a close rival of Mark Twain in terms of his renown in nineteenth-century France, only Twain has continued to grow in reputation and popularity up to the present time. Translations and reprints of Twain's work have been numerous, and the number of critical estimates has been such that we can only sample them here. Among his far-reaching studies of American letters, Cyrille Arnavon has examined Twain's French fame before 1917. "We have not," wrote Arnavon in 1951, "had access to the respective publication figures, but it seems certain that Whitman or Lafcadio Hearn—if they have aroused in France some much more arresting and new interpretations than Mark Twain, if they have had more points of contact than he with our contemporary letters—have never met his almost popular success. We will wager that even today his name is one of the best known in American letters, familiar to many who know nothing of Emerson or Longfellow."[10] A historical summary of Twain's reputation in France may be found in Roger Asselineau's *The Literary Reputation of Mark Twain from 1910 to 1950* (Paris, 1954), and the bibliography in that book includes the French criticism of Twain since his death in 1910.

But although Twain was known he was not always admired. Asselineau, the foremost French authority on Twain today, seemed almost to contradict Arnavon when he said: "Mark Twain was never popular there in his lifetime. . . . The French readers of those days failed to appreciate his humour in spite of the fervour of Michel Epuy who had translated some of his tales."[11] And as late as 1935, the hundredth anniversary of Twain's birth, Maurice Le Breton reported: "Twain is hardly read in France; he has never been much read."[12]

The attitude that was to dominate the early French criticism of Twain was established in an introductory essay by Th. Bentzon in the *Revue des deux mondes* in 1872. Mme. Bentzon concerned herself chiefly with *The Innocents Abroad,* and, as might be expected, she was offended by Twain's offhand treatment of Europe and his "mistakes" in history. His proper subject matter, she believed, was the Wild West.

> With his energetic instincts that carry him into difficulties and adventures, with his explosions of hearty mirth in the middle of the most terrible circumstances, he has free rein, he is absolutely himself only in this far West, where, with a laugh, he clears a rude path among the bandits and the Indians, the wilderness and the snow, wielding either a revolver or the tools of a miner, in order, after having brandished the pick and shaken the gold pan, to seize the journalist's pen with a hand no less vigorous. Towns like Virginia City suit his pioneer temperament a thousand times better than our feudal and gothic capitals of Europe—fallen queens sometimes who wrap themselves in mourning with a silent majesty that only the initiated can comprehend.[13]

As described in Chapter 1, Mme. Bentzon had translated in the same essay "The Celebrated Jumping Frog of Calaveras County," which Twain had translated back into English with such comic effect. Mme. Bentzon was aware of the difficulty of translating the language of Twain's narrator Simon Wheeler. She also recognized the impact of Twain's style, even though she did not entirely approve of it. "What is especially untranslatable," she said, "is what makes the principal merit of these medleys [Twain's travel sketches], the original and caustic style, the idiomatic turn, the bizarre and often picturesque mixture of neologisms, dialect, and argot that is called slang. English remains the mother language fundamentally, but she is an old nurse whose breasts are often dry; she can express only European civilization, and is at a loss before the superabundance of ideas, inventions, and discoveries that young America prides herself on. . . . The audacities of Bret Harte and the grosser temerities of Mark Twain astonish us still, but soon we will be accustomed to an American language, the racy freshness of which is not to be disdained, while we await qualities which are more delicate and exalted and which time will bring without doubt."[14]

Despite her own national prejudice, misinformation, and preciosity of style, Mme. Bentzon was both perceptive and farsighted, considering that her criticism was written when *The*

Celebrated Jumping Frog, The Innocents Abroad, the *Burlesque Autobiography,* and *Roughing It* were the only books Twain had produced. She noted his importance as a representative voice from the United States, she foresaw the significance of his indigenous language, and she recognized the emergence of an American humor that she admittedly only partly understood and that she considered, perhaps rightly, to be almost untranslatable. In a review of *The Gilded Age* in 1875, she was even more complimentary, though recognizing the difficulties of the joint authorship of Twain and Charles Dudley Warner.[15] In 1885 she spoke for most French critics up to World War I when she said: "Psychological preoccupations, the analysis of passions that are common to all humanity will take the place of this painting—rude enough sometimes but always expressive of local manners that the genius of Bret Harte can render strikingly, who becomes joyous with the exotic joy of a semi-barbarian child, and yet witty under the facile pen of Mark Twain, who, with Cable, bears such a strange color of passionate melancholy. . . . They have exploited the vein that has given them celebrity until nothing is left for anyone who would follow them."[16] Although Twain and some of his contemporaries had perhaps risen above the category of popular literature, to French critics they were still primitives, and their manner would give way to a more sensitive literature as America outgrew its childishness. Such a conclusion seems dimsighted in view of Hemingway's assertion that *Huckleberry Finn* is the source of all twentieth-century American literature, and in view of Faulkner's utilization of even earlier material in the crackerbox tradition. On the other hand, it is true that Twain cannot be surpassed in his own vein.

Representative of the adverse criticism of Twain was an article by André Theuriet (1833-1907) in *Parlement* as early as 1881. A highly respected novelist and critic and a member of the Académie Française, Theuriet was profoundly offended by American vulgarity:

> It is evident that this coarse-grained comedy has nothing in common with attic salt. If one insisted, I would avow that on my own account I find only a mediocre charm in this kind of humor. Humor—that special product of the Anglo-Saxon imagination— attracts and enchants me only when it is ably mixed with poetry and truth, with laughter and tears, as in the work of Dickens, Holmes, or Bret Harte. This rude and vulgar

> irony of Mark Twain always strikes me rather as those gross country pleasantries that consist of punches and blows on the back or in the sides of the sufferer, applied "for fun."

The critic revealed his own conservative, romantic orientation when he exclaimed:

> Alas! it is the destiny of democratic societies, this betrayal of the literary domain by violent and crudely painted works where the art of composition, the purity of language, the delicacy of sentiments, the science of taste and nuance no more count for anything. We can already perceive it here at home, where, under the pretext of naturalism, certain novelists have substituted for psychological analysis the minute description of the purely bestial appetites and passions of the human animal.

Theuriet concluded with the prophecy: "Great art is dead!"[17]

On the other hand, Henry Gauthier-Villars had a different view of Twain's worth in the 111-page monograph on Mark Twain developed from an earlier lecture. He wrote:

> Some critics have persuaded themselves that the vogue of the humorists was only the result of momentary infatuation; they believed it agonizingly and profited from it by lampooning it disdainfully; others maintain a shrewder jealousy and combat relentlessly the success of this young school that dares to declare its independence. They count its blunders, underline its failings, note its imperfections, and, gleefully lining up a long column of errors that they have uncovered in spiteful detail, they will cry out with a most chauvinistic joy:
>
> Ah! how fortunate to be a Frenchman,
> In regarding this column!
>
> Let us say without insisting: our epoch was, more than any other, incapable of comprehending this off-handed literature; in fact, who are the writers in vogue? Refined stylists, tyrants of words and syllables, composing a phrase with the minute labor of a mosaicist, after the manner of Théophile Gautier, Flaubert, or Goncourt, they seek the tortured, the over-subtle, and the precious, and care nothing for naturalness except to hunt it down; it is all too evident that for them American productions would be a closed book. On the contrary, I do not believe that we should, like them, disparage gaiety, spontaneity, and what I shall call *literary healthiness,* which blooms so freely in the work of Mark Twain. Let us allow the modern critics, those sly foxes, to find these qualities proper for boors,

> and let us try rather to grasp them; let us make our reservations, but let us not strain ourselves to find dung in the pearls of Ennius.

Furthermore, Gauthier-Villars understood the underlying seriousness of Twain's writing, even at this early date. "What is Mark Twain trying to do?" he wrote.

> Simply to inculcate some notions (not too subtle) of justice and goodness to men who were not otherwise disposed to receive it; now, it is no mystery that our poor human nature is so made that it deliberately yawns at sermons, and repeats:
>
> A naked moral means boredom.
>
> It is necessary to wrap the moral in a happy story which will make it pass with them; such was the role of Mark Twain.[18]

Though the explanation of Twain's greatness was an oversimplification—and Gauthier-Villars was well aware of that—still it accords remarkably with Twain's own statement many years later that "humor must not professedly teach, and it must not professedly preach, but it must do both if it would live forever."[19]

In the following year, 1885, L. Lionel Radiguet wrote an essay on Twain that was laudatory but also epitomized the French impressions of America's childishness, vulgarity, and commercialism. "By the time the American race felt strong enough to shake off the tutelage of the English, there still remained much to do to consummate its independence. The British flag no longer waved over the territory of the Union, but the commercial and moral influence of the mother country was no less intact in the colony that had become a nation," he began. But America was finally asserting its independence, and Mark Twain represented the raw experience of American nationality. "Representing most completely and remarkably the national literature of the United States is M. Clemens, better known under the pseudonym of 'Mark Twain,' by which he signs his principal works." Radiguet's essay considered only Twain's sketches and short tales, though *The Gilded Age, Tom Sawyer, The Prince and the Pauper,* and *Life on the Mississippi* had already appeared. Further, he misread Twain in several instances. (He had the stranger giving Jim Smiley's jumping frog a drink of whiskey instead of a handful of quail-shot.) Yet he recognized, as early as

1885, Twain's significance as a critic of society; and he cautioned French admirers of American society to note the implications of Twain's picture.[20]

One of the most significant reviews of Twain in the nineteenth century was that of Eugène Forgues, son of Eugène-D. Forgues who reviewed Poe, Hawthorne, and Holmes in the mid-century. Reviewing *Life on the Mississippi* in the *Revue des deux mondes* in 1886, the younger Forgues surveyed the current French attitude toward Twain and, like Gauthier-Villars, came to the American author's defense. He recognized the difficulty of translation; several people had tried it and "the result of their efforts was an almost complete failure." His own translation of parts of *Life on the Mississippi,* which made up the most part of his article, was intended as a kind of paraphrase in which he tried to capture the spirit of the original. But the French public, he said, was quick to form opinions and showed a "remarkable tenacity in not changing them." Twain was considered barbarous: "They found his pleasantry grim, his wit brutal, his temperament bald. His deliberate exaggerations were taken for symptoms of mental alienation." Furthermore, "one could say that at the basis of all French readers there is an academician sleeping; now the talent of Mark Twain has nothing in common with the academic kind." But above all Twain had the temerity to ridicule the French. "In a word," Forgues continued with irony, "he made the very great mistake of not always taking seriously the most intelligent nation in the world."

In contrast with the notions of the French reading public, Forgues saw imposing merits in Twain's work:

> Mark Twain is not simply an incorrigible and perpetual entertainer. There is in him another nature, a truly pungent originality and some definite talents and qualities. He is a wise and penetrating observer, who sees well and narrates accurately, a tireless traveler who sometimes places before us strange and unknown countries and sometimes brings to our well-worn lands an element of unforeseen novelty. His descriptions are almost always interesting and full of exactness, his judgments marked with good sense and free of all banal influence and all conventional barriers. Conventions count for nothing in this independent and ardent nature in which all the resources are new. When he decides, more often than one thinks, to treat a subject seriously, his information is sound and precise, drawn from the best sources, and with an irreproachable authenticity.

> But at the very time that he interjects a bit of comic fancy, as he often does and as he seldom completely refrains from doing, the chief concern of his narrative is always his first consideration and never disappears behind empty and pointless pleasantry.[21]

Although Twain was not as popular with the French public as with the American, British, and German publics, he was not without his influence in France. The novelist Alphonse Daudet—now known to have borrowed from many authors—borrowed the plot and structure of part of Twain's *A Tramp Abroad* (1889) for his *Tartarin sur les Alpes* (1885). And, according to the critic René Doumic (1860–1937), writing in 1899, Twain and other American writers had influenced a whole school of French humorists. "Humor is a 'specialty' of MM. Courteline, Jules Renard, Alphonse Allais, Capus, Georges Auriol, Tristan Bernard, Pierre Veber, Willy, and Grosclaude; they have a monopoly of it, such as the State has on the manufacture of matches, and the refiners on the sugar industry." But the critic did not feel that they were successful. "They have been able to take from American humor only its exterior methods and its mechanical means. They have remained themselves, but they have contracted some habits of insistence in pleasantry, of heaviness and slowness, a certain embarrassment, awkwardness, and uncomfortableness, such as we feel when we put on clothes that were not made for us." The trouble was, the critic contended, that American humor could not be transplanted in French culture, and he repeated with emphasis the notion that Mark Twain was untranslatable: "To taste perfectly the work of Marck [*sic*] Twain is a joy that ought to be renounced by those who do not know the English language wonderfully well or indeed those who do not have a little English blood in their veins."[22]

The most ambitious French criticism of Twain before World War I was published in the *Revue du mois* on April 10, 1910, just eleven days before Twain's death. The critic, Régis Michaud, emphasized Twain's Americanism: "Mark Twain is exclusively, aggressively American." "The American," he continued, "is fundamentally serious. The frequently boundless jokes of the humorist are a sort of reactivating or relaxing of his overtense nerves." And "humor is perhaps the only kind of fiction of which [the American] imagination is capable." But Mark Twain was more than just a popular humorist.

> The best of Mark Twain's humor is, even more than his jokes, the character that he gives men and things. To view them through his spirit (Isn't humor above all a point of view?) one perceives them on the one hand completely disfigured, as in the concave or convex mirrors that gazers see themselves in at the fair, and on the other hand discreetly and wittily altered and lightly exaggerated. In satisfactorily holding them at more or less distance from reality, the humorist transforms men and actions into types, into allegories which equal the classic creations of caricature and burlesque.

In conclusion, Michaud seemed to rank Twain among the greatest writers.

> The humorous stories of Mark Twain apprehend the ideal American just as the speeches of Roosevelt and the lectures of William James. From the artistic point of view, Mark Twain is, after Dickens, one of the greatest caricaturists in English letters. Like the authors of Gargantua and of Don Quixote, he has more than once given to satire the form of an epic. Smallnesses and greatnesses, limitations and extent, American democracy is all there in his stories. Mark Twain is its Homer, more serious than one thinks, under his disguise of humorist.[23]

Two months later the critic and translator Gabriel de Lautrec (1867–1938) echoed Michaud's approach in an article in the *Mercure de France,* comparing Twain with Swift, Molière, and Dickens. Twain's work, he said, had "achieved a very remarkable success in France." In fact, most Frenchmen knew little more than Poe and Twain in American literature. Yet Lautrec perpetuated the notion that America was an infantile land, and that Twain's writing reflected American naïveté.[24]

After World War I, interest in Twain gradually increased. In 1919, R. Bosc wrote: "In reading the lively analyses of M. Régis Michaud and his well chosen quotations, in seeing the droll and vivid types portrayed in his [Twain's] extensive work, perhaps the French reader, who has frequently declared Mark Twain unintelligible to him, will get over his first impression and put himself on guard against the sin of philistinism, never more grave than when it is committed against humor."[25] But in 1920, Jean Richepin repeated the charge that Twain was puerile, vulgar, and basically ferocious. Americans, he said, "are a people childish, young, hardly advanced beyond youth."[26] And at least as late as 1935 the notion of Twain's barbarism survived. John Charpentier, for example, characterized the humor of Mark Twain, in contrast with the comic spirit of the French and the English, as purely destructive.[27] In the same year, the centennial of Twain's birth, one of the foremost scholars of American literature in France, Maurice Le Breton, summed up the French attitude:

> The greater part of his work has not been translated; the public at large knows him here by some extracts that certainly do not show him in the best light. As to the critics who have pursued their curiosity further, they have generally treated him without indulgence and with a marked degree of disdain: his humor has seemed too gross to have a rightful place in respectable literature, his portrayals of American life have been judged too crude by a timorous criticism which has lately seen others like them. Mark Twain has not excited the interest in France that is attached to writers more respectful of conventions, a Fenimore Cooper or a Bret Harte. Even his originality and his sincerity have harmed him; we have preferred talents more conformable to our ideal, more romantic painters of the America of pioneers and prospectors; we have not been able to see under the somewhat unruly humorist the most shrewd observer of the society of the Middle West and the most American of the writers of his time.[28]

Even as late as 1945 the reproachful attitude toward Twain continued, and from no less than the first great academic scholar of American literature that France was to produce, Charles Cestre (1871–1958). Concerning *The Innocents Abroad,* he wrote: "The tone of disparagement spiced with gross pleasantries toward the art galleries of Italy and the palaces and cathedrals of France and England, which amused the farmers of the Mississippi valley, seems unfortunate to us."[29] Shades of Th. Bentzon! And the remainder of his commentary on Twain, though not entirely uncomplimentary, showed no improvement over Mme. Bentzon's criticism of 1872.

In spite of the sympathetic criticism of Eugène Forgues, Régis Michaud, and Maurice Le Breton, the French contributed little to Mark Twain scholarship until almost the 1960s. An exception might be claimed for Léon Lemonnier, who in 1946 explained Twain's humor as basically pessimistic: "He has the huge, boisterous laughter of one who expects nothing of the world and who wishes at all costs to make others laugh in order to make himself laugh."[30] But even the sympathetic critics were so much concerned with combatting what they considered the prevailing antipathy toward the American humorist that they failed to offer insights or ideas that were not already commonplace in America. The situation is all the more regrettable in contrast with the frequently brilliant perceptions of French critics toward the work of Edgar Allan Poe, for example. Critical views began changing in the 1950s and continued especially in the 1960s, when Mark Twain scholarship as well as criticism came of age in France. But the discussion of twentieth-century scholarship belongs in the next chapter.

One more late nineteenth-century view of American humor remains to be considered—a critical essay written about Henry James by Th. Bentzon in the *Revue des deux mondes.* As Mme. Bentzon had noted the melancholy humor of George Washington Cable, she also relished the quiet wit of Henry James. In her introductory review of James's work, May 1, 1883, she chose to study especially the related stories "The Pension Beaurepas," "A Bundle of Letters," and "The Point of View"—three of the author's most comic writings. Her essay included her translation of most of "The Point of View," in which James impartially satirized the critics and defenders of America—French, English, and American. After pointing out that James did not write for "the gross public, who wish to be served ready-made emotions and to find at the end of the volume that all is for the best in the best of all possible worlds, thanks to the marriage of M. X and Mlle. ***," Mme. Bentzon praised the comic characterizations of Mlle. Nioche in *The American* and Henrietta Stackpole in *The Portrait of a Lady.* She also admired the gentle satire of the French aristocracy in the character of Valentin in *The American.* She characterized James's comic sense as "traits of *esprit* that make only discreet borrowings from the humor that one hears in America." She spoke wisely and accurately of the three short stories that were the particular subject of her review:

> To analyze this kind of work, so marvelously appropriate to the genius of M. James, will be indeed difficult; all the charm, subtle as the brilliant powder on the wing of the butterfly, being in the original and familiar tone of the letters, the vivacity of the conversations, the amusing contrast of judgments about the same thing or the same person by a ped-

> ant of Göttingen, an enterprising Parisian, some Americans eager to buy everything and learn everything, some scandalized Englishmen, etc. . . . The author embodies himself in each of his personages and takes one by one their prejudices, passions, and absurdities with a prodigious suppleness and ability.[31]

Mme. Bentzon did not of course make Henry James a popular writer, nor was he ever a popular writer. But he did achieve the respect of a choice few. A few of his novels and novelettes were translated during his lifetime, and some of his short stories appeared in translation in the magazines, but their selection appeared to be haphazard. A scattering of critical articles also appeared. Unlike Twain's, however, James's fame did not spread in France following his death.[32]

The "Age of Twain" brought forth no great burst of understanding or enthusiasm for American literature. In many ways the critical opinions expressed were merely a continuation of those of Chasles and Tocqueville, which had their origins in the post-Revolution era. On the other hand, the tradition of native American humor was discovered and recognized, particularly in the work of Th. Bentzon, as the beginning of a new truly American literature. And once again French criticism noted the comic element in a major "serious" writer, Henry James.

7

The Twentieth Century, First Half

The French reception of American literature in the twentieth century has been fairly clearly divided into three stages by the two World Wars. In the period from 1900 to 1920, future appreciations were only foreshadowed and the period could best be characterized perhaps as one of transition between nineteenth-century aloofness and twentieth-century admiration. Between the wars, admiration was not wholesale, but an understanding of the major contemporary American writers developed that was greater, both qualitatively and quantitatively, than that of the nineteenth century. Since World War II American literature has been almost totally accepted in France—more than any other foreign literature there, and more there than in any other European country with the possible exception of Great Britain. Today the American novel is widely believed to be the greatest in the world and William Faulkner the greatest twentieth-century novelist. Even American poetry has been widely and sensitively appreciated. Further, there exists today a significant scholarly recognition of earlier American literature.

The reception of American humor has slowly followed that of American literature in general. Today, the French people see the humor in American movies and comic strips, and they may read Robert Benchley, James Thurber, and Ogden Nash in translation. Art Buchwald, during his residence in Paris, was a kind of French institution. In university classrooms and in bookstores one finds the novels of John Updike, Ralph Ellison, and Joseph Heller. And French television is full of American material, including humor, and French imitations of it.

Perhaps the first sign of all this new understanding was the appointment of Barrett Wendell as the first visiting professor of American literature in 1904.[1] Wendell's appointment was part of an exchange with Harvard, and in the following years increasing numbers of French professors and scholars spent some time in the United States. Among the most important of these were Gilbert Chinard (1881-1972), who became a professor at Brown University in 1908 and continued to live in America; Jean Jules Jusserand (1855-1932), who was Ambassador to Washington during World War I; and Charles Cestre (1871-1958), who held visiting professorships at Harvard, Michigan, Wisconsin, Illinois, California Wesleyan, and Bryn Mawr. These men and others contributed immensely to Franco-American understanding on both sides. Furthermore, they laid the foundations for a scholarly approach to American studies in France.

Meanwhile, the number of *revues* that dealt with American literature had greatly increased, and they were both a result and a cause of the new interest. In addition to the *Revue des deux mondes,* the following periodicals were active in the field between 1900 and 1920: *Correspondant, Mercure de France, Nouvelle revue française* (beginning in 1909), *Revue bleue, Revue du mois* (beginning in 1906). According to Delbert L. Gibson, who studied thirty-three of the major literary reviews for their opinions on American culture, "The importance of the *revues* in the artistic, literary, and intellectual life of the French people cannot be questioned: throughout the span of their lives, the *revues* mirror the many aspects of the life of the nation with more breadth, with more precision, with more conscience, than creative literature itself and the frantic journalism from the pens of hired propagandists."[2] The general attitude of the reviews toward American culture was not very favorable. The fears and antipathies that had built up during the nineteenth century were still there, and all the old presentiments flourished. "This immense nation," wrote the young Bernard Faÿ in 1920, "which has civilized a whole world from the Atlantic Ocean to the Pacific, seems never to have had time to devote to its spiritual welfare what it offers to bodily comfort. Literature and the arts have no life of their own there."[3] In the preceding year, Georges Batault had summed up French fears in an article in *Mercure de France,* in which he maintained that American literature had fulfilled all the worst predictions of Alexis de Tocqueville:

> At the time when the United States deliberately takes its place at the head of the nations and peoples who constitute history in progress toward the future, the impotence of American literature—its subordinate and mercantile

> character, its aspects of democratic industrialism, its servile acceptance of the law of number, its strong desire to please at all costs, and its readiness to bend to the least caprices of an enormous and mediocre reading public—all these abdications, these defeats, these capitulations are signs that can hardly fail to disturb us.
>
> More clear and striking and therefore more visible overseas—are not these characteristics, with all the shades and nuances that one might wish, the indicators of the actual state of affairs—the actual state, more and more, of *Universal Civilization*?
>
> Under this pompous title, what bleakness and what negation![4]

Yet at least the reviews published an increasing number of articles on America from 1900 to 1914, and they reflected a growing recognition of America's importance.[5]

According to Félix Ansermoz-Dubois, Europe in 1914 "did not yet take America very seriously." "In matters of literature as in those of civilization," he continued, "it was America who turned her eyes toward Europe. Five years later, the roles would be reversed."[6] On the other hand, Charles Cestre, writing in 1920, saw the beginnings of French interest in American literature before the War: "The latest brand of 'exoticism' was American literature and thought, which was beginning to be imported just before the war, in the shape of translations and a few literary articles in magazines. The movement may have slackened a little, but it has not stopped; it will recover all its force when the pressing preoccupations, which for the present engross our minds, have ceased to raise a screen between us and the outside world."[7] Both writers were right, though Ansermoz-Dubois was speaking retrospectively from the 1940s and in broad terms, while Cestre spoke at the moment. If Gibson's count of the number of articles on the United States in the French reviews is an accurate index, there was a peak of interest in 1918 and then a slump until the early twenties.

In 1918, the year of the American Expeditionary Force in France, three important works on American humor appeared: A.-L. Jeune's "L'Humour anglo-saxon" in the *Correspondant,* Régis Michaud's *Mystiques et réalistes anglo-saxon,* and a translation of Stephen Leacock's "American Humour," from his *Essays and Literary Studies,* published in London in 1916. Though all three considered American humor as a form of

Anglo-Saxon humor, they also attempted to distinguish it from British humor—as a new and original contribution. All noted the violence of American humor and all cited Mark Twain as the exemplar.

Leacock's essay, though written by a Canadian, seems to have made an impression on French views. He emphasized the prevalence of exaggeration in American humor, the use of the innocent pose, and the "outside" view of European ideas and institutions. He also saw a "cheap vulgarity" in much of it, and referred to that favorite bad example of the French critics, Mark Twain's "Cannibalism in the Cars." He concluded that while English humor arises from literature, American literature arises from humor—a conclusion perhaps more epigrammatic than sound, but one worth considering in view of the comic impulse to be found in Irving, Poe, Hawthorne, Melville, and James and the tremendous impact of Twain on subsequent American writers.[8]

Michaud's discussion of humor repeated some of the ideas on Mark Twain that he had stated in his 1910 essay in the *Revue des deux mondes.* But by 1918 he had further refined his notions of American character. "The American is grave and serious by nature," he wrote. "The often unbounded jokes of the humorist are healthy gymnastics for his overtense nerves—a release. . . . However outrageous they may be in their unexpected blasts, they respond to his need to be overstimulated. In the humor of Mark Twain, the elements of violence and excess are made to order to satisfy the need." According to Michaud, *l'humour* is an art of contrasts, and American humor is particularly so. Furthermore, humor is didactic. "By means of contrast," he said, "it serves to attract attention to some important point. . . . To introduce into a description, a portrait, or a narrative an element that contradicts another idea and throws us back to a third point of view which is that of the humorist—that is the purpose of the stratagem." And he cited Twain's account of gladiatorial contests in the Coliseum as reported in the *Roman Daily Battle-Ax* (from *Innocents Abroad*), where the humorist compared ancient spectacle with modern commercialism and at the same time mocked sentimental rhapsodizing over historic ruins.

Michaud recognized a tradition of American humor and noted its basis in oral storytelling. "During his life, Mark Twain achieved some veritable triumphs with the humorous story, in which a number of narrators continue the tradition across the sea. It is indeed a national genre, a popular literature in the true sense of the word, a rich folklore exploited by a whole line of humorists from Artemus Ward to that prince of deadpan Americans of today, the very modern Mr. Dooley."[9]

A.-L. Jeune, in his essay "L'Humour anglo-saxon," subtitled "Les Jeux d'esprit de nos alliés d'outre-mer," again took up the problem of defining *l'humour*—with admirable perspicacity. Humor involves, he said, a manner of speaking in completely concrete terms of something that has abstract implications, or, on the other hand, a use of abstract or sentimental terms for something that is brutally concrete. Humor "sometimes spiritualizes the material; it often materializes the spiritual. In general, it is the pleasantry of a man who pretends not to see the psychological and moral scope of the facts that he reports." The deadpan manner, or, more properly, the innocent pose, is thus the essential element of *l'humour.* "To his gift of objective observation, the humorist seems to join a particular mastery of himself. . . . All passion is permitted to the humorist, but all direct expression of a passion is forbidden. Like a living statue, he pretends to imitate impassible matter."

Though its roots were in England, Jeune said, American humor has developed its own individuality as shown in such writers as Artemus Ward, James Whitcomb Riley, and especially Mark Twain. "Like English pleasantry, American verve is robust, but with a savor often less bitter." And, despite the claims of modern criticism, bitterness is not to be mistaken for profundity, nor pessimism for wisdom. American humor is sometimes childish—we hear it again from Jeune—but it represents a healthy vigor. It is the "youthfulness of the American soul, no doubt, but also it seems a sudden release of an energy too constantly active. In the country of the strenuous life, the need for release can be more necessary than elsewhere."[10] A relaxation of tension or an explosion of pent up energy—Jeune's thesis was very like that of Michaud. It also showed, possibly, an influence of Freudian theory but without the negative implications of humor as disguised aggressiveness. Rather, humor was an evidence of vital force, and especially in America was that force characteristic.

Then came the twenties. To American readers the France of the 1920s is the France of Ernest Hemingway, F. Scott Fitzgerald, Sherwood Anderson, and the rest of the Lost Generation—the

France of Gertrude Stein's Saturday evenings at 27 rue de Fleurus and of the writers who congregated at Sylvia Beach's bookstore, Shakespeare and Company. But the impact of these writers on French literature and criticism was long delayed. Hemingway and Fitzgerald did not become well known until late in the decade. Gertrude Stein was a personality among artists and collectors as early as the first decade of the century, but her writing made little impression until the late twenties and the thirties. Her *Three Lives* was, of course, known in its American and British editions (1909, 1915, etc.). *The Making of Americans* was first published in Paris in 1925 but not translated into French until 1929. In 1927 and 1928 she contributed several short works, in English, to *transition,* the avant-garde magazine founded in Paris by Eugène Jolas and his American wife, Maria. And finally, in the June 1930 issue of *Echanges,* Marcel Brion wrote a long, appreciative essay entitled "Le Contrepoint poétique de Gertrude Stein." Perhaps her most immediate contribution to Franco-American understanding was her steadfast friendship with Professor Bernard Faÿ (1893–?), one of the foremost French spokesmen for American culture between the wars—a friendship that began in 1926 and lasted to the final day of her life, despite the ignominy of Faÿ's collaboration with the Pétain government in World War II.[11] In 1932 Faÿ was appointed to the chair in American civilization at the Collège de France, and he was assisted in his lectures by Gertrude Stein. Of course, any appreciation of Stein meant an appreciation of her humor, for, regardless of her still-questioned status in American literature, she was a humorist. In 1944, André Maurois, loyally supporting the French cause in New York, paid tribute to her courage in remaining in France throughout the War: "In this universal confusion, she has remained intelligent; she has maintained her sense of poetry and even her sense of humor."[12]

But in the period following World War I, it was Sinclair Lewis who really grasped the attention of French readers and critics. When Lewis visited Paris in 1921, he was disappointed to find himself neglected. His *Main Street* (1920) was not yet known to the French. Furthermore, he did not improve his reputation when he received André Siegfried (1875–1959), professor of political science at the Collège de France, in a false white beard and pretended to be Dr. E. J. Lewis, come to Paris to see his son. Siegfried was not amused with this example of American humor, though Lewis later told Lewis Galantière that Siegfried had called Lewis the American Flaubert. The interview with Galantière, however, was similarly inauspicious as Lewis was in a fit of drunken self-pity.[13]

Within two years, however, his reputation in France was established. No less a critic than Régis Michaud compared *Main Street* to Flaubert's *Madame Bovary,* and he continued in glowing terms to praise *Babbitt:* "With a consummate art which is joined with a marvelously engaging sensitivity and of which we have few examples in fiction since Balzac and Dickens, Lewis has been able to collect and classify the features of a portrait that compares with Grandet, Mr. Micawber, Tartarin, or Don Quixote."[14] In fact, Lewis rapidly became the most highly reputed contemporary American author in France in the twenties, and it was not surprising to the French that he should receive the Nobel Prize for literature in 1930. Further, he was hailed as a symbol of America's literary coming-of-age.

But the reasons for Sinclair Lewis's popularity—and well known he was, both in terms of reprints and translations and in terms of critical notice—reflected the continuance of French skepticism about American society. Lewis was applauded as the supreme critic of all that was disgusting and frightening in the New World: commercialism, vulgarity, conformism, mechanization, "the strenuous life." "In an egalitarian society, originality is impossible," said Michaud in summing up his evaluation of Lewis's picture of American life. Yet he modified that dictum a dozen lines later. "The sharpness with which Sinclair Lewis's heroes are conscious of their miseries is motive for indulgence and hope. Let's speculate with optimism on the literary future of a country where *Main Street* and *Babbitt* could be written."[15] In his *Panorama de la littérature américaine* in 1929, Michaud developed the same thesis further:

> A hundred million Americans live a life of one mind. The immense democracy has to prosper and defend itself. It imposes disciplines, laws, "standards." That is its right, its duty, but a danger awaits it. Sacrificed to commercial imperialism, must a hundred million individuals let themselves be regimented without warning? The church, the school, the state, the press, and the tyranny of opinion proceed toward a leveling without precedent in the history of the world. A hundred million different beings are rendered similar under the weight of the most formidable steamroller that has ever been known. But there is

> resistance. Individualism is dear to the Anglo-Saxon. There are always apostles of "self-reliance," of full mastery of the self, in the United States. Uneasiness, protest, inquiry, denunciation mark the end of the epic named after "the strenuous life." The new generations rebel against the enforced moral militarism. And here the courage of an inspired satirist comes to their rescue.[16]

Thus, "Red" Lewis, from Sauk Centre, Minnesota, became for Europeans the champion of the finer things against the menace of Americanism.

Michaud was by no means alone. Lewis's satires of American life were taken as stark realism, and his "revolt" was his great attraction. We heard it in 1923 from Léonie Villard (1878–1970), one of the early professors to specialize in American subjects, and in 1946 from Pierre Brodin (1909–), critic and author of many books on American literature who in 1938 emigrated to the United States, as well as in criticisms by André Levinson, R. de Villeneuve, Bernard Faÿ, and Joseph Mainvard between those dates. Faÿ wrote in 1939: "I have never been able to read his novels without being bored, I admit. They are so long, so slow, so true (so extravagantly true, one might say)."[17]

But Lewis's humor was not totally overlooked. Michaud correctly placed the American writer in the tradition of local color and native humor: "Portraits and caricatures of the average man have abounded for thirty or forty years in the American novel. Around the beginning of the new century, the moment seemed to have arrived to attempt a synthesis, and it is Sinclair Lewis who undertakes it. Mark Twain had prepared the way of the inspired caricaturist, but his portraits were exaggerated. The satirist Sinclair Lewis presses closer to the real."[18] And fifteen years later Pierre Brodin, in summarizing American literary achievement between the wars, developed the point further:

> Here is a humorist. None of the naturalists of the preceding period were humorists. And it is perhaps this which most distinguishes Lewis from Dreiser, Norris, or Crane. He has rediscovered and put to use in his work the humor of Mark Twain, the humor of the American "frontier," the humor lost by the sad naturalists. . . . This kind of humor, one can see, is not necessarily either bitter or light. It can be ferocious, but most of the time it is the good-natured humor of the Middle West.[19]

Thus, while the French critics relished Lewis's attacks on the evils of American society, they recognized that he himself was a product of that society, which could not, therefore, be all bad. Further, they realized that his humor was more often sympathetic than bitter and that it derived from the native American tradition.

Although Lewis was probably the best known American writer of the twenties, and certainly the best known humorist, the French noticed other humorists, particularly Finley Peter Dunne (Mr. Dooley), H. L. Mencken, and George Ade.[20] Earlier humorists, too, such as Artemus Ward, Petroleum V. Nasby, and Joel Chandler Harris were discovered or rediscovered, and the humor of O. Henry, Jack London, and Edward Streeter was recognized. But this was only a symptom of growing interest, and the more or less casual reference to these writers neither effected nor reflected any great general change in French attitudes toward American humor. It may have foreshadowed such a change, however.

Meanwhile Léon Bazalgette (1874–1929), lately called the "discoverer of American literature," was fostering an interest in nineteenth-century American writers by means of translations and new interpretations of Emerson, Thoreau, Whitman, and others. Bazalgette, an internationalist and one of the founders of the review *Europe* in 1923, though not primarily interested in American humor, did much in both France and America to change the image of Henry David Thoreau from that of a "poet-naturalist" to that of a sarcastic critic of conformism and hypocrisy.[21] Likewise, the study of Benjamin Franklin was forwarded greatly by the work of Gilbert Chinard and Bernard Faÿ, though neither focused on him as a humorist. Chinard's many short studies of Franklin extended from the 1920s to the 1950s. Faÿ's *Franklin: The Apostle of Modern Times* (1929) remains an important biography.

The 1920s also saw the publication of two anthologies and an analytical survey of American literature. Charles Cestre's *Anthologie de la littérature américaine* contained a special category of writings under the heading "L'Humour." The writers represented were Irving, Holmes, Lowell, Twain, George Ade, and James Branch Cabell. James Whitcomb Riley was not represented because of failure to receive permission to reprint. Other writers, such as Bret Harte, O. Henry, and Joaquin Miller, who might be considered humorists, were included under other headings. In 1927 the dramatist and man of letters Maurice Dekobra (1885–) compiled *Le Rire dans le brouillard,* an anthology of British and American humor, and included the following Americans: Twain, Mencken, Dunne, O. Henry, London, and Streeter. Stephen Leacock, the Canadian humorist, was also included. Régis Michaud's *Panorama de la littérature américaine* contained a ten-page section on humor, in which the author traced the American tradition from Benjamin Franklin to Mark Twain, devoting half his space to the latter. These works provided no more than a minimal introduction to American humor; but they went beyond Michel Epuy's *Anthologie des humoristes anglais et américains* which included only Irving, Hawthorne, Holmes, Frank Stockton, Gelette Burgess, and Twain as American humorists. Furthermore, they recognized American humor as an important and distinctive element of American literature.

By this time, French interest in American literary humor was being reinforced by the mass media, especially the movies. Charlie Chaplin was popular in France, and he was afforded serious consideration by critics and artists, as were the productions of director D. W. Griffith. In fact, some critics felt that American movies were generally better than French, and that the popular arts were the place where America could excel. American cartoons and comic strips were also beginning to have an influence. Matthew Josephson told of introducing George Herriman's Krazy Kat to the French in the twenties and reported that cartoons and other forms of American popular arts were influencing French artists, particularly the Dadaists.[22] Clearly, a broader appreciation of American humor was evolving in France.

Meanwhile, the universities were beginning to show interest in American literature and culture. Exchanges of both instructors and students gradually became more common. A few American books were included in the program of study for the Agrégation d'Anglais, the highest competitive examination open to students of languages. In addition to the professorship in American literature and civilization at the Sorbonne, there were, by 1933, similar professorships at Lyons (Léonie Villard), at Aix-Marseille (Marcel Clavel), at Lille (Maurice Le Breton), and at Grenoble (Jean Catel). At the Collège de France, Bernard Faÿ occupied the new chair in American civilization.[23]

A general interest in the American novel was developing

throughout the period between the wars, so that by the time of World War II it was agreed in France that John Dos Passos, Ernest Hemingway, Erskine Caldwell, John Steinbeck, and William Faulkner were not only great American writers but were among the greatest contemporary writers in the world. These five, "les cinq grands," became, during and after the War, the focus of attention, to the neglect even of contemporary French writers.

The French critic who was probably most responsible for the interest in "les cinq grands" was Maurice Edgar Coindreau (1892–). Coindreau, a professor at Princeton from 1923 to 1961, translated works of all five of these American writers between 1928 and 1939. Some of his prefaces and articles in Spanish and French were eventually published in book form (all in French) in *Aperçus de littérature américaine* in 1946. Another sympathetic critic of American culture was Bernard Faÿ. With two years of postgraduate work at Harvard after World War I, and numerous visits to the United States, Faÿ was a well-known authority by the time of his appointment to the chair of American civilization in 1932. Although his concerns were not strictly literary, he did much to bring an appreciation of American culture to France. His *Civilisation américaine* (Paris: Sagittaire, 1939) contained a brief survey of some fifteen twentieth-century American authors, but his interpretations seem outdated in 1939 by comparison with Coindreau's. Neither Faÿ nor Coindreau had much to say about American humor, though the latter at least recognized its existence and the need perhaps for further understanding of it.

From the viewpoint of American humor, the only one of "les cinq grands" of great importance to the French was Erskine Caldwell. Strangely enough, although Faulkner was properly appreciated in France in the thirties and forties, a time when he was considered merely a regionalist and a naturalist in the United States, the French showed no real sensitiveness to his humor. They noted an undercurrent of black humor in his fiction but they ignored his strong ties with the tall tale and dialect humor of the Southwestern tradition of American humor.[24]

As for Hemingway, one critic went so far as to see him as a comedian, among other things, and his satire was duly noted; but, according to at least one critic, "the satire is too expected, too systematic, too banal."[25] Certainly Hemingway was not one of our great comic writers, and the French criticisms seem just.

Of the other two writers, Steinbeck and Dos Passos, very little was said about humor or even a lack of it. That is not surprising with the latter, whose trilogy *USA* was the work by which he was best known, a work rather notably lacking in humor, except for the coarse, unfunny humor of some of its characters. Steinbeck's humor was recognized but not explicated, even though it is an important element in the writer's work. The slight mention it did receive seems rightly to connect it with Steinbeck's human sympathy. Again, no connection with the tradition of native American humor was noted.

Erskine Caldwell became popular in France in 1936, with the publication of Maurice Coindreau's translation of *God's Little Acre,* including a preface by the critic and popular biographer André Maurois (1885–1967). As with Lewis, Dos Passos, and Steinbeck, Caldwell was appreciated for his bold exposé of the evils of American society, while at the same time, that society was beginning to be respected for the freedom it allowed its own critics. As Caldwell's critical reception in America dwindled, it increased in France, reaching its peak after World War II.

To French readers and critics, Caldwell was a humorist: "Caldwell laughs at human stupidities. He is both an observer and a satirist. His book [*Tobacco Road*] is really a farce in spite of the constant atmosphere of tragedy."[26] The humaneness of his humor was noted: "As a humorist, he is delightful because, never trying to be comical, he becomes irresistible, and because he has a genuine gift of sympathy."[27] Caldwell's humor was neither black nor cynical; it was a result of health and vigor: "This humor is the magnificent proof of the health and youth of America. The reader's laughter never mocks but pays homage to the vitality of the characters, to their ruggedness, to their rage to live." Finally, Caldwell's humor was seen as part of the native tradition. His "is a humor *pince-sans-rire* whose American forebear is Mark Twain."[28] Not only was Caldwell considered a humorist, but he was placed by many critics among the great humorists. Frequently compared to Rabelais, he was considered superior to Maupassant.[29]

By 1939, American literature was very much in vogue in France. According to one commentator, "it was becoming [difficult] to discuss contemporary French literature with enlightened Frenchmen, since all the young and enthusiastic intellectuals would much prefer to talk about American literature."[30] American writers were featured in the *Nouvelle revue française,* in *Europe,* and in *Mesures. Etudes anglaises* frequently published criticisms of American literature by such scholarly writers as Maurice Le Breton, Léon Lemonnier, and Jean Simon. And *Cahiers de Paris* and *Mesures* published special issues on the literature of the United States. The number of translations of American books was increasing, and the purchasing and borrowing of books in English reached remarkable proportions. Even the universities were beginning to make room, and a small but increasing number of doctoral dissertations on American writers was coming forth. The time was arriving when the serious study of American literature would be done by soundly trained scholars, rather than by journalistic critics alone. It was not surprising to find Léon Lemonnier, in the May 1939 *Cahiers de Paris,* characterizing contemporary American literature as "one of the great literatures of the world."

Although France was still far from assimilating the humor of America into its own culture, perhaps the way was being prepared. André Maurois, traveling in the United States in the fateful year 1939, remarked: "One sign of the political health of the Anglo-Saxon nations is not only their respect for essential liberties but their invincible sense of humor."[31] Looking back from the vantage point of today, we can view Maurois's words as prophetic of the arrival of the GIs in 1944—bringing, among other things, their invincible sense of humor.

8

Today

World War II and the fall of France put a stop to most of the publication and distribution of American books and to public criticism of them. In 1940, Germany forbade the sale or translation of any books from the Allied countries, including all recent books in the English language. But French enthusiasm for American literature was simply stimulated by attempts at suppression. The reading of American books became a symbol of resistance. A lively black market grew up. A number of presses continued underground publication of forbidden literature. Some American works were translated and printed in Switzerland; and a number of magazines were published in Algiers—most notably *Fontaine,* which did a special issue on American literature in 1943.

As soon as Paris was liberated, in August 1944, the rage for American literature was on. *L'Arbalète* published a special autumn 1944 issue of selections from American novels. The 1943 number of *Fontaine* was reissued in Paris in 1945. Special issues on America were brought out in 1946 by *Cahiers des langues modernes, Esprit, Renaissances,* and *Les Temps modernes.* Book publishers, whose number tripled immediately after the liberation, were scrambling to produce American books both in English and in translation. And despite the inflation of the franc and the shortage of dollars, American publishers were busy keeping up with the demands for their books.[1]

As early as 1945, Albert Guérard, on leave from Harvard University and in France with a U.S. Army Psychological Warfare unit, described the rather indiscriminate enthusiasm for American writers and the limitations of French knowledge of the American literary scene:

> Ignorance of all but a few writers leads them to assume uniformity where none exists; they will be disappointed if they do not find in *Forever Amber* some of the qualities of *Sanctuary* or *Tortilla Flat.* Faulkner, Hemingway, Steinbeck, Dos Passos, Erskine Caldwell—these *are* the American novel: *"l'école d'outre-atlantique."* The simplification is so great that

> they see only minor divergences in the other authors they know and admire: Saroyan, Henry Miller, Pearl Buck! They are victims of the barrier of language which selects a few titles and rejects others; the same barrier which leads us, for instance, to make wide generalizations about "French symbolist poetry"—as though all the poets were alike.[2]

Still there was no denying the enthusiasm, or the probability that it would lead to a less simplistic understanding as more American writing became available.

Maurice Coindreau continued to lead in the evaluation of the American novel. His *Aperçus de littérature américaine,* although made up largely of previously published material, was not published as a book until 1946. It was probably the most important book on American literature published in France in the forties. But Coindreau's voice was joined by the voices of André Maurois and Jean-Paul Sartre. Both had recognized American literature before the War. In fact, Sartre (1905–), already well known as a philosopher and novelist, wrote in 1939: "The greatest literary development in France between 1929 and 1939 was the discovery of Faulkner, Dos Passos, Hemingway, Caldwell, Steinbeck."[3] And Maurois showed a sensitiveness to American humor in his praise of J. P. Marquand in 1939, of Gertrude Stein, Dorothy Parker, and J. Frank Dobie in 1945, and of *The New Yorker* humorists, especially James Thurber, in 1946.[4]

The Yale professor Henri Peyre diagnosed the rage for American novels as a recognition that European literature had become too effete, too abstract, and too analytical. The American novel appealed not to the "unhappy few" but to the healthy millions. It aspired "to take the place left vacant by the disappearance of the epic." Its "willful intensification of life" and its "power to move heroes through ordeals and battles and to relate adventures with convincingness [have left] French (and other European) literature profoundly transformed."[5] And more recent critics have pointed out the impact on French writers of the innocent and primitive focal character who abounds in the American novel. One can, in fact, draw a direct line of influence from the innocent pose of Artemus Ward and other crackerbox humorists, through Mark Twain and Ernest Hemingway, to Albert Camus's *L'Etranger.*[6]

But the French did not know about this influence. *L'Etranger* is not a humorous novel. French readers took American literature seriously—too seriously. Absorbed in social and philosophical concerns, they overlooked the "lighter" side of American literature. They expected too much, and some began to become disillusioned. As early as 1947, the philosopher-novelist Simone de Beauvoir (1908–), writing for the *New York Times Book Review,* felt that a reaction had set in against the great popularity of the American novel—for it was the novel, primarily, that was read in France, although poems and occasional short stories were brought in on the basis of the prestige of the novel, and they were handier for magazine publication. But what was really happening was that the French were taking a more critical and balanced view of American literature. Previously, the reception had often been notably undiscriminating. "We made best sellers of such books as *Gentlemen Prefer Blondes* and *Show Boat,*" wrote Professor Jean Simon of the University of Lille. "We attributed genius to Bromfield, and mixed up Melville, Upton Sinclair, Sinclair Lewis, Tarkington, Hawthorne, London, Hemingway in a frightful 'Irish stew.' "[7] The light comedy of Anita Loos and Booth Tarkington were hardly distinguished from the deadly seriousness of Upton Sinclair and Ernest Hemingway. It was only natural that after such an orgy there would be some taking of stock. A series of interviews with sixteen French writers and critics in *Combat,* early in 1947, revealed a certain skepticism, but that skepticism itself was a sign of how deeply American literature had been felt. "If the reading of Faulkner, Hemingway, Steinbeck and others affords an unusual shock, so that some would say that it is impossible to write today in a valid way without reference to them, then there are several reasons more or less unconfirmed, a certain snobbery, among others," said André Bay. The popularity of American literature might well be a fad, he continued, but even a temporary infatuation can have valid causes.[8]

The critic Maurice Nadeau (1911–), in reply to the criticisms in *Combat,* went even further:

> The new patriots feel bound to believe that the world still comes to us for the fashions of life and thought. Actually, our literature—we say it sadly but sincerely—no longer interests the world. American literature is preferred. For the present and for

> an unforeseeable length of time, American literature expresses most forcefully "the moral, social and metaphysical problems of our epoch."[9]

Literature was expected to express the "problems of our epoch"; there is no mention of the comic spirit.

But the disenchantment was not to be casually brushed away. Jacques Tournier, in 1948, took Maurice Coindreau to task for his overenthusiastic preface to William Maxwell's *The Folded Leaf,* in which, he asserted, Coindreau contradicted himself by affirming the validity of Maxwell's "public schools novel" as opposed to the violence and raciness of Faulkner, Caldwell, and others. Tournier wondered if the American novel had not reached a dead end, in that no new young writers of any merit had appeared. An even stronger protest came from Jean Kanapa, representing a Communist point of view. Kanapa maintained that there was a conspiracy between French publishers and American capitalist-imperialists to suppress the "revolutionary" writers of America and promote Hemingway, Caldwell, Faulkner, and others:

> Who speaks of Dreiser (who was the real pioneer of the American novel) or of Upton Sinclair or Sinclair Lewis; who speaks of Whitman? There have been some bewildered articles on K[enneth] Patchen (the [Henry] Miller of poetry), but Carl Sandburg has been properly buried. In fact, it is nothing more nor less than a systematic literary assassination.[10]

Lewis and Sandburg probably never saw Kanapa's essay, but if they did they probably smiled at its humorlessness.

Actually, the indiscriminate enthusiasm of the early forties was simply replaced by a sounder appraisal and a more serious intellectual interest. The "cinq grands" were still admired—are still admired—and have influenced a generation of French writers.[11] But other Americans began to find places in the appreciation of both the French public and the intelligentsia. In 1957, Professor Raymond Las Vergnas (1902–) listed the following authors as receiving some of the largest recent printings in translation: Thomas Merton (107,000 copies), Frank and Ernestine Gilbreth (200,000), Betty MacDonald (100,000), Pearl Buck (85,000), Mary O'Hara (350,000), Marjorie Kinnan Rawlings (70,000), Mazo de la Roche (140,000), Louis Bromfield

(109,000), John Steinbeck (220,000), Ernest Hemingway (280,000). But he was quick to point out that this list did not reflect the permanent values placed on these and other writers:

> There have been without doubt some shifts of reputation, but they are not reversals, and in fact our public is much better informed on American literary matters than on those of England. At the same time that there is a scarcity of guides for England, there is an abundance here. Alfred Kazin, John Brown, Claude-Edmonde Magny, Michel Mohrt, Cyrille Arnavon, Jean Simon, Maurice Coindreau, to cite only some of the best recent commentators, native as well as French, have brought into perspective the American novel, traced the avenues of approach, analyzed and defined the tendencies of the times, and enlightened our progress even among the youngest of our contemporaries. With the result that, in spite of the inevitable differences in viewpoint and reaction, it is no longer easy to be misinformed.[12]

As early as 1951, Harvard professor Perry Miller saw the influence of American writers as a notable movement in intellectual history, not alone in France but in Europe generally: "In the intellectual history of Europe the impact of these writers during the last two decades is comparable to the domination of the *philosophes* in the eighteenth century, to the contagion of the German romantics in the early nineteenth, or to the later influence of Turgenev, Tolstoy, and Chekhov."[13]

American literature and culture were making a greater and greater impression on the conservative but slowly changing French educational establishment. A few American writers had long been included in the readings in English literature in the schools, but there was almost no study of American literature as such, and, until the 1960s, no required courses in American literature for majors in English. Today such courses are required and specialization in American literature and American studies is officially recognized. A great deal of interest was generated by the United States Information Service, with its libraries and its assistance in sponsorship of programs involving American culture. The Fulbright program was an important force in promoting a true understanding of America, both with its opportunities for French professors to visit America and its provision for American professors in France. The Institute d'Etudes Américaines, founded in 1959 and now under the joint sponsorship of the State University of New York and the University of Paris, has provided and encouraged extracurricular study and discussion of all phases of American culture. In 1967, the Association Française d'Etudes Américaines was founded, and French Americanists now have their own scholarly organization, clearinghouse, and annual conferences.[14]

A roster of the members of the AFEA is a list of the important French scholars of American culture who are on the faculties of the universities. The number of such scholars has increased notably since the early 1960s and will continue to increase. Along with the increase in the number of specialists went an increase in the offerings that the universities could make in the study of American literature. In 1968 twenty-one French universities had 143 programs in American literature under the direction of forty-five faculty members. An indication of the academic activity in the subject is the approximately 155 theses written between 1945 and 1968 at the Sorbonne.[15] The numbers have continued to increase since 1968, though figures are not immediately available. At the 1977 meeting of the AFEA, more than eighty academic specialists in American studies were present, and of course there are others who did not attend.

The generally increasing cordiality toward American literature gradually brought with it an increased acceptance of American humor. The basis for a scholarly and historical understanding of American literature had been set in the ten years following the liberation of Paris with the publication of three histories of American literature in French by French scholars. The last and most comprehensive of the three was by Cyrille Arnavon, one of the foremost authorities on American literature. All three were noteworthy in their recognition of the importance of American humor, though none was very original in its treatment of the native or crackerbox tradition. In fact, all three were so briefly comprehensive that they often did little more than catalogue. They all offered, nevertheless, a good place for the student to begin more intensive studies. "At least we have given the titles," wrote Cestre, "of [the American] works that cultivated French readers would find pleasure or profit in reading."[16]

The first of these histories, and perhaps the one that laid the groundwork for the other two, was by the venerable Charles Cestre—*La Littérature américaine* (1945). Cestre devoted six pages to *l'humour* under the general heading of nineteenth-century realism:

> *L'humour* is not realism, but often it accompanies or favors it. Under the disguise of pleasantry hide observation and good sense. The swirl of drollery is the seething of a candor, of a clear-sighted satire, of a moral intention, of, in fact, truth. The Anglo-Saxon comic spirit, in America as in England, generally implies "*l'humour*" in the precise sense of the word, that is, the laughable expressed in an apparently grave tone; the shock that causes laughter is augmented by the contradiction between the basis—full of exaggeration, absurdity, comicality, grotesqueness—and the form—ably maintained under a mask of seriousness, reason, logic, and technical precision. The men of the West deliberately practiced this deadpan comedy, as relaxation during the evening with their glasses of whiskey. They were the first to applaud the professional humorists, whose reputation flowed back from the banks of the Mississippi toward the East and became national.[17]

Aside from the myth that native American humor began in the West and "flowed back" east—a myth originated in America—Cestre started out well. Unfortunately, the rest of his six pages, except for one paragraph, had to be devoted to Mark Twain. The one paragraph attempted to characterize John Phoenix (George Horatio Derby), Artemus Ward (Charles Farrar Browne), Petroleum V. Nasby (David Ross Locke), and Josh Billings (Henry Wheeler Shaw) in one sentence each. Furthermore, his treatment of Twain was conventional, including some of the conventional French misinterpretations.

In addition to the passage on nineteenth-century humor, Cestre dealt at some length with Benjamin Franklin and very briefly with the twentieth-century humorists Ring Lardner, Irvin S. Cobb, Don Marquis, and George Ade.

In 1950, Jacques Fernand Cahen published a book with the same title as Cestre's *La Littérature américaine,* in the Collection que sais-je?—an encyclopedic series of handbooks on all kinds of subjects. Cahen's book was very opinionated, sometimes superficial, and sometimes quite perceptive. For example: "If one could say of Franklin that he was the first civilized American, one could say of Irving that he was the first American who was solely a man of letters. Moreover, this is his only claim to true originality." On the other hand, he had flashes of insight that are worth considering. Of Emily Dickinson he said: "Her themes are not new, but she always shows a vivacity, a spirit of satire and a humor that make them original in spite of everything." Or of Erskine Caldwell's *Tobacco Road:* "It is indeed a caricature of the literature of despondency, all its characteristics being carried to excess." And of John Steinbeck: "Steinbeck has . . . a tendency to believe that the bad boys have the most goodness, as he shows in his amusing *Tortilla Flat* (1935) and *Cannery Row* (1945) which are a kind of collection of fantastic tales for grown-ups, with a most delicious humor."[18]

Cahen also pointed up the satire and sarcasm of Stephen Crane and the humor of Ellen Glasgow, and gave special mention to Joaquin Miller, Bret Harte, and John Hay. And of course he paid proper respects to Mark Twain and Sinclair Lewis. On the whole, his book was the most eccentric and the most provocative of the three literary histories.

Cyrille Arnavon's *Histoire littéraire des Etats-Unis* (1953) attempted a balanced but not an impersonal judgment of American literature, and relied—sometimes heavily—on standard American sources, such as Walter Blair's *Native American Humor.* His coverage of American humor was quantitatively sound. Of his 438 pages, he devoted two good paragraphs to Augustus Baldwin Longstreet and Davy Crockett, as representative of the beginnings of backwoods humor in literature. Five pages were assigned to "La Littérature de l'humour," including a few sentences apiece on Seba Smith, James Russell Lowell, William Tappan Thompson, Johnson Jones Hooper, George Washington Harris, George Horatio Derby, Henry Wheeler Shaw, David Ross Locke, and Charles Farrar Browne. Bret Harte received almost four pages, Mark Twain almost seven, and Ambrose Bierce a page and a half. Three and a half pages on "La Poésie humoristique" considered John Hay, Irwin Russell, Charles Godfrey Leland, Eugene Johnson, and Langston Hughes. And there were references to humor, wit, sarcasm, and satire in the works of the "serious" writers.

Arnavon characterized Anglo-Saxon *humour* as a realistic reaction against excessive romanticism:

> *L'Humour* has always been and will be again, since the 1840s, in the Anglo-Saxon countries (as with Thackeray, for example), the enemy of passionate effusion. When lyric intensity ex-

hausts itself through lack of sincerity, there will be inevitably some wits prompt to laugh at the ridiculousness that attaches to inspired or grandiloquent attitudes. In America, as we see, romantic poses—Byronesque particularly—were never truly prevalent because they offended the egalitarian convictions of militant democracy. This spirit of simplicity goes along, on the other hand, with the tonality of the humorists, who speak more or less directly from a popular level. Humor, which in one sense is the negation of sad reality—and therefore an evasion—can also, by introducing common everyday matters into literature, prepare the way for realism. With story-tellers and novelists, humor and the stock-in-trade of realism are concomitant.

And, according to Arnavon, American humor differed from English only in its extravagance:

> It is not necessary to try to define American humor too strictly. The contrast that is often made with the English variety of humor is artificial. Meanwhile, it can be said that the blustering buffoons of the "frontier" often go beyond—in an enormous farce—the limits which a very British sense of decency in regard to emotion would allow for a humorous effect.[19]

Arnavon's characterization of native American humor persists, but his history of American literature has been in part superseded by Jean Béranger's and Maurice Gonnaud's *La Littérature américaine jusqu'en 1865*. Published in 1974, the book recognized the humorists of the old Southwest, that is, Augustus Baldwin Longstreet, Thomas Bangs Thorpe, Johnson Jones Hooper, and George Washington Harris, with a five-page chapter but ignored the New England humorists. Perhaps the authors mean to include the humor of Haliburton, Smith, Shillaber, Whitcher, and others in their next volume. At any rate, they perceived a "profound cleavage between two varieties of [nineteenth-century American] literature, one noble, serious, conforming to the traditional canons of taste, the other popular, lively, exuberant, but breaking all the rules, ridiculing the proprieties and confusingly disorganized."[20] Further, they gave reasonable space to such early humorists as Franklin, Royall Tyler, the Connecticut Wits, Joel Barlow, and Washington Irving.

Besides the histories of American literature, several attempts to survey twentieth-century American literature came in the wake of Coindreau's *Aperçus.* Even before Coindreau's book was published and presumably before the presses of Paris were back in full swing, Nelly Vaucher-Zananiri published in Cairo *Voix d'Amérique: études sur la littérature américaine d'aujourd'hui* (1945). Despite its title, the book was little more than a list of authors with brief biographies and capsule summaries of selected works. The list of forty writers included the "humoristes" Ring Lardner, Christopher Morley, William Saroyan, and James Thurber, although the author was reluctant to call most of these "true humorists":

> In modern American literature, we find few true humorists. It seems that the difficult postwar period and the years of depression have especially developed in the young writers a sense of mordant criticism or of incisive irony. Sinclair Lewis branded harshly the whole spectrum of parvenus and materialists. Dos Passos took part with passion in the social and political battles. As to fantasy, the burlesque parodies of Erskine, the stories and sketches of Thurber reveal a bitter pessimism. They have none of the easy grace of Saroyan nor the imaginative verve of Christopher Morley, who, in his stories, introduces us into an enchanted domain where poetry and humor are mixed up together and transport the reader into a utopian sphere and sometimes a fairy illusion.[21]

Christopher Morley, then, appears to have been Vaucher-Zananiri's ideal of the true humorist, but regardless of the semantic hair-splitting, there was an honest attempt to discriminate between different facets of the comic spirit in America. The author's inclusion of such predominantly comic writers as Booth Tarkington, Thornton Wilder, James Branch Cabell, and J. P. Marquand is to be commended, though we might lament the omission of Robert Benchley, Ogden Nash, Will Rogers, and George Ade.

In 1949, André Rousseaux published a three-volume study of modern literature, *Littérature du vingtième siècle,* and included some American writing. In his otherwise quite sober work appeared the following passage on Hemingway, which perhaps illustrates the problem that French readers sometimes had in accepting the apparent banality of American realistic dialogue:

> A truly natural human dialogue is often exhaustingly banal. I know that Hemingway fills his dialogue with his abundant experience as adventurer and humorist: the other war on the Italian Front, Paris in the twenties, hunting in Africa, the

world of boxers, jockeys, sailors—not to mention Spain. The technique, well mastered, of all the occupations that his characters take part in, of all the sports that they practice, serves their purpose with true substance. The author's irony and easy frankness cause this harvest of unrefined human truths to fall amusingly into place. Yes, such is the tumult of life, but it makes a lot of useless noise, expecially when the speakers are drunk, as in certain of Hemingway's novels almost from beginning to end. And the dialogue of men is valuable, on the contrary, not only when it projects their exterior reality but when it reveals—perhaps in a chance word—the essential truth of man, the unique key to the farce, the drama, and the diorama.[22]

It is difficult to think of Hemingway as a humorist, yet Rousseaux seems to have been reaching for the key to his dead-pan manner—his surface objectivity—which is a conscious inheritance from Mark Twain and the whole tradition of native American humor.

Jean Simon's *Le Roman américain au XXe siècle,* though published only a year later (1950), showed an altogether new and sophisticated understanding of American humor. Beginning with the sources of twentieth-century fiction in the late nineteenth century, he noted that the style of William Dean Howells, "not lacking in humor and liveliness, makes his books agreeable to read." He found in Henry Blake Fuller, H. C. Bunner, and others a genre "humoristique" that was popular in America before World War I, and he ranked O. Henry as "the master of the humorous story." He noted the humor of John Erskine and James Branch Cabell and, later, of J. P. Marquand and Stephen Vincent Benét, while he likened William Saroyan's "mixture of clowning and tears" to that of Charlie Chaplin. He perceived the "rather sad humor" of John Dos Passos in *Journeys Between Wars,* the "virile laughter" of Hemingway, the "macabre buffoonery" of Faulkner in *As I Lay Dying,* the "rich range of comic effects" in Erskine Caldwell, and the picaresque element in John Steinbeck. He recognized also the notable lack of humor in Theodore Dreiser and James T. Farrell. But perhaps his most perceptive comments, in regard to American humor, are those on Sinclair Lewis:

What has perhaps made the fortune of Lewis the satirist is his sense of humor. The books of Frank Norris and Stephen Crane were sad. The novels of Dreiser are so humorless that it is

> painful to read him. Lewis seems to have rediscovered the tradition of Mark Twain. And to understand his success, it is necessary to realize how this easy, good-natured humor, usually without particular significance, is typically American. There is not an orator, in a ceremony or official banquet, who would hesitate to slip into his discourse an anecdote to provoke laughter, despite the solemnity of the occasion. Lewis goes all the way. Joking is continuous under his pen. There is humor in the situations, in the awkwardness of the actions, in the ridiculous titles or the mock extracts from newspapers, in the aims of the most insignificant characters or of the most serious ones. And the whole work of the novelist is lightened; it is amusing, absorbing. Whatever most irritates him can hardly efface his smile. This is without doubt the secret of his success.[23]

Although humor was brought in only incidentally and no section of Simon's book was devoted to humor, the author recognized its underlying importance in American literature and especially in the tradition of Mark Twain.

On the other hand, when the editors of *Europe* published a volume on American literature in 1959, the result was remarkable for its lack of almost any consideration of humor, with one important exception. Ogden Nash was one of the sixteen best American poets to be represented by a brief biography and a selected poem or two. The headnote on Nash stated: "He is essentially a humorist and perhaps the most dynamic of the American humorous poets. . . . Let us add that Nash, a veritable jongleur, has utilized all the possible and imaginable techniques to convey his humor, which goes from bitterness to the most unbridled fantasy."[24]

By the 1960s, a new generation of American writers had begun to fall into place, and French scholars and critics were generally as up-to-date and perceptive in their criticisms as were American scholars and critics. Furthermore, their recognition of American humor and its recent developments was sound. Pierre Brodin's *Présences contemporaines: écrivains américains d'aujourd'hui* (1964) comprised sixteen American novelists, each chapter containing a brief biography and summaries of some of the works of the author, with a few critical comments. Brodin (1909–) was a French critic residing in the United States and dean of the French school in New York. Basically a simple introduction to the contemporary American novel for the general

French reader, his book provided enough criticism to allow the reader to make his own estimates. For example, Brodin noted the "undercurrent of humor and irony" in Saul Bellow; the "first-class humor" of Truman Capote; the "pain twisted into humor" of Bernard Malamud; the "humor and tenderness" of Flannery O'Connor; the "predominant quality" of humor, over and above the satire, in James Earl Powers; the "incontestable comic gift" of Philip Roth; and the rather different "gift of humor, satire, and irony" of J. D. Salinger.[25] Of John Updike, Brodin said: "The humor and irony, already quite apparent in his poems and stories, burst forth joyously in *Rabbit, Run.*" He considered the novel to be Kafka-esque except for its humor. His remarks on Ralph Ellison were even more discerning: "Strictly bound to the triple notion of clowning, absurdity, and foolishness, his humor is not above the use of word play, the pun, the grotesque slogan ('If it's the Optic White, it's the Right White'), and it uses freely the joke, as expressed in the blues, which reconcile violence and human dignity through irony."[26]

Brodin saw American humor as more than an element in modern American novels; the comic tradition—the innocent pose, the irony, the absurdity—was their basis.

> Their heroes are "innocents" who feel guilty (or "sinners" who feel innocent), free men who are also slaves, *victim-rebels* like Prometheus, like Oedipus, like Don Quixote, like so many other representatives of the great myths of literature and art, martyrs, anarchists, clowns, dreamers who dream of immortality in a world delimited by suffering and death. These are heroes of the *absurd,* but the absurd envisaged with *irony* rather than rancor. They live in a state of tension or alienation in regard to society. They are "strangers," a little like that of Camus, but with a whole specifically American tradition of innocence behind them—the innocence of a new country which has rejected, or thought it had rejected, the sins of the Old World and is always astonished and scandalized to see them reborn in a virgin land.[27]

The following year, 1965, Pierre Dommergues of the University of Paris in *Les Ecrivains américains d'aujourd'hui* developed further the theme of innocence, absurdity, and irony in post-World War II American literature. He divided American writers into those who revolt, such as Norman Mailer and Arthur Miller; those who accept, such as J. D. Salinger, Robert

Lowell, and Richard Wilbur; those who escape into innocence, such as Carson McCullers, Truman Capote, Tennessee Williams; those who disengage themselves into beatitude, such as Jack Kerouac and Allen Ginsberg; and finally those, such as Richard Wright, Edward Albee, Joseph Heller, Ralph Ellison, and Saul Bellow, who face life with a healthy desire for personal lucidity in spite of the absurdity of the universe. The latter and most modern group, according to Dommergues, belongs to the "era of the possible," and represents "a creative convergence" of the previous attitudes. "The writers of the possible . . . conscious of the diverse 'attitudes' that they have sometimes incarnated in the course of their literary career . . . attempt a supreme synthesis where, this time, the dominant idea is that man is a being, if not free, at least capable of a certain number of choices." These writers, he said, are undertaking a new exploration of the universe, an exploration that "implies, for their characters, certain qualities, of which the most important are lucidity—indispensable for self-direction; love—which leads to others; the taste for liberty—which incites to discovery; a certain kind of passivity—which encourages resistance to the absurd; and a sense of humor—which allows one to extricate himself without too much difficulty." The result is a literature in which "the traditional distinctions between the comic, the tragic, the satiric, and the lyric shade into each other."[28]

Thus, the mythically innocent and Edenic American, created in part by the French philosophes of the eighteenth century, found in the nineteenth that an innocent pose paid off in terms of freedom to observe and to criticize—à la Mark Twain. With the disillusionment of the twentieth century, Americans still pretended to be innocent, or longed to be innocent, or attempted to return to innocence. Today they have managed to retain the wonder and the joy of life and liberty that innocence implies, while their sense of humor modifies and protects them from the absurdities of an otherwise chaotic world. This is the American image today—projected by American writers, as seen by America's friends abroad.

Attempts to survey the contemporary American scene continued to be popular. *La Prairie perdue: histoire du roman américain* (1966) by Jacques Cabau, another professor at the University of Paris, was a conventional analysis of sixteen American novels, with no emphasis on humor. However, the analyses of John Updike's *Rabbit, Run* and *The Centaur* rank among the best criticism of that author. Pierre Dommergues's *Les U.S.A. à la recherche de leur identité* (1967) took a new approach. It was a series of "encounters" with forty American writers—mostly in their own words, though translated into French. Dommergues gave due proportion to "la folie" as part of the American search for identity, and to humor as a concomitant of health and optimism. Another survey of the American novel was Marc Saporta's *Histoire du roman américain,* which was notably lacking in attention to humor. In *Panorama de la littérature contemporaine aux Etats-Unis* (1971), John Brown, who described himself as an American "going and coming between New York and Paris for the last twenty years," combined an encyclopedic history of modern American writers, a representative selection of their writings, and a number of essays on America by American writers. He had little to say about humor except for his comments on the novel of the absurd—from Joseph Heller to Terry Southern. But he concluded his criticism of the absurd manner in fiction by pointing out the danger of its becoming mere formula: "The sick yellow smile and black humor can end up being as monotonous and gratuitous as the rosy optimism of certain feminine literature."[29]

Two anthologies of American literature for French students of English show the increasing interest in the subject in the schools. They are Maurice Le Breton's *The Student's Anthology of American Literature* (1955), and Pierre Deflaux, Jean-Paul Martin, Daniel Royot, and Jean Guiguet's *American Trails: An Anthology of Representative Works* (1970). Both are characterized by very brief selections from a large number of American authors. The book by Le Breton, one of the first French professors of American literature, covers sixty-eight authors in the first volume, 1600-1865, of 458 pages—an average of considerably less than six pages per author when the table of contents, indexes, and appendixes are subtracted. Such an approach, however, makes possible the inclusion of Abigail Adams, John James Audubon, Hinton Rowan Helper, and others who are important in American culture if not in literature strictly defined. Further, it allows relatively fair space to the more or less humorous writers Sarah Kemble Knight, William Byrd, Thomas Morton, Royall Tyler, Nathaniel Ward, Hugh Henry Brackenridge, Augustus Baldwin Longstreet, and John Pendleton Kennedy, not to mention Benjamin Franklin and Washington Irving. It is to be hoped that such a quick taste will encourage students to look more deeply into individual American writers.[30]

The more recent anthology by Deflaux and his coeditors, all faculty members in universities outside of Paris, is in two volumes of approximately 400 pages each. (A third volume covering 1910 to 1970 was not published because of the publisher's reluctance in view of French copyright law concerning American authors.) It gives somewhat more space to fewer authors—thirteen in the first volume, 1620-1850, for example. The aim, according to Jean Giguet's foreword, was "to provide students, not with a bird's eye and secondhand view of the literary landscape nor with a series of negotiable abstracts of biographies or works they could produce on request without caring in the least for what the résumés or critical definitions stand for, but with a choice of texts which are generally accepted as representing the American tradition."[31] Unfortunately for the cause of American humor, the limitations of space in the first volume restricted the representation of anything comic to two works: Franklin's satire "An Edict of the King of Prussia" and Irving's humorous tale "Rip Van Winkle." It is a well-chosen but tiny sampling for the beginner.

At least three anthologies of humor deserve to be mentioned in regard to post-World War II impressions of American humor. The first of these, *Anthologie de l'humour noir,* by the famous critic André Breton (1896-1966) was published immediately before the War, in 1940, but presumably made its impression later. A collection of translated humorous writings that satisfied the editor's Freudian definition, the book contained two American works, O. Henry's "While the Auto Waits" and Poe's "The Imp of the Perverse."[32]

Un Siècle d'humour anglo-américain, edited by Michel Chrestien and Jacques Sternberg, was composed of translations of humorous writings in English, about half of which were American, from Poe to Perelman, Bierce to Benchley. The volume was finely printed and bound, with a brief but thoughtful preface by André Maurois and numerous cartoons by Ronald Searle, Saul Steinberg, and others—evidently meant for the leisurely entertainment of a fairly well-to-do reading public.[33]

An even more handsome volume was *Les Chefs d'oeuvre du sourire,* edited by Jacques Sternberg, Jacques Bergier, and Alex Grall in 1964. Besides a more lavish collection of cartoons—English, French, and American—it contained some ninety brief selections by late nineteenth-century and twentieth-century humorists of different nationalities. America was represented by Ambrose Bierce, Mark Twain, Ring Lardner, Robert Benchley, James Thurber, and Art Buchwald.[34]

The list is representative of French recognition of American humorists in the 1960s. All these writers, with the exception of Twain, were more or less "discovered" during the decade; translations of all of them and English-language editions of some were published in France. Bierce's *The Devil's Dictionary* was translated by Jacques Papy in 1964. The introduction by Jacques Sternberg pointed out that Bierce had been awarded the Grand Prix de l'Humour Noir, an award of which he was eminently deserving. And, in further characterizing the somewhat neglected American author, Sternberg defined *l'humoriste* in general as "a deliberately neurasthenic spirit whom nothing can console."[35]

Benchley was translated by Paulette Vielhomme in 1963. Again, the introduction was by Sternberg, who characterized Benchley as "one of the most vigilant and most virulent humorists that the United States has ever known."[36]

Jacques Sternberg (1923–) deserves credit as possibly the most important popularizer of American literary humor in France. In addition to his impressive anthologies and to his edition of Bierce, which was a selection of the Club des Chefs-d'Oeuvres, he was the general editor of the series "Humour Secret" which included not only *Benchley* but also *Thurber,* translated in 1963 by Christiane Potesta and Claude Dalla Torre. According to the jacket blurb of *Benchley:*

> There has been no book series in France consecrated to humor—at least not to that which contains cruelty, coldness, poetry—and which is called English humor—the only humor, the pure humor, the true humor, according to its devotees.
>
> The series Humour Secret aims to give to this humor the letters patent of nobility that it has not yet acquired in France. There exists in the world, but especially in the United States and England, a number of writers of great value whose virulent humor is generally unknown outside their own country. This series proposes to explore, then, a practically unexplored domain. It will uphold a certain kind of humor which is perhaps nothing more than a certain smile, and certainly not a foolish laughter.[37]

Sternberg's preface to *Thurber* concluded with a general comment on the humorists of the first half of the twentieth century, of whom Thurber was the outstanding representative:

> When we finally reach an evaluation of the contribution of the literature of this century, when we seek to know which authors have best described this twentieth century, those who have felt it most acutely, it is not impossible that these humorists will have more importance than all the subtle analysts who are so amply rewarded in literature. Then only they will take their revenge.[38]

An acknowledged partisan of "English humor," Sternberg brought up a point that was not new perhaps but that bears serious consideration. Will James Thurber someday be remembered along with Hemingway and Steinbeck? Is American humor indeed one of our greatest achievements?

In addition to the translations promoted by Sternberg, the 1960s saw Ring Lardner, *Dix nouvelles (Haircut and Other Stories),* translated by Jacques Guicharnaud (1963); two books by Art Buchwald, *N'oubli pas d'écrire (Don't Forget to Write)* (1960), and *Combien ça fait en dollars (How Much Is That in Dollars)* (1962), both translated by France-Marie Watkins; and Ogden Nash, *Envers et contre tous,* "adapted" by Renaud de Jouvenal (1963).

While general histories and anthologies, critical journalism, and popular publications revealed an increasing interest in American humor in France, scholarly research on specific topics developed more slowly. Until the 1960s, Franklin and Twain dominated the attention of those university scholars who were inclined to look seriously into American humor. Gilbert Chinard's work on Franklin continued through the 1950s. The studies of Mark Twain increased with the years, and Roger Asselineau's definitive bibliography, *The Literary Reputation of Mark Twain from 1910 to 1950* (1954), could be considerably extended in terms of French scholarship alone. Cyrille Arnavon's *Les Lettres américaines devant la critique française, 1887–1917* (1951) examined French criticism of American literature and included a chapter entitled "Les Humoristes: Mark Twain," in which, though Twain's comic predecessors were acknowledged, the French critics and translators of Twain himself were well covered. Georges Remords's monograph, "Les Lettres américaines devant la critique universitaire française" (1956) extended Arnavon's study to a more recent period and emphasized the more scholarly studies, but had virtually nothing to say of American humor.

In 1957, Edgar Edgeworth MacDonald wrote a doctoral dissertation, "Les Sources étrangers du roman épique de James Branch Cabell" at the University of Paris under the direction of Maurice Le Breton, which showed the influence not only of Provençal poetry on Cabell but also of Rabelais, Molière, and especially Voltaire. Another dissertation under the same director was Reine Kruk's "Un Siècle de magazines californiens," 1962, which, along with mention of Mark Twain, Bret Harte, and Joaquin Miller, signaled Ambrose Bierce as the supreme representative of "the satire of caustic wit, of a certain humor" that was notably Californian.

In the same year appeared René Rémond's study of the formation of the French image of America, *Les Etats-Unis devant l'opinion française, 1815–1852.* It, along with two works by Americans, Durand Echeverria's *Mirage in the West: A History of the French Image of American Society to 1815* (1957) and Simon Copans's as yet unpublished study of French opinion toward America in the middle nineteenth century, afford a profound accounting of the historical basis of French attitudes toward the United States.

Two books on individual American writers were published in 1964. Jean Normand's *Nathaniel Hawthorne: esquisse d'une analyse de la création* (Paris: Presses Universitaire de France) has been translated into English and is a significant contribution to Hawthorne scholarship. Though Normand stressed the black side of Hawthorne's creative spirit, he also pointed out the obverse side, that of the "protean joker with a delight in mystification" and of the self-deprecating storyteller. Maurice Gonnaud's *Individu et société dans l'oeuvre de Ralph Waldo Emerson: essai de biographie spirituelle* (1964) had little to say about humor, but his recent article, "The Humane Seer: Humor and Its Avatars in Emerson's Writings" in *American Transcendental Quarterly* (1974), demonstrated convincingly that elements of native American humor existed especially in Emerson's early and late works.

In 1965, Bernard Poli showed a real understanding of the tradition of native American humor in his *Mark Twain, écrivain de l'ouest.* Pierre Weisz's doctoral dissertation, "James Thurber"

(1965), made no attempt to place the humorist in the tradition but rather analyzed his approach in the light of French theories of humor. Weisz saw the basis of Thurber's humor in human eccentricity and defined his humoristic point of view as one of complicity with the reader. Jean Wagner's *Runyonese: The Mind and Craft of Damon Runyon* (1966) examined Runyon as a philosopher-humorist, linked him with the crackerbox tradition, and explicated the artistry of his use of the present tense and the causal clause. Guy Jean Forgue's *H. L. Mencken: l'homme, l'oeuvre, l'influence* (1967) was a solid study of Mencken, characterizing him as a veritable humorist in the Jonsonian sense. In the same year, 1967, Gilbert Debusscher provided a traditional French analysis of Edward Albee's work in *Edward Albee: Tradition and Renewal,* translated into English by Anne D. Williams. Although humor was not a primary concern of Debusscher, he noted a combination of satire and farce in Albee's early work, and felt a tone of "pity and sympathy" that distinguished him from Strindberg, especially in *Who's Afraid of Virginia Woolf.*

In *La Genèse de l'esprit de révolte dans le roman américain, 1875–1915* (1968) Marianne Debouzy considered the spirit of revolt in William Dean Howells, Hamlin Garland, Stephen Crane, Frank Norris, Theodore Dreiser, Jack London, Upton Sinclair, and others; but it was Mark Twain, especially in his late years, who most purely represented the revolt of the individual against a hostile universe. Twain's humor was black, according to the author, and hence destructive, but it was also liberating.

Jean Béranger, in 1969, published a thorough and much-needed study of one of America's earliest humorists, *Nathaniel Ward (ca. 1578–1652),* in which he praised the variety of Ward's humorous techniques. In *Francis Scott Fitzgerald*—published that same year by Bernard Poli, André Le Vot, Geneviève Fabre, and Michel Fabre—Le Vot contrasted the lyric hyperbole of Gatsby in *The Great Gatsby* with the comic distance of the narrator Nick, while the Fabres pointed out Fitzgerald's parodies of himself and his acquaintances in *Tender Is the Night.* Also in 1969, Robert Silhol published what he called a combination of Freudian, Marxist, and traditional literary analysis of Sinclair Lewis in *Les Tyrants tragiques.* Lewis's style, according to Silhol, alternated between cliché, quantitative realism, and satiric contradiction—though the author seemed often to miss the irony of Lewis's use of clichés. In 1971, Maurice Coindreau's significant study of William Faulkner, *The Time of William Faulkner: A French View of Modern American Fiction,* recognized Faulkner's humor, especially in *The Reivers,* but did not develop that recognition.

In the 1970s, scholarly activity has intensified, especially in American humor. Roger Asselineau continues to work with several American writers. His introduction to a 1973 edition of Baudelaire's translation of Poe's *The Adventures of Arthur Gordon Pym* and his "Walt Whitman's Humor" (1974) demonstrate again the French awareness of humor in serious American writers. Jean Harzic considers William Faulkner as a humorist in his rounded analysis *Faulkner: présence littéraire* (1973). Maurice Gonnaud's study of humoristic techniques in Emerson (1974) has been noted already. Jean Béranger extends his work on Nathaniel Ward with "Voices of Humor in Nathaniel Ward" (1975). Daniel Royot continues his research in nineteenth-century New England humor—Seba Smith, Matthew Whittier, John Neal, James Russell Lowell—but he is also concerned with the chronological range of American humor, as his analysis of Thomas Berger, "Aspects of the American Picaresque in *Little Big Man*" (1977), attests. His essay is part of an anthology of French criticism of recent American fiction, *Les Américanistes* (1977).

In addition to the traditional historical and analytical approaches, some of Royot's work reflects the recent concern with linguistic approaches to American literature and humor. His "Eléments phonologiques du dialecte noir dans 'Huckleberry Finn'" (1972) is a step toward a much-needed study of Twain's use of American dialects. He has in progress a semiotic study of Franklin's sayings in *Poor Richard's Almanac.* Violette Morin's "L'Histoire drôle" (1976) analyzes jokes from the point of view of communication theory. And Robert Escarpit, the foremost French scholar on the nature of *l'humour,* has turned his attention to the communication code that is shared by the humorist and his audience. His book *L'Ecrit et la communication* (Paris: Presses Universitaires, 1973) is not concerned with humor but indicates the basis of his current thoughts on the subject.

Finally, there is today a return to the psychoanalytic or neo-Freudian approach to literature, using psychological techniques to analyze, for example, the humor in individual works. This approach is represented in a recent issue (July 1973) of the *Revue française de psychanalyse* and particularly in an article by Paul Racamier, "Entre humour et folie."

In 1976, the Association Française d'Etudes Américaines (AFEA) began publication of a semiannual journal, *Revue française d'études américaines,* which provides an outlet for scholarly work in American studies. Until then the French student of American studies was limited to book publication, university monographs, the popular media, the journals on British language and literature, or the journals published in America. The first issue of the *Revue* centers on contemporary American fiction: William Burroughs, Stanley Crawford, Richard Brautigan, Vladimir Nabokov, Robert Coover, Ishmael Reed, John Hawkes, Kurt Vonnegut, Flannery O'Connor, and James Purdy. The editor of the first issue, André Le Vot, notes a shift in American fiction from the use of language as an instrument to express realistic or psychological truths to its use for its own sake, "apprehended in its materiality, its opacity, recognized as an autonomous force" in a sense until now reserved for poetry. The serious examination of the language of the American writers considered necessarily involves word play, figures of speech, far-fetched imagery, exaggeration—devices that are often comic in their contemporary usage.

French understanding of American humor achieved a kind of apotheosis in the 1977 conference of the AFEA on the theme of American humor, and in the subsequent special issue of the *Revue française d'études américaines* (Number 4), composed of talks delivered at the conference. The conference began with Jean Raynaud's structural analysis of jokes and puns, "Les Mécanismes de l'humour." Daniel Royot, Giliane Morell, and James Austin demonstrated the distinguishing characteristics of Yankee, Southwestern, and Western humor respectively. There were papers on S. J. Perelman by Rolande Diot, Erskine Caldwell by Michel Bandry, Frank Baum *(The Wonderful Wizard of Oz)* by C. Johnson, and Vladimir Nabokov by Maurice Couturier. A symposium on "Feminine Humor in American Literature: An Anatomy" reached a tentative conclusion that there is no psychological difference between male and female humor, though of course differences in subject matter are apparent. The conference concluded with Escarpit's analysis of humoristic codes.

There are still obstacles to the study of American culture in

France, the most important being the high costs of obtaining American books and articles, either through libraries or bookstores, and the dwindling support of the United States government for international exchanges of books and scholars. But American literature and American humor have been fully received in France since mid-century. French criticism, both negative and positive, can no longer be discounted. The influence of the literary reviews of the nineteenth and early twentieth centuries has given way to that of movies, newspapers, and television, on the one hand, and universities on the other. American culture has penetrated—for good or evil—the lowest to the highest levels of French society.

9

American Humor and the French Psyche

DANIEL ROYOT

For generations, French students in Anglo-American literature have been taught subtle distinctions between wit, humor, and irony. Indeed, it seems that the sense of humor is a basic component of the Anglo-Saxon character but any discussion about it often sounds like a debate on the sex of angels. Besides, why should Americans be privileged with that special gift? Was it a bonus given over by God to the puritanical happy few?

In *Tristram Shandy,* Laurence Sterne stated: "Everything in this world . . . is big with jest and has wit in it, and instruction too, if we can but find it out." French people might feel proud to know that they can be humorists occasionally, just as Monsieur Jourdain in Molière's *Le Bourgeois Gentilhomme* was delighted to learn that he talked in prose. Yet it is customary to hear friends say about an American comedy: "It is incomprehensible, it must be humor." If "the feeling of relativity is the very soul of humor," as Louis Cazamian put it, it follows that France never received a fair share of objectivity and humility. Fortunately, Americans are sufficiently creative and profuse to offer us the kind of good laughs that we need so badly.

When I was teaching a seminar on Yankee humor in California, I thought it convenient to refer to Bergson, Freud, and Kierkegaard. As I was painstakingly engaged in analyzing such notions as playfulness, exuberance, overstatement, and understatement, my puzzled students reminded me that they first expected the teacher to crack some good jokes. Once again, I realized with hurt pride that Frenchmen are too often enslaved to categories and fight hard to make material fit into previous definitions, instead of enlarging definitions according to material. As the graduates' final evaluation of my performance was not unfavorable, I guess that, after all, we did not do a bad job together.

For this reason, I am fully aware that James Austin's study fulfills a double task. It teaches Americans about their own attitudes as seen by uncommitted foreigners but also brings to light sophisticated research methods. Now that American humor has invaded European culture, it may be rewarding to complement Austin's work by suggesting modern responses that critics have not dealt with for want of references. Millions of lowbrow French people enjoy American comedies, cartoons, and serials, but most papers, TV guides, or motion picture magazines carefully avoid objective criticism about those productions. The following pages simply outline a comparative study of French and American popular humor since World War II.

Sociology teaches us that acculturation results from a direct and prolonged contact between two cultures of unequal strength. Yet one might also discover similarities in our national tempers that facilitate that process. Though it is hazardous to seek comparisons between French and American folk humor, it is clear that they both have a common European heritage. Furthermore, we now identify with Americans in many ways and tend to love and hate the same things. Should we still believe that our taboos are different, that American humor is all inclusive whereas French humor remains selective, that Americans are pragmatists and Frenchmen ideologists? The fact that we now laugh for similar reasons is meaningful but, ultimately, a syncretic vision of the universe could endanger our sense of humor. Let us remain as dissimilar as possible!

While enraptured French crowds were welcoming their liberators after four years of German occupation, dispassionate observers could already notice that the GIs also brought in their train the tawdry paraphernalia of the American way of life. The summer of 1944 thus marked the beginning of a steady Americanization of the long frustrated "hexagon."[1] In the late forties, jazz became the musical support of existentialist folklore at Saint Germain des Prés while graffiti relentlessly denounced Yankee imperialism in suburban back streets. Today, the slow emergence of the affluent society, the impact of the mass media, and especially the dumping of Hollywood movies concur to establish the United States as the major cultural model for the new generations. Naturally, this challenge does not fail to arouse mixed feelings. In fact, few French people realize how paradoxical their attitudes may be toward this alteration of national tastes and habits. Both admiring and critical, young radicals readily succumb to transatlantic faddism but also condemn the materialistic urges bred by big business. In May 1968, many leftists wished universities to emulate the American college system while still favoring a centralized organization supported by government funds. The middle class now worships management and marketing but would gladly experiment with life in communes. American humor pervades magazines and countless imitations of Broadway musical comedies unsuccessfully attempt to sweep the time-honored "opérette" off the Paris stages.

In our age of confusion, patterns of thought imported from the New World are constantly liable to distortion. However, no serious efforts have been made to expose unabashed plagiarists and counterfeiters. Within the last few years, we have had Celtic pop songs and a rock opera about the French Revolution while pseudo-women libbers who buy dresses from Cardin's give hints about successful adultery during winter sports.[2] Admittedly, both comic distance and militancy would be necessary to unmask exploiters of public gullibility. When it comes to genuine productions, to what extent can American humor survive once transplanted, as social conditions are different in the host country?

On that score, France would seem to be an exceptionally favorable soil, owing to its folk traditions and reputation of long standing as "most intelligent nation in the world." Yet strong nationalistic trends have developed in the last decade and, now, foreign observers feel impelled to compare "Eternal France" to a morose old lady who deplores the pranks of restless neighbors, though secretly tickled by the playboys of the Western World. So far, the deep-rooted Gallic spirit appears unimpaired and still apt to assimilate whatever may enrich the lore of native humor. Yet the very number of American productions flooding the French market makes it a formidable task to evaluate the response of the general public. It seems that any such attempt should first point to similar trends in folk humor.

France probably enjoys the greatest variety of landscapes and regional characters in Western Europe. Along each of the five state boundaries, idiosyncrasies owe something to the neighboring country while still retaining national traits. In the Southeast, Occitanie claims cultural independence, endeavoring to recapture the humanism of medieval troubadours. Farther west, Brittany proudly revives her legendary Celtic past. Not so long ago, the Breton girl was often identified with Bécassine, a thick-headed maid hired by the Paris bourgeoisie, who delighted readers of comic strips. Popular humor still resorts to the treasury of folk material even though so-called regional narratives, jokes, or puns often turn out to be more akin to fakelore. Anyway, such pluralism has always been serenely accepted and genuinely enjoyed throughout the country. Popular humorists have nevertheless been denied access to the pantheon of literary achievements. A powerful cultural elite still imposed strict linguistic standards long after the Genteel Tradition had died out in the United States. However, oral tradition has evolved stock figures easily recognizable in novels or movies. People will exorcise their foibles by transferring them to such comic demigods as the Parisian, the Corsican, or the Gascon, who become substitutes for self-mockery in local yarns or folk motifs.

The Paris-born "titi" appears as the spearhead of native jingoism. Though distrustful of institutions, this petulant youngster takes good care to appear as a law-abiding citizen. At times, he thrills at the thought of challenging whomever enforces law and order and, accordingly, tests his bravery provided there is no great peril. Resourceful but cautious, individualistic and irreverent, he epitomizes the French "débrouillardise" or expediency, sometimes called "System D." "Resquille," that is, gatecrashing, constitutes the utter refinement of that congenial trickster. Besides, his glib monologue entitles him to remain the unrivaled peddler or "camelot." Gavroche is probably the earliest example of this Paris folk hero. In Victor Hugo's *Les Misérables,* the young boy searches corpses for bullets on the barricades during the 1848 riots and dies bravely while singing:

> Je suis tombé parterre, c'est la faute à Voltaire.
> Le nez dans la ruisseau, c'est la faute à Rousseau.

Less heroic but equally demonstrative is the central character in Raymond Queneau's *Zazie dans le Métro,* of recent date. Living in a time of penury, she becomes roguish out of necessity. Huck Finn's comments would sound sanctimonious compared to Zazie's crude, abusive language. Shrewd but innocent, she unconsciously punctures the pretensions of adults while remaining pure at heart whenever she seriously discusses sex. She is no perverse French Lolita, but rather is exclusively intent on rationalizing the subject. In the same vein, Poulbot (1879–1946), a famous cartoonist, imagined the daily lives of chubby urchins on the sloping streets of Montmartre. Those young tramps' self-sufficiency contrasts with Charlie Brown's obsessive fear of inadequacy in *Peanuts.* While the American boy cultivates self-pity in a cozy environment—or rather in blank space—Poulbot's brats make fun of their destitution and triumphantly survive in the gutter.

In the thirties, Maurice Chevalier was grabbed by Hollywood producers and sufficiently reconditioned to suit the American public. A formerly low comedian of the Café Concert, he then embodied the dapper, winking Parisian in saccharine comedies when the Gay Paris still had the flavor of forbidden fruit. Today, the sophisticated striptease of the Crazy Horse Saloon definitely overshadows the painstakingly scabrous jocularity of the Concert Mayol.

The Parisian titi is still a popular figure in comics and films. Goscinny has turned a Gaul into the unruly, shifty Parisian in *Asterix* while another of his famous characters, Lucky Luke, "the man who shoots faster than his shadow," is dressed as a Westerner but talks like a titi. In movies, Louis de Funès, a middle-aged actor, embodies the grumpy, ill-tempered Paris comic hero, a kind of French "Uncle Scrooge." Incidentally, the latter, renamed Picsou (pick-cent), is becoming more popular than his nephew among children, as an American cousin of Molière's Harpagon.

Away from the capital, northern provinces have fostered the lusty, wisecracking "chtimi," a native of mining towns as revealed through the "Petit Quinquin," once a lullaby, now converted into a marching song. "The Giant of the North," a local stock figure, could well be Paul Bunyan turned hard hat and impersonating the loudmouthed, tough heroes of the coalpit. For instance, he will tell you that rape is impossible up there because women with skirts up run faster than men with trousers down.

It was, however, rural France that naturally produced the greatest number of comic folk characters. The countryside of Normandy still harbors the arch, cautious peasant who affects ignorance through his widely known noncommittal retorts. In

Contes normands and *Rustres et terriens,* Jean Revel, a contemporary writer, has depicted this European counterpart of the Down East crackerbox philosopher, a type that shows equal distrust of strangers. Strikingly, French folklore does not abound in examples of reluctant eloquence. The salty humor and racy idiom of its multifaceted stout fellows are more in the storyteller's tradition of the American West.

South of Paris, Burgundy gave birth to the epicurean vine grower, a dedicated gourmet who holds gaiety as the prerequisite of dinner table enjoyments. Though most generally a bon vivant, he can be brimful of aggressiveness and shamelessly treacherous. Did not Charles the Bold wage war on Louis the Eleventh and the Burgundian army sell Joan of Arc to the English? Gaston Roupnel's *Nono* is a realistic tale of buoyant drinking and frantic peasants' loves. Yet it has never been a best-seller like *Clochemerle* by Gabriel Chevalier, another interwar regional novelist. In a mock-heroic tone, the author portrays the Rabelaisian characters at war with self-righteous bourgeois in the Saone Valley, close to Lyon. Hilarious episodes involve an outraged though sex-obsessed spinster who spies on youngsters engaged in a urinating competition against her house, and the pompous inauguration of the village urinal. Though more chauvinistic and sometimes bitterly antidemocratic, Marcel Grancher, another Beaujolais writer, also relies on heavy-handed vaudeville to glorify an innate lust for life through hyperbolic evocations of sexual prowess. His *Charcutier de Machonville* (the pork butcher of Chewcity) has been a best-seller for decades. Equally typical of a province close to the Saone Valley is Louis Pergaud's *La Guerre des boutons,* published in 1912. A native of Franche Comte, a province close to the Swiss border, the novelist stresses local rivalries illustrative of life during the Third Republic. The crux of the story is the stern opposition of the profane public school to the proselytizing Catholic church. Through mock-epic battles in defense of democratic ideals, schoolchildren vigorously assert their intellectual independence in face of bigotry and self- interest.

French people have always been suspicious of German attempts at humor. As the saying goes, a Prussian takes three days to understand a joke and then laughs for three consecutive days. This side of the border, the Alsatian does not completely share the earnest, uninspired "Kolossal Finesse" of his neighbor across the Rhine. Erckmann Chatrian's *Ami Fritz* (1864) constitutes a piquant description of a stubborn bachelor's experiences. Fritz enjoys the camaraderie of plentiful banquets before he is tricked into marriage by the plump, rosy daughter of his tenant farmer.

It has become harder for regional characters to escape standardization, and among French provinces it is Provence which has yielded the most enduring and original kind of folk humor to this day. The native "méridional" has been able to keep alive the tradition of tall tales ever since liars' contests involved crusaders on their way to the Holy Land. Just as in the big talk of the American West, Marius draws the longbow and uses a rhetoric that hypertrophies life. Naturally, his artful mendacity is intended to ascertain the limits of his listeners' gullibility. However, he cannot easily refer to natural wonders or Herculean deeds. Provence has little in common with the American frontier. Mobility and versatility are not the forte of French Southern society. Davy Crockett could improve on actualities and tell outrageous falsehoods with a straight face. At least part of his fame was justified. Marius counts only on his imagination and expansive eloquence. His tall stories have nothing to do with the reverse bragging of pioneers who comforted themselves by belittling the dangers that confronted them. Although his attitude may entail sectional pride, it is not obvious that his hoaxes originate in a need for social compensation as Jesse Bier has suggested in *The Rise and Fall of American Humor*. Though less industrialized than many other provinces, the South has always felt privileged geographically and culturally. The Marseilles "galéjade," that is, the art of stretching facts, is still thriving. The well-known sardine that blocked the old harbor is as popular in France as sea serpents in Maine or the jumping frog of Calaveras County.

Alphonse Daudet gave a literary form to the tall tale tradition in *Tartarin de Tarascon* (1872). For want of game, the inhabitants of a small city on the Rhone River meet on Sundays to shoot at hats thrown into the air. Tartarin, the most distinguished member of the hunting club goes to North Africa on a safari to test his skill. Though the trip proves a complete failure, he is capable of transfiguring his misadventures into a glamorous epic on his return home. But blissfully engrossed in his storytelling, he finally believes in his own hoax. Anyone familiar with "The Big Bear of Arkansas" cannot fail to discern striking similarities between Daudet's and Thorpe's calculated extravagance. From the same premises, Marcel Pagnol developed a

Provencal comedy of manners in his trilogy entitled *César, Marius,* and *Fanny,* especially stressing the combination of verve and tenderness in Southern temperaments. Jean Giono also seasoned his lyrical portrayals of simple lives in Haute Provence with a touch of native humor in *Regain* and *Un de Baumugnes.* Both writers relied on Fernandel, who impersonated the shrewd ignoramus from Marseilles, and Raimu, an actor with protean gifts for parody, when movies were made from their novels in the thirties and forties.

This picture of "méridional" humor would be incomplete if no mention was made of the famous cartoon by Dubout, born in 1905, of a pétanque game, or local bowling, in downtown Marseilles. As a huge crowd assembles round the players, a streetcar stops for the driver and passengers to watch the final throw more closely. It is true that a game of pétanque amounts to a Greek drama when played by Southerners, who generally prepare themselves for the contest as carefully as bullfighters.

The bulk of Provence yarns tends to overshadow a few other raconteurs from the South. Yet one should also single out Corsican folktales in which the central actor-narrator is the touchy, insular wisecracker with a tribal instinct and a strict code of honor. Most yarns center around mock feuds or ritual indolence. Having to emigrate, the Corsican finds himself in Paris, either a gangster or a policeman, but in both cases he considers work with too much respect to touch it.

Across the Mediterranean, the French settler in Colonial North Africa or "Pied Noir" became a familiar type during the war with Algeria. Clannish, boastful, and quarrelsome, the poor white from the populous Bab El Oued area in Algiers was popularized in "La Famille Hernandez" sketches. More verbal than physical, his violent outbursts bore no small resemblance to those of the two ring-tailed roarers in a chapter of *Life on the Mississippi* which Twain had first intended to include in *Huckleberry Finn.* Such braggadocio is also displayed in the self-assertive soliloquies of the Gascon, an expert fencer and big talker from Guyenne, in the Southwest. Similarly, in *Cyrano de Bergerac* (1897), Edmond Rostand staged a dashing, swaggering Gascon, a kinsman of the three musketeers, Alexander Dumas's world famous heroes.

There is no doubt that France owes her expansive eloquence to her Latin heritage. Corneille portrayed the swashbuckler of the commedia dell' arte in *L'Illusion comique* in the seventeenth century. His comic hero, Matamore, remains the archetype of the big talker whose verbal art conceals a funky nature.

French regional humor is naturally ethnocentric. It glorifies the mercurial, self-sufficient countryman who either ignores or ridicules the stilted Paris bourgeois. Today it is more and more superseded by the nationwide entertainments provided by mass media culture. The bistro, like the country store or saloon, has partly lost its function of storytelling center. After World War I, massively diffused Hollywood burlesques conveyed a silent message universally comprehended and the French public turned to Harold Lloyd's acrobatics and Buster Keaton's poker face. Charlie Chaplin owed his success to the adroit combination of slapstick and sentimental comedy. Audiences could easily identify with a character whose weakness appeared as a saving grace. He taught them that no one is a complete fool, that fooleries may be a pretence. "Charlot's" movies appeared while a class-conscious proletariat was confusedly striving for political power. Accordingly, the French underdog saw him as an accomplice and thus took a vicarious revenge on social injustice.[3] Meanwhile, films produced in France in the late thirties, at the time of the Popular Front, exemplified the confusion prevailing in minds intensely committed to socialistic ideology. Frequently, tragedy loomed large in stories depicting romantic outlaws victimized by the police, as in *Pepe le Moko*. Other motion pictures, on the contrary, showed formerly enslaved workers suddenly given access to a world of freedom and fantasy. On that score, *A nous la liberté*, by René Clair, constituted a deliberately optimistic version of Chaplin's *Modern Times* by exalting the laborer deserting the assembly line to become a blissful hobo.

In the meantime, the worlds of Lubitsch and Capra appeared as exotic rarities but also gratified the dreams of evasion of an expanding middle class. Yet the delicate balance between mild satire and sophisticated emotion was bound to baffle a public more familiar with farcical situation comedies or uncompromising social criticism.

As Hollywood movies monopolized French screens after World War II, *The Great Dictator* and *Duck Soup* appeared strangely prophetic in retrospect. The Marx brothers' belated appearance suffered from mediocre subtitles that could not render the pace of witty verbal exchanges. Groucho's deflationary punning was mostly lost on the public. But Harpo's innocuous sex mania seemed reminiscent of the moonfaced Pierrot, the pathetic sucker of French pantomime. The nonsensical flamboyance of *Helzapoppin* was acclaimed in Paris, but until today Laurel and Hardy have remained the favorites of filmgoers. Their extravagant anarchy and complementary inadequacies expressed through primitive gags benefited from excellent dubbed versions, sometimes made by the American actors themselves and later by French comedians who retained an American accent. After the war, Bob Hope and Danny Kaye appeared too clearly as average American citizens through their effete impersonations and could not compete with Laurel and Hardy's zany shows. Now, Hollywood trademark gags are shamelessly looted by second-rate French comedians who claim to be original but do not even improve on their models.

In recent years, Jerry Lewis has become the favorite of several film critics. Benayoun, his devoted hagiographer, sees him as the all-American boy who successfully blunders through life. Jerry Lewis's humor seems to be closely related to a new trend that in the last decades evolved parodies of the teenager's self-consciousness. Yet France never worshipped youth as much as America did in the past and the French public was not in a position to see into the motives of an American humorist who made fun of mass media culture heroes. For identical reasons, I am not sure that *Mad*'s satires are within the grasp of the French reader.

Jerry Lewis publicly considers Pierre Etaix as his French lineal descendant. *Le Soupirant* and *Tant qu'on a la santé* echo the clownish, blundering manner of their American models but cannot overshadow the first productions of Jacques Tati, an acknowledged emulator of Hollywood burlesques in this country. *Jour de fête* and *Les Vacances de Monsieur Hulot* reveal an inexhaustible flair for incongruities, a talent for contriving anticlimactic situations. With his loping walk and high-strung trousers, his persona debunks modern absurdities such as a person's obsession with his own image or the French citizen's summer madness as crowds rush to beaches. But in his own way Tati also ridicules the Gallic devotion to the American way of life. Why shouldn't we turn right against a red light as in California? In France, it would result in mass murder.

In *Jour de fête,* Tati stages a postman who, introducing a new type of fast delivery, imitates American high-pressure salesmanship. Riding a 1911 Peugeot bicycle just as John Wayne would mount a mustang, the naïve villager unconsciously parodies Hollywood treatments of the pioneer spirit. Tati relies on gags that owe much more to American burlesque movies than to French vaudeville. Mimicry supersedes comic dialogues and witty repartees, while the sound track simply underscores the visual quality of the scenes through all kinds of onomatopoeia and scraps of conversation. Yet the villagers seem perfectly true to life even in the most discordant juxtapositions of American style with French homeliness. A good example is afforded when a young mechanic in his tarred overalls comes across a sloppy farm girl pushing a wheelbarrow. They face each other at the entrance of the local cinema while a glamorous Hollywood motion picture is being shown, at the moment of the big love scene. When they talk, it is only the sound track of the movie that is heard. Through comic reversal, the French couple seems to be dubbed by American film stars speaking in their native language.

Tati's recent movies, *Mon oncle* and *Play Time* have been judged insufficiently derisive of our contemporary mania. Strikingly, replays of W. C. Fields's comedies attract more people now in Paris. The misanthropic, resigned American Falstaff appeals to spectators who feel as despised and disoriented as he was but remain confident that detachment is the only way to preserve one's sanity.

Both in motion pictures and TV serials, present French productions testify to a scarcity of new talents. Long before Hollywood gagmen, the Lumiere brothers had shown the way by observing comic scenes through their "cinématographe." They delighted in filming a baby eating breakfast or a gardener with his hose suddenly turned against him. In the meantime, Americans were still busy taking pictures of plays or shows. Since then, there have been few original contributions to the comic tradition in France. The state-controlled television has its homemade Ed Sullivan shows which display insincere cordiality through mutual congratulations and spurious playfulness. Jean Christophe Averty, a talented producer, once indulged in black humor by showing, through special effects, a baby thrown into a mixer. Within a few weeks, his show was banned from the programs.

Among serials now offered to public taste, *Bewitched* and *Get Smart* seem to be fairly popular, though critics repeatedly point to their insipidity. Fortunately, the extreme prudery of French TV has induced another former producer to turn to motion pictures. Jean Yanne clearly emulates Woody Allen by debunking the Jesus freak, women's lib, and South American revolutions in *Tout le monde il est beau, tout le monde il est gentil.* However, there remains a gap between the seemingly iconoclastic Parisian and the insecure Jewish persona. The former appears more cynical and aggressive than the latter but finally lacks the humorous impact that the innocent pose provides.

At this juncture, it seems obvious that American humor inspires comics and moviemakers more and more directly in France. The mass media have certainly diffused this peculiar Yankee quality with more success than generations of publishers. Anyhow, the popularity of Hollywood gags and comic strips appears justified in a country that has always relished rambling, digressive stories, baroque adornments, and a physical lack of proportion as a source of fun. Gags correspond to a deep-seated urge to manipulate reality gratuitously and perturb it so as to disclose the fragility of norms. They are thus perfect elements of disruption. American cartoonists brutally reveal the nonsensicality that underlies everyday life and seem to dynamite conventions in the least expected manner. The French cartoonist Sempé, in turn, adroitly combines cartoons and comic strips in his devastating caricatures of bourgeois who behave like the sheep of Panurge in *Gargantua*—that is, like blindfolded asses.

Communication, the foremost review of semiotics, devoted one of its 1976 issues to analyses of comic strips, with articles on *Peanuts* and Cathy Berberian's *Stripsody.* Guy Gauthier entitled his contribution "*Les Peanuts,* un graphisme idiomatique." Throughout his demonstration, he attempts to link the "graphic code" to the "narrative code," both text and pictures seen as a coherent system of signification. As far as graphics are concerned, he views lines, dots, surfaces as organized in a basic code which amounts to circles, rectangles, and trapeziums. Such figures make up all the characters. Charlie Brown, Schroeder, Linus, Sally, or Lucy have undistinguishable profiles but can be recognized through hairdress (black or simply blank). Every single item of the strip has a function so that "lines become features." In addition, the narrative involves a "code of identity," a "code of attitudes" corresponding to feelings, emotions, or moods (for instance, anger is not produced in the same way for Lucy as for Charlie), and finally a "code of motion," especially through movements suggested by eyes. Gauthier concludes that such simplified graphics are relevant to humor and satire because of the clear-cut aspect of the pictorial narrative. He contrasts Schultz's art with a Western tradition that relies heavily on shades of light providing "realistic illusions."

Similarly, the classic burlesque movies afforded a cinematic presentation of reversed values and proportions that gratified a desire to break away from long-time habits. Maybe this was also in the tradition of Anglo-Saxon behaviorism, a philosophy that prefers valid data provided by observation to tentative explorations of the mind. There is no doubt that the custard pie trick appealed to French audiences who trusted their eyes more than their intellects. Moreover, wild chases and street fights attracted spectators already familiar with the "Images d'epinal," age-old comic strips that depicted a series of disasters resulting from an initial blunder, as though the Watergate case was shown by installments in Sesame Street. However, the early French cartoonists did not spare elements of cruelty such as bleeding noses and amputated limbs. Walt Disney also influenced our comics by his sentimental animal stories, but he may just have satisfied a basic need of our time. At any rate, the French public almost unanimously responded to the persistent moral impulse and the romantic nostalgia for a lost paradise. In the world Disney created, everything had a plastic quality; it absorbed shocks and returned to its former shape after duly shrinking or dilating. His stories of victimization or sadism probably appealed to basic emotions but, as things finally ran smooth, it seems that the Disney opium could anesthetize the harshest reality—hence the feeling that his cartoons also subverted human responsibility.

Generally, French critics both admired the technicalities and decried the complacency of most American comedies after World War II. Yet it is clear that they had only a fragmentary view of American humor. Their judgments were thus necessarily biased. Furthermore, they were not familiar with such important humorists as Thurber and Benchley. Hasty generalizations were made by reviewers who often judged in terms of their own political commitments. André Bazin in *Les Cahiers du cinema* and George Sadoul, the best historian of motion pictures in France, wrote reliable criticisms. Roland Barthes especially concentrated on popular satires in *Mythologies* (1956). He remarked that *From Here to Eternity* began as a seemingly uncompromising lampoon, but after the initial exposure of the U.S. Army, the author introduced somebody who could hopefully redeem the system. Barthes then used a well-known caption of radio commercials to illustrate his thesis; it said about someone who was disgusted with margarine without ever having tasted it, "Once he has tried it, he will be rid of a ridiculous and costly prejudice." For Barthes, the American reader was invited to see the army more closely and eventually abandon any misconception about it.[4] Humor could also be a weapon of conservatism against dissidence.

Strikingly, *Catch-22* belies such an interpretation. In a recent issue of the *Revue française de psychanalyse,* Paul Racamier quotes passages from Heller's book. Mentioning Yossarian's attempt to skip missions, he develops an analysis of what he calls "circular reasoning" on the part of the authors of the standing regulations: if a man is mentally sane he does not want to fly, but if he is sane there is no reason for not having him do his duty. Racamier concludes, "Throughout the story, death and madness dance a ballet endlessly repeated. Moreover, there are not only strategies of madness; there are also foolish mistakes. . . . Thus, reasons, regulations, claims, and conduct, strictly followed, lead to the heart of a situation that arranges the relentless and ambiguous mechanism of the absurd, in the immanence of death."[5] It seems a far cry from James Jones's vindication of tough maleness. Heller's uncompromising exploration of the military mind evinces both laughter and dizziness.

In France, political commitments to the Right or the Left have certainly given a special flavor to native humor. Satirists have been more prone to castigate institutions than the average citizen. Generally more malignant than didactic, they have inherited from the eighteenth-century libertines the habit of cynically jibing at the clergy or the parliament. Meanwhile, succeeding regimes brought disillusion and skepticism. Indeed, France has always wavered between anarchy and despotism. "La République était belle sous l'Empire" simply means that you miss the freedom provided by republics once you have chosen another form of government. Individualism prevails when everywhere people behave like pack rats for fear of what may happen next. In fact, scarcely any institution remained unscathed by the humorists in the last hundred years of French literary history. Alphonse Daudet railed at the educational system in *Le Petit Chose,* Anatole France unmasked adamant judges in *Crainquebille,* Jules Romains made fun of quack doctors in *Knock.* In the same vein, Marcel Pagnol portrayed degenerate politicians in *Topaze* and, more playfully, Robert de Flers made fun of the Académie Française in *L'Habit vert.*

A long tradition of comic muckraking is perpetuated in *Le Canard enchaîné,* a weekly paper specializing in the exposure of lobbies and militarism. Like *Mad* it also demonstrates the vacant quality of approved entertainment, but its rationalistic stand appeals to the intelligentsia rather than flatters the lowbrow public. For instance, during de Gaulle's presidency, André Ribaud held a chronicle of the "Court" in perfect imitation of Saint Simon's style. *Le Canard enchaîné* thus appears to fill the role of Beaumarchais's Figaro, the barber who tricked noblemen, and to carry on the tradition of Georges Courteline, a satirist of the early twentieth century who portrayed sly lawyers and zany officers as well as all the red-tape zealots.

So far, few magazines have specialized in parodies of mass media culture. French critics of the establishment always direct their shafts at political powers but, unfortunately, pay too much respect to the average citizen's tastes. Therefore, no equivalent of *Mad, Help,* or *Humbug* has appeared. Kinky pictures of ugly candidates in a beauty contest are not the kind of humor that our cartoonists could offer indiscriminately to the general reader. Yet in recent years the development of a semiunderground press indicates that cartoonists are more and more concerned with grownup readers.

Charlie Hebdo, first issued after the 1968 riots, essentially anarchistic and always engaged in a freewheeling treatment of controversial issues, overstates its cases with the purpose of shock. Being committed to an ideology, *Charlie Hebdo* ascribes all evils to bourgeois society, the police, and the soporific action of mass media culture. Some of its strips seem indebted to Robert Crumb's *Zap* comic books but do not share the tone of despair transpiring through the morbid humor of the latter.

So far, France has not fully enjoyed the advantages of advanced technology and few of our humorists are engaged in ridiculing its dehumanizing aspects. *M*A*S*H* and *Catch-22* are more devastating criticisms of war than any French production, and it seems that open-minded satires cannot have easy access to the general public in France for lack of financial support. The present contribution of the American underground press to humor is probably as significant as Alfred Jarry's invention of *Ubu Roi* in 1896. This truculent phantasmagoria about a screwy despot had the same liberating effect by exploding the convention of bourgeois culture in a manner that foreshadowed surrealism. After World War II, Boris Vian appeared as a Franco-American Janus. In a subtle combination of Parisian impudence and American sick humor, he tumbled bourgeois taboos, foreshadowing a mad, mad world. His "philosophy fiction" showed old-timers serving as toys for children *(L'Arrache Coeur),* and, when he signed his books "Vernon Sullivan," he half parodied Faulkner in *J'irai cracher sur vos tombes,* a story of racism in the American South, and he imagined what our planet would be if only Mr. America and pinup girls were allowed to procreate *(Et on tuera tous les affreux).*

Another significant field of humor is sex. Traditionally the French comedy of manners seemed unprejudiced to foreigners. Jules Renard portrayed the professional mistress or "cocotte" in an indulgent, slightly condescending manner at the turn of the century. In the meantime Feydeau showed "le Dindon," the sucker, as a prey to feminine cunning but his situation comedies were more akin to ballets than to pamphlets on decadent manners. In the thirties, Sacha Guitry produced his own life story through his versatile, casual comedies about women's trickeries. Numbers of fashionable playwrights have enlarged upon the triangle of the original vaudeville and discovered new plots to stage the husband, the wife, and her lover. Sacha Guitry said that the word *cuckold* is never used in the feminine, at least in theaters. This tradition has gained French people a worldwide reputation and it seems that for many American teenagers French is still the language of love. In America, adultery has always been a serious matter and we cannot imagine O'Neill hesitating between a comedy or a tragedy on that theme. What was considered as a breach of faith by Americans could well be viewed as a welcome revenge by French women whose freedom of choice was probably narrower regarding matrimony.[6] Besides, Leslie Fiedler makes it plain that American folklore and literature are filled with males fleeing from females. Unfamiliar with transatlantic obsessions, the French public was first baffled by comedies showing ridiculous guys in baggy pajamas confronted with overpowering beauties like Jayne Mansfield or Marilyn Monroe. Male self-consciousness could hardly be humorous here. Gallic ribaldry implies sexual realism but no morbid concupiscence: Marcel Aymé crudely depicted the love life of farmers in *La Jument verte* and Alexandre Breffort idealized a prostitute and a pimp in *Irma la douce* long before *Portnoy's Complaint* made sex humorous.

However, a growing permissiveness now contributes to make woman less a dream creature or a plaything than an object for satire. Heffner's *Playboy* still attracts French readers who seek fun in titillating but vicarious sex. *Lui,* a French replica of *Playboy,* also combines satire with charlatanry but in no way improves on its model. Only recently, *Hara Kiri,* a weekly magazine self-styled as "the stupid and vicious journal," appeared as an offshoot of the American underground. Like S. Clay Wilson in the *Zap* comic books, its cartoonists challenge conventions of taste and judgment and indulge in fantasies of depraved sex and violence with a kind of scathing humor directed against the reader himself. The cover of *Hara Kiri* may represent a woman smeared with the blood of a pig, or a cop with a big moustache and voluminous breasts, suckling his baby. Most often women and love are ridiculed through mechanical analogies or degrading metaphors. This is far removed from Rabelaisian ribaldry and indicates that pornography may be in the long run destructive of sexual humor. After the last taboos are tumbled down, there is nothing left for the humorist to attack in human nature.

The mass media provide our contemporaries with such a bulk of data that their reactions depend more on the way information is given than on its content. On French TV, a commentator judging the conflict in the Middle East recently said with a smile, "Let the best win." Wars are now presented as top competitions. After the semifinals between Israel and Egypt, North and South Vietnam, the public anticipates the big finale. If humor results from the pleasure derived from sparing oneself emotional release, as Freud put it, it seems that the benumbing of sensitivity caused by the mass media should make humorists of any one of us. However, I believe that ideologies are still taken too seriously by the French and Americans to allow them to laugh guiltlessly. People say that we now understand why Nasser died suddenly. One day he received a secret message from Mrs. Golda Meir saying, "Let's make love, not war," and he could not survive the shock. I do not believe that this joke would cause bursts of laughter everywhere today.

If Americans seem more gifted than French people in seeing the incongruities of life they probably owe it to their well-known self-reliance, which tends to give them a sense of invulnerability. Besides, the American system is capable of absorbing all contradictions and the individual, invited to adjust himself, finds in humor a deterrent to suffering. Instead of weighing the pros and cons of human predicaments, Americans simply go ahead, but then wear masks to protect themselves. This longtime habit of masquerading often takes foreigners off their guard. In *Ni Marx ni Jesus,* Revel tried to justify his idea that the next revolution would happen in the United States. He reasoned in terms of political commitments to the Right or the Left but did not realize that those words cover different concepts across the Atlantic. Most French people are unaware that modish attitudes and sinless exhibitionism are part and parcel of American folklore. To oversimplify the case, we might say that Americans readily convert ideas into images whereas the French toy with the concepts and love to earmark new trends to fit them into their old European categories. A Frenchman would feel committed for a lifetime if once he ventured to put a bumper sticker on his Renault.

The French attitudes are more akin to irony, the type of romantic irony that Jankelevitch, a prominent philosopher, calls "intellectual nomadism." It asserts individualism, deprecating whatever does not belong to the self while glorifying the unique and despising the general. The elitist French culture encourages people to have a philosophy of their own, which should, preferably, appear as a mature Cartesian synthesis. Innocents unable to attain a coherent vision of life are derided because they are too soon self-confident. Bouvard and Pecuchet stand for the acme of stupidity in Flaubert's satirical novel (1881) because they aim at encyclopedic knowledge; Homais, the well-to-do chemist in *Madame Bovary,* appears as a fool when he displays superficial ideas about religion and politics. Similarly, Jean-Paul Sartre ridicules the "autodidacte" who, in *Nausea,* sets himself the task of learning every bit of the encyclopedia.

The American humorist fights the smug conformity of his fellow citizens. Moreover, he now tends to desecrate approved models of behavior by showing the seamy side of life with morbid exaggeration. To degrade the American superman, he uses an overdose of horror simply for fun. The French humorist, knowing how aggressive his contemporaries can be when they trust abstract notions, always directs them to "Juste Milieu," the middle of the road, as a refuge from pernicious vanity, "the French disease," as La Fontaine already underlined in the seventeenth century.

However, even though one may not directly influence the

other, both French and American humorists project the phantasms of their societies and show the way to escape from humbug. Pynchon, Barth, and Hawkes appeal to French intellects filled with what they condemn and conscious that simulation prevails in our baroque age. There is a long tradition of nihilistic and absurd humor in American culture. Such writers as Melville, George Washington Harris, Poe, Twain, Bellow, and Vonnegut, to cite only a few, rapturously describe, each in his own way, the disintegration of an American dream, thus finding pleasure in their ability to survive the loss. Indeed, such exorcism offers narcissistic comfort to an injured self. But there is also some giddiness in the humorous attitude, for Thanatos is never far removed from the American humorist's vision in which sanity and morbidity coexist. Hence the basic ambiguity of today's humor. In frontier days, it was an outlet to fear and often emerged as a therapy for diseased minds. In our time, frustrated imaginations conjure up danger or horror and play with phantasms, thus converting nightmares into funmaking. This attitude French readers may now more readily respond to than in the past. Also torn between hope and despair, faced with decadence or confronted with deadlocks, French intellectuals need an outlet to their manifold psychoses. However, some tend to lose the satiric edge that goes along with protest or militant progressivism. They seek refuge in grim humor if only to preserve a safe distance between a fragile self and a world deemed hostile. On the other hand, the average citizen has gone through so many changes in the past decades that he may more easily identify with Herzog or even Archie Bunker. He probably had grandmothers who dreamed like Madame Bovary but now finds himself with children who resemble *Mad* or Flakey Foont. Yet there is still something lacking in the gradual Americanization of France. Our average citizen should learn to transcend his own fears through self-mockery as the American humorist is able to do. This way of acknowledging some partial weakness in order to dispel anxiety and gain self-assurance is undoubtedly a saving grace of the Yankee character, even though it may appear cynical at times. But French people should also be wary of taking too seriously the pervasive gloom in American humorous fiction. Isn't the morbid pose the favorite trick healthy people use to hoax the insecure sucker?

Notes

CHAPTER ONE

1. René Rémond, *Les Etats-Unis devant l'opinion française, 1815–1852,* p. 2. Rémond acknowledges a debt to the American writer Oliver Wendell Holmes for this idea. See Holmes, *The Autocrat of the Breakfast-Table* (Boston: Houghton, Mifflin, 1890), pp. 53-54.

2. Robert Bush, "Grace King and Mark Twain," p. 48. See also Mark K. Wilson, "Mr. Clemens and Madame Blanc," which appeared after my commentary had been written and which adds to our understanding of Mme. Bentzon's contribution to American Literature in France.

3. Durand Echeverria, *Mirage in the West.*

4. Rémond, pp. 473-480 and *passim.* The French picture of the American owed much to Frances Trollope, *Domestic Manners of the Americans* (London:Whittaker, Treacher, 1832) and probably to Charles Dickens, *American Notes for General Circulation* (London: Chapman and Hall, 1842).

5. "Qui mange à table d'hôte son chapeau sur sa tête, et vous dit dogmatiquement en vous soufflant au nez la fumée de son cigare: 'Un misérable vieux monde, votre Europe! Un ramas de laquais et de pourris. Mais la libre Amérique balaiera toute cette vermine.' " Cited in Simon Copans, unpublished research in progress on the French image of America during the last half of the nineteenth century—the source of my comments on this period.

6. Charles Farrar Browne, *Artemus Ward: His Book* (New York: Carleton, 1862), pp. 17-19; James C. Austin, *Artemus Ward,* p. 40. See also Copans.

7. The subject of the economics of authorship deserves a great deal more study than it has yet received. The only literary scholar who has gone deeply into it is the late William Charvat, whose posthumous *The Profession of Authorship in America, 1800–1870* (Columbus: Ohio State Univ. Press, 1968) is sadly incomplete. See also his chapters in *Literary History of the United States,* ed. Robert E. Spiller et al. (New York: Macmillan, 1948).

8. See Jean-Alexis Néret, *Histoire illustrée de la librairie et du livre français des origines à nos jours* (Paris: Lamarre, 1953).

9. Erskine Caldwell, *Tobacco Road* (New York: Modern Library, 1960), pp. 106-107; *La Route au tabac* (Paris: Gallimard, 1947), pp. 104-105.

10. My analysis of Coindreau's translation owes much to Professor Claude Francis, Department of Foreign Languages and Literature, Southern Illinois University, Edwardsville.

11. "Caldwell est particulièrement difficile à traduire parce que c'est un auteur hardi, dont le comique douloureux est obtenu par l'union d'une forme impossible et d'une licence toute rabelaisienne. Conserver en français la violence de l'expression sans tomber dans l'obscénité était malaisé. Maurice Coindreau y a réussi parce qu'il a transposé plus que traduit." *Etudes américaines,* p. 191.

CHAPTER TWO

1. Tony Mayer, ed., *L'Humour anglais,* pp. 11-12. Voltaire's quotation from Corneille is from the *Suite du menteur* (1643): "Cléandre: Cet homme a de l'humeur. Dorise: C'est un vieux domestique/Qui, comme vous voyez, n'est pas mélancolique."

2. "L'humeur des Anglais est quelque chose qui est indépendant de l'esprit et en est distingué. . . . Cette humeur est distinguée de la plaisanterie et n'est point la plaisanterie; c'est plutôt le plaisant de la plaisanterie." Fernand Baldensperger, "Les Définitions de l'humour," p. 183.

3. "De notre mot d'*humeur,* les Anglais ont fait celui d'*humour*; mais ils lui ont donné une signification toute différente de celle qu'il a dans le français. Le mot d'humeur, pris absolument dans notre langue, emporte une idée de tristesse et de mécontentement. *Avoir de l'humeur,* c'est être fâché. Celui d'*humour,* au contraire, ex-

prime l'idée d'une joie singulière, et peut-être un peu folle. L'*humour*, dit un de leurs auteurs, *est l'extravagance ridicule de la conversation par laquelle un homme diffère de tous les autres.* C'est quelque habitude, quelque passion, ou quelque affection bizarre et particulière à une seule personne. Mais ce n'est pas là le seul sens que ce mot, qui leur est très familier, ait dans leur langue; il se dit aussi bien au sujet d'un ouvrage d'esprit qu'au sujet du caractère d'une personne, et signifie toujours dans l'un et l'autre cas un certain tour de plaisanterie qui ne soit pas trop près du ton naturel, et qui cependant n'y soit pas totalement opposé." Baldensperger, p. 184.

The French term *humeur* is still quite opposed to *humour.* See, for example, Emile Chartier (Alain) in *Propos sur le bonheur,* pp. 53-54, who defines *humeur* as follows: "Selon le système de l'exaspération, rien n'est meilleur que de se gratter. C'est choisir son mal; c'est se venger de soi sur soi. L'enfant essaie cette méthode d'abord. Il crie de crier; il s'irrite d'être en colère et se console en jurant de ne pas se consoler, ce qui est bouder. Faire peine à ceux qu'on aime et redoubler pour se punir. Les punir pour se punir. Par honte d'être ignorant, faire serment de ne plus rien lire. S'obstiner à être obstiné. Tousser avec indignation. Chercher l'injure dans le souvenir; aiguiser soi-même la pointe; se redire à soi-même, avec l'art du tragédien, ce qui blesse et ce qui humilie. Interpréter d'après la règle que le pire est le vrai. Supposer des méchants afin de se condamner à être méchant. Essayer sans foi et dire après l'échec: 'Je l'aurais parié; c'est bien ma chance.' Montrer partout le visage de l'ennui et s'ennuyer des autres. S'appliquer à déplaire et s'étonner de ne pas plaire. Chercher le sommeil avec fureur. Douter de toute joie: faire à tout triste figure et objection à tout. De l'humeur faire humeur. En cet état, se juger soi-même. Se dire: 'Je suis timide; je suis maladroit; je perds la mémoire; je vieillis.' Se faire bien laid et se regarder dans la glace. Tels sont les pièges de l'humeur."

4. *The Essence of Laughter,* title essay trans. Gerard Hopkins, p. 130. For the succeeding quotation, see p. 124.

5. "Ce mot, que la critique française a depuis longtemps accepté, mais dont la valeur est loin d'être clairement determinée." "L'état d'une âme qui a l'habitude de s'abandonner entièrement à son *humour,* ou plutôt aux différents *humours* ou aux dispositions naturelles qui se succèdent en elle. . . . On appelle *humoriste,* dans ce sens, un écrivain qui laisse son imagination se porter sur les objets les plus différents, aller du bas au sublime, du triste au gai, et qui rapproche, par conséquent, les choses les plus éloignées. . . . l'humour triste ou la mélancolie, en tant qu'elle se réalise dans sa forme la plus élevée et la plus frappante, c'est-à-dire quand 1° elle existe d'une manière continue dans un individu et forme le fond de son caractère; 2° qu'elle a pour cause la connaissance des facultés humaines, des imperfections des sociétés et des misères de la vie; 3° et qu'elle s'exprime dans la forme qui commande le plus l'attention, c'est-à-dire avec la plaisanterie. . . . C'est la mélancolie d'une âme supérieure à qui il arrive de plaisanter." "La plaisanterie n'a de valeur que dans la bouche des gens sérieux." *Des Causes du rire,* pp. 115, 116-118, 133.

6. Hippolyte Taine, *Notes on England,* p. 257.

7. Taine, pp. 253-254.

8. "Si nous avions à définir l'humour, nous dirions que c'est la raillerie dans l'observation ou la représentation directe et concrète de la vie, — ou au moyen d'elles." "Il se peut que la définition qui vient d'être proposée paraisse vague au premier moment. On reviendra peut-être sur ce jugement et on reconnaîtra qu'elle renferme bien les éléments constitutifs de l'humour, si l'on prête attention à la remarque suivante. C'est qu'il suffit de préciser chacun des deux termes dont elle est formée, de les particulariser au moyen d'adjectifs, suivant la marche ordinaire des définitions, pour serrer chacune des variétés de l'humour, et même pour tenir la formule individuelle de chaque humoriste. Si nous mettons une raillerie amère, sombre, presque haineuse, avec une observation impitoyable d'exactitude nue, n'aurons-nous pas défini l'humour de Swift? Si nous joignons une raillerie attendrie à une observation minutieuse, et, comme on l'a dit, microscopique, n'aurons-nous pas celui de Sterne? Le rire joyeux, débordant, torrentiel, ivre et heureux de son propre bruit, avec une observation grossissante qui exagère les dimensions des objets et les tord en mouvements forcenés, n'est-ce pas Rabelais? La gaîté et la bouffonnerie dans le rire, avec la tristesse et les larmes dans l'observation, n'est-ce pas l'étrange contraste de Dickens? La raillerie pleine de bonhomie et l'observation souriante, n'est-ce pas Goldsmith? Le rire niais et finaud, avec l'observation intéressée et grossière de la vie, n'est-ce pas Sancho Pansa?" *Robert Burns,* pp. 116, 117-118.

9. *Revue des deux mondes,* October 15, 1899, pp. 924-935.

10. "C'est une tournure d'esprit vers toutes les impressions. C'est une disposition égale et soudaine à la tristesse comme à la joie; mais la joie est souvent mélancolique et la

tristesse s'échappe en des gestes bouffons et rassurants. Des recherches subtiles de pensée fatiguent presque le lecteur. Des naïvetés profondes le désarment. Le même écrivain flétrira rigoureusement les cruautés banales de l'existence, puis se complaira avec indulgence et sans arrière-pensée aux joies faciles de chaque jour. Certes, il n'est pas aisé de noter les qualités essentielles qui font qu'un auteur est un humoriste, car cette fantaisie diverse est chez les uns cruelle, chez les autres triste, bouffonne chez celui-là, correcte et discrète chez celui-ci. Il faut donc trouver pour les rapprocher une disposition qui soit la même pour tous, malgré les formes opposées qui la manifestent. Il semble qu'on la peut trouver dans une sensibilité extrême, en prenant ce mot au sens le plus large. Cette sensibilité fait que nulle impression, même légère, ne passe inaperçue. Un observateur aux nerfs vibrants, à la curiosité sans cesse éveillée, ressentira fortement. Pour se satisfaire, s'il écrit, il faudra qu'il trouve une forme égale en intensité. Il sera ainsi conduit, volontairement ou non, au style concret et capable, par ses recherches, ses tours imprévus, et ses exagérations, de suivre fidèlement le mouvement de la pensée." Gabriel de Lautrec, ed., *Contes choisis, par Mark Twain,* pp. 28-29.

11. In *Diderot: oeuvres,* pp. 1033-1088.

12. Henri Bergson, "Laughter," trans. Cloudesley Brereton and Fred Rothwell, pp. 142-143.

13. Bergson, pp. 105, 121, 181.

14. *Jokes and Their Relation to the Unconscious,* p. 228. See also "Humour," pp. 160-166.

15. "Il n'y a pas d'humour, il n'y a que des humoristes." Baldensperger, p. 217.

16. "L'humour est plus une disposition particulière de l'esprit qu'un genre littéraire susceptible de définition complète. . . . Ce serait la disposition de l'homme qui a reçu une éducation austère, qui a eu une enfance ingrate et une jeunesse dure et triste: Il s'aperçoit qu'après tout, il y a des choses amusantes dans ce monde. Il s'enhardit d'abord à sourire avec un peu de contrainte des grosses mésaventures dont il est spectateur, puis il ose en rire et ce rire, qui ne lui est pas familier, est fort, sonore, gros, bruyant. Après cela, il apprend à discerner et à goûter le comique plus fin, celui qui ne fait que sourire et qui, au début surtout, est plus près des larmes que du rire. Mais en tout cela cet homme n'oublie jamais son passé et ne saurait négliger la voix de sa conscience, et même lorsqu'il arrive à connaître la tranquille douceur de l'enjouement d'esprit, il se garde du *mal.* De là, souvent, une retenue, une gêne, une difficulté de parler de tout avec grâce, mais par contre une grande loyauté, beaucoup de franchise et de sincérité. Et enfin, comme il faut avoir souffert pour pouvoir réellement sympathiser avec les malheureux, il y a dans cette disposition d'esprit une compassion chaleureuse, brûlante même, pour les misérables, une compassion qui ne se borne pas à plaindre, mais qui, dans sa force et son orgueil, se retourne pour châtier les coupables." Michel Epuy, ed., *Anthologie des humoristes,* p. xiii.

17. "C'est une sorte d'épice dont on retrouve le goût particulier, *sui generis,* dans *toutes* les oeuvres anglo-saxonnes. Il peut y en avoir imperceptiblement, mais il y en a." Epuy, pp. xiii-xiv.

18. "Un soir, à travers la foule bariolée de la vieille Angleterre, le Rire rencontra la Bonté. Ils ne se connaissaient point. Ils étaient très différents l'un de l'autre. Ils s'aimèrent. De leur baiser naquit un fils. On l'appela l'humour." "La Naissance de l'humour," p. 307. See Jean Jules Jusserand, *A Literary History of the English People,* 1: 219, 225.

19. *The Development of English Humor,* p. 39, also pp. 40-41, 5-6.

20. "Humour et amour," pp. 141-147. Cazamian had been developing his theory of humor since at least as early as 1906 when he published "Pourquoi nous ne pouvons définir l'humour" in the *Revue Germanic,* later published as "Le Mécanisme de l'humour," pp. 97-160.

21. "L'humour, cette attitude mentale qui est devenue l'un des traits dominants du génie britannique, est la manifestation d'une contrainte spéciale, d'un arrêt, chez l'humoriste, du flot normal de ses sentiments et de ses idées, d'une réserve consciente dans l'énoncé des réactions instinctives de l'individu." "Sur une théorie nouvelle de l'humour," p. 534.

22. "La catégorie de l'humour, telle qu'elle est ici délimitée, ne demeure-t-elle pas assez voisine du paradoxe, de l'esprit, de l'ironie surtout, ces autres variétés du comique dont l'effort délibéré semble bien, comme dans notre définition nouvelle de l'humour, la caractéristique principale? Ne pourrait-on point estimer, d'autre part, que la présentation volontairement transposée de nos idées et de nos sentiments constitue, non pas la *matière* de l'humour, mais sa *forme,* son procédé seulement, et que sa réalité positive réside, au

contraire, dans 'la présentation directe que se découvre au fond de l'expression indirecte'? Ainsi que l'écrivait naguère M. Cazamian, n'est-ce pas, 'la leçon de tendresse, d'amertume, de pitié, de colère, d'obligation plus haute, de noble tristesse ou d'optimisme', n'est-ce pas, en d'autres termes, 'la résonance émotionnelle', 'les suggestions morales et philosophiques' émanant de l'humour qui en semblent constituer, bien plutôt, 'l'arôme essentiel'?" Ibid., p. 535.

23. "Et pourtant pour moi, aussi brillant, aussi clair soit-il, l'humour anglais se détache toujours sur un fond nettement sombre, tel un feu d'artifice brodé sur le manteau de la nuit." Mayer, p. 20.

24. "Pour moi, l'humour est un masque." Mayer, p. 13.

25. "Il y a deux manières de lutter contre ces craintes. L'une, c'est d'en combattre ouvertement les objets par satires, pamphlets; l'autre c'est de les anéantir par le ridicule. L'humour emploie la seconde méthode. Il ne s'irrite pas; il ne condamne pas. Il imite, mais il imite en exagérant assez pour que le dictateur cesse d'être un vrai dictateur, et devienne un personnage comique." Michel Chrestien and Jacques Sternberg, eds., *Un Siècle d'humour anglo-américain*, p. 9.

26. "Sinon, l'esprit du lecteur se détacherait d'un récit trop évidemment faux." Chrestien and Sternberg, p. 11.

27. "M. Dulck: Vous concevez l'Humour comme essentiellement engagé c'est-à-dire prenant parti sur un point de morale, de sociologie, de métaphysique. M. Escarpit: En effet je ne crois pas que l'Humour puisse être purement mécanique. M. Dulck: Je définis au contraire l'Humour comme un procédé mécanique. Sinon vous devez admettre avec Delattre l'existence d'un 'Humour charité.' M. Escarpit: Mais bien sûr." Jean Dulck et al., *Humour anglais*, p. 8.

28. "C'est cette conscience naturelle, intuitive, mais lucide et déliberement souriante de son propre personnage caracteriel au milieu d'autres personnages. Des lors ce *sense of humour*, qui est un des biens les plus précieux transmis par l'éducation anglaise depuis la Renaissance, apparaît comme la condition fondamentale du compromis sur lequel repose toute la vie nationale anglaise. Il est l'equivoque par excellence, le *no man's land* des valeurs où, de même que l'excentricité avec l'équilibre moral, le conformisme joue à cache-cache avec la révolte, le sourire avec l'amertume, le sérieux avec le scepticisme.

"C'est ainsi que le mot, proposé par Ben Jonson pour ses héros de comédie, en arrivera à désigner pour les Anglais de chair et d'os une attitude sociale, un réflexe national. . . ." Robert Escarpit, *L'Humour*, p. 26.

29. "Depuis le XVIe siècle, le mot *humour* a constamment accompagné le phénomène, lui donnant une cohérence sinon rationnelle, du moins empirique, et le liant à un phénomène tout aussi empirique, d'ordre à la fois psychologique et social." Escarpit, pp. 63-64.

30. "On voit tout ce qui sépare Mark Twain des mécaniciens du rire que sont devenus les humoristes bien élevés d'Angleterre, frères de Jerome K. Jerome et de P. G. Wodehouse. Le compagnon d'escapades de Tom Sawyer, l'ouvrier typographe, le pilote du Mississippi, le chercheur d'or, le journaliste se soucie fort peu du confort intellectuel de ses lecteurs. Mais aucune des leçons qu'ont enseignées les grands maîtres du XVIIIe siècle n'est oubliée. Il y a du Sterne, du Smollett et du Fielding dans ce voyage sentimental d'excentriques Américains en Europe qu'est *Innocents Abroad*. Il y a aussi chez Mark Twain beaucoup de la sombre métaphysique swiftienne." Escarpit, p. 58.

31. "1° Le paradoxe ironique, qui est le premier temps de l'humour, est obtenu par la mise en contact soudaine du monde quotidien avec un monde délibérément réduit à l'absurde;

2° La réduction à l'absurde est obtenue par la suspension volontaire d'une évidence accompagnée d'un comportement mental par ailleurs parfaitement normal et surtout parfaitement logique;

3° L'évidence suspendue est propre à un groupe social donné et le paradoxe humoristique n'existe que pour les membres du groupe social acceptant cette évidence, ce qui, par parenthèse, explique pourquoi l'humour d'un pays donné est souvent inaccessible aux habitants d'un autre pays."

"1° La situation créée par la réduction à l'absurde obtenue au moyen du paradoxe humoristique est invivable et appelle un deuxième temps de l'humour qui fasse succéder l'affirmation à la négation;

2° Ce deuxième temps, qui intéresse surtout la sensibilité, comporte essentiellement un acte de foi, de confiance ou tout au moins de solidarité affective envers l'humoriste et, à travers lui, envers l'ordre du monde que son ironie vient d'ébranler et qu'il a, seul, le pouvoir de rétablir;

3° L'humoriste invite son lecteur à ce 'rebondisement' hors de l'absurde par des indications plus au moins subtiles, parfois implicites, mais qui, créant une complicité d'homme à homme, ne sont intelligibles que dans un groupe social donné, ce qui impose à l'humour un deuxième niveau de 'localisation' humaine." Escarpit, pp. 89-90, 92.

32. "Il semble . . . qu'au bout de cette étude il soit possible d'entrevoir une forme générale, un mouvement, une intention—ce que la langue anglaise appellerait un *pattern* (mot pour lequel, n'en déplaise aux puristes, il n'y a pas de traduction). C'est une volonté et en même temps un moyen de briser le cercle des automatismes que, mortellement maternelles, la vie en société et la vie tout court cristallisent autour de nous comme une protection et comme un linceul. L'homme sans humour vit de la vie des larves, sous leur enveloppe de soie, sûr d'un avenir sans durée, mi-conscient, inchangeable. L'humour fait éclater le cocon vers la vie, le progrès, le risque d'exister. Le plus souvent, il n'en sort qu'une mite ininteressante et vulgaire, mais parfois jaillit le papillon multicoloré d'un rire pareil à celui des dieux, ou bien on devine dans l'ombre le déploiement mystérieux des ailes de quelque phalène couleur de nuit." Escarpit, p. 127. Escarpit has recently modified and expanded his view of *l'humour,* especially in the light of his current interest in communication theory.

33. "L'humoriste reproduit la réalité, non sans la déformer plus ou moins, mais toujours en feignant avec une certaine complaisance d'être parfaitement objectif . . . il se met *du coté* de cette prétendue victime, qui, finalement, n'en est pas une. Il la caricature à gros traits, ou si finement qu'on s'en doute à peine: dans tous les cas, l'humoriste s'assimile à elle. Quand il l'attaque, c'est de l'intérieur, comme on s'en prend à soi-même. Le style impossible cache une profonde sympathie. . . . Son *il* apparaît comme un *toi,* et finalement, comme un *je*. . . . L'expression imperturbable de l'humoriste montre que la passion vengeresse est chez lui, au moins en apparence, mieux que dissimulée: dominée. L'humour *reconnaît* l'existence, tout à la fois au sens où l'on reconnaît quelqu'un que l'on a déjà vu; de la manière aussi qui nous fait dire qu'une patrouille a reconnu un petit bois; et enfin, comme on déclare d'un père qu'il reconnaît son enfant. Le connu est retrouvé, exploré, et finalement, accepté. . . . L'humour fait ressortir, en l'accompagnant d'une sorte de satisfaction intime, l'incoherence des hommes et des événements. Il n'est pas rationaliste dans son principe; il se complaît, bien au contraire, dans la profonde absurdité des choses. . . . Dire l'*absurdité* du monde, c'est peut-être mal parler. Pour ce qui est de l'existence, il serait plus exact de retenir le mot *irrationnel,* en regrettant qu'*a-rationnel* n'existe pas, qu'exprimerait mieux l'insuffisance de toute explication raisonnable." *Anatomie de l'humour et du nonsense,* pp. 82-83.

The succeeding definition of *l'humour* is on p. 47: "l'humour est une manière volontairement impassible et d'une minutie quasi scientifique, de décrire le bizarre, l'insolite ou le ridicule, avec l'arrière-pensée de faire ainsi accepter son propre particularisme sous l'effet d'une tolérance réciproque."

34. Lautrec, p. 26.

35. ". . . a découvert qu'on peut se délivrer du réel, non seulement en le *diminuant* par l'indifférence du ton, mais au contraire en peignant plus grand que nature." In Chrestien and Sternberg, pp. 12-13.

36. "New-York a le sens de l'humour. Elle laisse dire l'étranger qui raille, et qui passe. Elle lui donnerait même volontiers raison: la tolérance n'est-elle pas la vertu des forts; l'Amérique n'a-t-elle pas le présent, et l'avenir?" "L'Humour de New York," p. 161. The essay was originally published in *La Revue anglo-américaine,* June 1929.

37. "C'est Homais, paré des plumes du Peau-Rouge, et dansant la danse du scalp autour du cadavre de Pallas-Athéné, après avoir accompli ses dévotions devant l'autel du Dieu-Machine." "Je vois en lui l'incarnation d'un art où le muscle participe autant que l'intelligence." "Humour anglais et humour américain," pp. 494, 500.

38. "Il existe une singulière corrélation entre l'humour et la terreur, que la plupart des grands humoristes furent également tentés par le fantastique et le cauchemar et qu'en définitive la constante commune à tous les humoristes, c'est tout simplement la lucidité, une terrible lucidité au premier degré qui se double tout naturellement d'agressivité. L'humour, dès lors, serait moins une littérature qu'une façon de *voir* les choses, une vision déformée, déformante, et la faculté de traduire cette vision, non avec des hurlements lyriques, mais avec un sourire, glacé de préférence, parfois méprisant. Mais poli. Un peu condescendant." Jacques Sternberg et al., eds., *Les Chefs d'oeuvre du sourire,* pp. 12-13.

39. "Ce n'est ni un hasard ni un besoin d'exotisme: c'est la preuve que les humoristes des Etats-Unis ont pris une certaine avance sur notre vieille Europe, encore sous le joug de l'analyse de l'Eternel humain, et, même en étant optimiste, il faut reconnaître que nous avons bien peu de chances de rattraper notre retard en quelques années, certainement pas en un seul volume." Sternberg et al., p. 13.

CHAPTER THREE

1. "Le peuple, chez nous aussi, est plein d'humour. Mais notre littérature fut, depuis le XVIIe siècle, aristocratique." "L'Humour anglais," 8: 1011, n. 1.

2. "Au moment où commença notre Révolution, l'Amérique n'avait pas cessé, depuis plus de deux siècles, d'alimenter l'esprit d'aventure de nos voyageurs, d'éveiller ou de stimuler l'attention du public cultivé, la cupidité ou la naïveté des speculateurs, la réflexion des philosophes, en même temps que son exotisme offrait ses thèmes et ses riches couleurs à l'imagination des romanciers et des auteurs dramatiques. Il existait donc chez nous, dans le domaine de l'esprit et en dehors de toute influence due aux vicissitudes politiques, une longue tradition qui était aussi une longue habitude d'intérêt et de dilection à l'égard de l'Amérique. S'appuyant sur des raisons diverses, cette tradition avait tiré de sa diversité même une persistance que les événements extérieurs allaient affaiblir sans cependant la faire disparaître." *La France et les Etats-Unis,* p. 347 and *passim.*

3. Durand Echeverria, *Mirage in the West.*

4. See, for example, Sylvia Kluth, "A Survey of Wit and Humor in Monthly Periodicals in America before 1776" (master's thesis, Southern Illinois Univ., Edwardsville, 1969). My conclusions as to the absence of any notable recognition of American humor in French newspapers was corroborated by Professor Durand Echeverria in a letter to me, August 31, 1969.

5. Cited in Alfred O. Aldridge, *Franklin and His French Contemporaries,* p. 50; Aldridge's translation. This work is my chief source for information about Franklin's reception in France.

6. Alfred O. Aldridge, "The Debut of American Letters in France," pp. 1-23.

7. "Random Notes on Two Bagatelles," p. 755. Three years after Chinard's statement, René Rémond devoted twenty-one pages of his *Les Etats-Unis devant l'opinion française, 1815-1852,* pp. 570-591, to Franklin's reputation in France in the first half of the nineteenth century.

8. "Qui ne paraît pas mal absurde, quoiqu'elle ne le soit peut-être pas plus au fonds, que celles des Egyptiens, des Phéniciens, des Grecs & des Romains, qui renfermoient des principes très sages & très vrais, sous une apparence de folie extrême. . . . *La Mithologie iroquoise* est plus simple, & nous pouvons dire plus *sauvage* que ne le furent celles de ces Peuples savants. Mais aussi elle est mieux liée avec la Morale; & c'est une chose assez surprenante, de voir que les Sauvages des bords de l'*Ohio* pourroient, sur *ce dernier point,* ainsi que sur les vrais principes de *la Politique* qui en dérivent, donner des leçons à la plupart des Nations européennes." Aldridge, "Debut," pp. 13-14. Franklin's authorship of "The Captivity of William Henry" is not certain. See *The Papers of Benjamin Franklin* (New Haven: Yale Univ. Press, 1972), pp. 145-148.

9. Echeverria, *Mirage,* p. 256. The hoaxes were included in Langeac's *Anecdotes anglaises et américaines.* See also Echeverria, " 'The Sale of the Hessians.' Was Benjamin Franklin the Author?" pp. 427-431.

10. Aldridge, *Franklin,* p. 182; Aldridge's translation. See Lander MacClintock, "Sainte-Beuve and America," p. 434.

11. Aldridge, *Franklin,* pp. 188, 191.

12. Claude-Anne Lopez, *Mon Cher Papa,* pp. 18, 346. Franklin's social success in France is detailed by the French Americanist Bernard Faÿ in his *Franklin, the Apostle of Modern Times,* pp. 453-500.

13. Quoted in Echeverria, *Mirage,* pp. 191-192; Echeverria's translation.

CHAPTER FOUR

1. Louis Auguste Félix de Beaujour, *Aperçu des Etats-Unis au commencement du XIXe siècle, depuis 1800 jusqu'en 1810,* cited in Durand Echeverria, *Mirage in the West,* p. 251; Echeverria's translation. See also Echeverria, "Antoine Jay and the United States," pp. 235-252. For a monumental study of French attitudes toward America in the early nineteenth century, see René Rémond, *Les Etats-Unis devant l'opinion française, 1815-1852,* especially pp. 283-309 on views of American literature, p. 186 and *passim* on the importance of politics even in purely intellectual concerns, and pp. 873-899 which is a

bibliography, arranged chronologically, of books on America published in France between 1815 and 1852.

2. "French Opinions of American Authors," 1: 76.

3. Echeverria, *Mirage*, p. 233.

4. Cited in Harold Elmer Mantz, *French Criticism of American Literature before 1850*, p. 69. See also George D. Morris, *Fenimore Cooper et Edgar Poe*, pp. 59, 60.

5. George D. Morris, *Washington Irving's Fiction*, 3: 6, 27. Echeverria, *Mirage*, p. 231. Stanley T. Williams, *The Life of Washington Irving*, 1: 437, n. 79.

6. Williams, 1: 454, n. 22, and *passim*. Morris, *Washington Irving's Fiction*, *passim*. Mantz, pp. 46–48.

7. The quotation from *Le Globe* is in Morris, *Irving's Fiction*, p. 6, Morris's translation. "Petit talent et d'un petit esprit," cited in Mantz, p. 57. "Assurément, nous le répétons, c'est un écrivains bien spirituel et bien élégant que l'auteur de l'*Alhambra*; mais plus on met de soin à l'étudier, mieux on s'aperçoit que l'originalité lui manque complètement. Il sait à merveille employer quatre ou cinq manières, mais toutes sont empruntées; il n'en a pas une à lui." Antoine Fontaney, "Littérature américaine: Washington Irving," 6: 548. The next quotation is from the same page: "Prenez le premier *Sketch Book*, les *Tales of a traveller*, *Bracebridge-Hall*. Qu'y rencontrez-vous? Bien souvent la grâce harmonieuse d'Addison, puis parfois la verve de Swift, parfois le caprice et les boutades de Sterne, parfois aussi la douceur aimable et la nonchalance sentimentale de Mackensie. Où est Washington Irving?"

8. "Ce sont du moins les seuls dont la réputation, traversant les mers et venue des Etats-Unis en Angleterre, la mère-patrie, se soit de là répandue et solidement établie dans le reste de l'Europe. Ce qui constate bien chez nous leur vogue et leur succès, c'est la promptitude que met notre librairie à publier les réimpressions et les traductions de leurs livres, et l'empressement avec lequel elles sont recherchées par le public." Fontaney, p. 515.

9. "Avant de juger 'l'Eutopie' en France, et de la faire passer dans notre langue, on fera bien de consulter nos voisins d'outre-mer. . . . Si les Anglais font à ce roman un accueil empressé, nos traducteurs pourront se mettre à l'oeuvre, mais si le public de Londres néglige la nouvelle production américaine, les Parisiens la recevraient plus froidement encore." From a review of the anonymous "The Humours of Eutopia" (Philadelphia, 1828), cited in Mantz, p. 45. See also Sidney-Lamont McGee, *La Littérature américaine*, p. 196.

10. "Le charmant style de Washington Irving se compose d'une élégante imitation d'Addison et d'une heureuse étude des vieux poètes. Il est difficile de pousser plus loin l'agrément et la douceur ingénieuse que M. Irving; ce n'est ni de la force ni de la profondeur. Son paysage est doux et velouté, sa lumière pure et bien disposée, ses personnages sont heureusement groupés comme ceux de Wouwermans; comme ce peintre, il n'est exempt ni de monotonie ni de manière." "Des tendances littéraires," p. 531.

11. Cited in Morris, *Irving's Fiction*, p. 7, Morris's translation. An 1826 translation of *Bracebridge Hall; or, the Humorists*, published by Corbet in Paris, was entitled *Les Humoristes, ou le château de Bracebridge*.

12. "Passages pleins de charmes," cited in Mantz, p. 42.

13. "Son mérite bien différent de celui de Cooper, consiste surtout dans la grâce et l'élégance du style, l'esprit et l'agrément des details. . . . Son histoire satirique de New-York est encore, sans contredit, le plus spirituel et le plus piquant de ses ouvrages. *Bracebridge-Hall*, avec ses humoristes exagérés et ses peintures forcées des vieilles habitudes anglaises, ne vaut pas assurément les précieux croquis et les charges curieuses de *Salmagundi*." Fontaney, pp. 517–518.

14. "Nous souhaiterions que, dans l'intérêt de la durée de son nom, Washington Irving eût appliqué plus souvent son savoir-faire et son talent à des sujets qu'il eût traités exclusivement et sans concurrence possible, à des fantaisies purement transatlantiques, comme l'histoire de *New-York* et *Salmagundi*." Fontaney, p. 549.

CHAPTER FIVE

1. Gilbert Chinard, *L'Amérique d'Abraham Lincoln et la France*. See René Rémond, *Les Etats-Unis devant l'opinion française, 1815–1852*.

2. Harold Elmer Mantz, *French Criticism of American Literature before 1850*, p. 155.

3. See Sidney-Lamont McGee, *La Littérature américaine*.

4. "L'Amérique, c'est l'exemple horrible des effets sur un peuple, de l'esprit mercantile et industriel que l'Europe commence à adopter." This is apparently a paraphrase of Chasles's words by the author, McGee, p. 23. See Margaret Phillips, *Ph. Chasles*.

5. "Qu'il embrassât sans effort et avec laquelle il mêlât son individualité propre." Mantz, pp. 126-127.

6. "La vrai critique, vigie perpétuelle, a mieux à faire que de peser les syllables et d'analyser les styles; c'est à elle de montrer dans quelles directions l'activité humaine est incessamment emportée." Philarète Chasles, "Littérature pseudo-populaire," p. 1109.

7. "Est-ce que la période grecque n'a pas eu son appendice et sa longue traînée de pâle lumière? Est-ce que la vaste domination de l'intelligence romaine n'a pas fléchi, pendant trois siècles, avant l'éclosion du génie moderne? A ne considérer les peuples européens et chrétíens que comme le faisceau de la civilisation moderne, à ne voir les institutions féodales et monarchiques que dans leur ensemble, ce vaste organisme ne s'en va-t-il pas de toutes parts en fragmens qui se dissolvent ici, qui là sont vermoulus, plus loin soutenus par des étais chancelans, partout fragiles? Enfin, l'expression définitive et complète de cette ruine des monarchies n'est-elle pas la société de l'Amérique du Nord? Et le retour invincible à la vie sauvage, que nous avons signalé tout à l'heure dans les faits et dans les livres de ce pays, n'est-il pas une des preuves évidentes de cette ruine?

Tout se présente donc sous une face nouvelle; l'étincelle de vie se cache sous les cendres. Les élémens de force surabondent, et parmi ces élémens qui jouent et joueront longtemps encore leur rôle de destruction ou d'abaissement, avant de parvenir à leur phase de création et d'organisme, il faut placer en première ligne cette matérialisation de l'intelligence, cette domination des procédés industriels, cette vulgarisation des idées et des faits, et cette assimilation générale des doctrines affaiblies." Philarète Chasles, "Des tendances littéraires," p. 545.

8. "Des deux sociétés nouvelles et menaçantes qui se forment, l'une sous la loi du czar, l'autre sous l'invocation de Washington, la plus intéressante par son énergie, ses traditions, sa filiation teutonique et sa forme libre, c'est l'Amérique septentrionale." Philarète Chasles, "Scènes de la vie privée," p. 325.

9. Alexis de Tocqueville, *Democracy in America,* pp. 174-175.

10. Tocqueville, p. 177.

11. "Je croirais volontiers que le premier homme de génie auquel ce peuple donnera naissance sera quelque grand satirique." Chasles, "Des tendances littéraires," p. 532.

12. Tocqueville, p. 174.

13. "Les Etats-Unis et l'Angleterre, en peu d'années, ont jeté sur la place, le terme commercial est ici le mot propre, plus de vingt ouvrages attribués à des gens du peuple, fabriqués par des spéculateurs en marchandise littéraire, et simulant les joies et les peines du pauvre, les plaintes de l'ouvrier, les remords du repris de justice. Ce sont quelques-uns de ces récens produits qu'il me semble bon de signaler comme les indices d'une nouvelle littérature aux prétentions populaires, incomplète et menteuse, pleine de désirs et d'aspirations, jusqu'ici fort stérile en résultats.

La dernière venue dans la route des civilisations, l'Amérique septentrionale, se montre hardie en ce genre; elle y met un sans-façon tout aristocratique; elle ne dissimule pas ses tendances anti-idéales et son amour des peintures matérielles et violentes. Elle outrage et maudit ouvertement le but spiritualiste de l'art." Chasles, "Littérature pseudo-populaire," p. 1107.

14. "Romans, *highly popular,* édités in-4° dans une publication périodique intitulée *Brother Jonathan* (*Jonathan* est le type national, le John Bull américain), avec d'horribles gravures sur bois, donnent pour douze cents et demi (à peu prés onze sous) la valeur de trois volumes in-8° de 300 pages chaque, un peu plus de trois sols [*sic*] et demi par volume." Chasles, "Des tendances littéraires," p. 532.

15. See Frank Luther Mott, *A History of American Magazines, 1741-1850* (Cambridge, Massachusetts: Harvard Univ. Press, 1957), pp. 358-363.

16. "Cette ironie est encore à l'état brut; elle se développe rudement, mais elle se raffinera; aujourd'hui la sève en est singulièrement âcre et grossière." "Les nations, à la fois jeunes et vieilles, qui, héritières d'une ancienne civilisation, voient devant elles un monde inconnu d'industrie et de politique à conquérir et à organiser, se trouvent environnées de si ridicules contrastes, qu'une pente naturelle les entraine à l'ironie." "C'est surtout pour la caricature outrée que les Américains de l'Union montrent du talent." Chasles, "Des tendances littéraires," pp. 532-533.

17. "Aujourd'hui, en France, comme en Amérique et en Angleterre, les hommes supérieurs qui prétendent aux grands honneurs craignent de se montrer humoristes. Il n'y a guère que deux ou trois téméraires qui osent encore rêver, méditer, ne pas dogmatiser éternellement. . . . Toute l'Amérique ne possède pas un humoriste, l'Angleterre ne compte que Carlyle." Chasles, "Des tendances littéraires," p. 542.

18. *The Clockmaker* was first published in a little known edition in Halifax, Nova Scotia, by Joseph Howe, in 1836, the year before the first London edition. A. H. O'Brien, *Haliburton ("Sam Slick"): A Sketch and Bibliography* (Montreal: Gazette Printing Co., 1909).

19. "N'y cherchez pas un roman, une histoire, un drame, un traité philosophique, un voyage, un récit, une déclamation; ce livre-patois, écrit par un colon d'Halifax, livre tout rempli d'adages à la Sancho Pança et de contes dignes de Bonaventure Desperiers, est tout bonnement le meilleur et le plus curieux ouvrage que la littérature anglaise, aujourd'hui si pauvre, ait produit depuis cinq ans. Il explique à la fois la civilisation ébauchée et vivante des Etats-Unis, la civilisation étiolée et nouée du Canada, et la profonde torpeur des possessions britanniques voisines. Il entre dans le détail secret des moeurs privées et fait comprendre tout ce que les voyageurs anglais laissent dans l'ombre." Chasles, "Scènes de la vie privée," p. 308.

20. "Depuis les personnages de Walter Scott, on n'a rien inventé de mieux que Samuel Slick. Ce marchand d'horloges du Connecticut est une excellente et spirituelle créature, n'ayant pas d'esprit à notre manière, de cet esprit déjà vieux, cent fois retourné, un peu rance, un peu usé, flétri par ses métempsycoses, ayant traversé le collége [*sic*], Rome, la Grèce, l'Egypte, et quelque trente siècles de filiations, mais un bon esprit naïf et natif, qui sort de l'expérience comme l'étincelle pétille en sortant du rocher; vif, bref, pénétrant, ne s'embarrassant pas des mots; quelque chose de Sancho Pança devenu homme politique, Sancho républicain. C'est le seul observateur sensé des moeurs américaines." Chasles, "Scènes de la vie privée," p. 311.

21. "Au lieu d'opérer sur des cadavres étymologiques. . . . Il ne s'agit plus ici d'hypothèses, mais de réalités, ni de conjectures inventées et superposées, mais de faits incontestables." Chasles, "Scènes de la vie privée," p. 307.

22. "Ce modeste peintre de moeurs est un philosophe aussi, d'autant plus philosophe qu'il ne fait pas de théories, qu'il n'a pas de systèmes; mais il est le miroir le plus fidèle de toute une portion de l'humanité et pourrait dire mieux que M. Clay lui-même vers quelles destinées marche l'Amérique." Emile Montégut, "Un Humoriste anglo-américain," p. 732.

23. "Ainsi Halliburton a toutes les qualités anglaises, la fermeté, la force, et aussi tous les défauts anglais, la minutie et la prolixité; mais il a surtout la qualité fondamentale du génie britannique, l'*humour*, et cette puissance d'expression et de trait, qui grave aussi solidement que sur l'acier les impressions que la réalité fait sur l'esprit et sur l'imagination. . . . Halliburton est encore un des écrivains anglais modernes qui excellent le mieux à faire la caricature, la *charge* d'un personnage; il la fait aussi bien peut-être que Dickens, et mieux à notre avis que Thackeray." "Spirituel, judicieux, profond Sam Slick!" Montégut, "Un Humoriste," pp. 735–746.

24. "M. Halliburton nous avait habitués à des écrits plus amusans et plus sérieux sous leur forme légère." Emile Montégut, "Du Génie de la race anglo-saxonne," p. 1037.

25. "L'une est la littérature sérieuse, celle qui survit au temps et au pays où elle a pris naissance; la seconde est la littérature qu'on peut appeler populaire, celle qui est condamnée à mourir avec les générations qui s'en sont nourries, et qui n'est plus ensuite exhumée de sa poussière que par la curiosité des chercheurs et les nécessités de la science historique." "Elle seule peut nous faire juger, en parfaite connaissance de cause, de ce qu'on peut appeler la *situation morale* de telle ou telle époque." Cited in McGee, p. 51.

26. "Il a bien l'allure lente, discursive des anciens *essayists*. Il sait comme eux, entant une idée sur une autre idée, enchevêtrant un sujet dans un autre sujet, imiter le vagabondage du rêve et de la causerie. Il sait aussi, quand il vous a égaré dans les régions sublimes de la philosophie transcendantale, vous en faire brusquement redescendre par quelque bouffonnerie sournoisement préparée. Ce ne sont là toutefois que les rubriques de l'humoriste et non pas l'*humour* elle-mêmes." "Chaque peuple aspirent plus spécialement aux succès pour lesquels la nature ne semble point les avoir faits. . . . Les Américains se sont vu contester les qualités, acquises ou innées, qui constituent la littérature de luxe, celle dont le vulgaire n'a pas la clé, celle qui passionne l'élite *des dillettanti*, et ils ont saisi le premier prétexte à peu près raisonnable qu'on leur ait fourni de protester contre cet humiliant arrêt. – *Ed anch' io son pittore.* 'Nous aussi, nous avons nos humoristes.' " "La Fantaisie aux Etats-Unis," p. 429.

27. "Il est fait une place à part dans la littérature américaine, ce que j'appellerais volontiers une place frontière; il touche à tout, aux sciences, au roman, à la philosophie, à la physiologie, à la médecine. Ajoutez à des connaissances techniques très étendues une dose extraordinaire d'imagination, à une exquise délicatesse de coeur, un goût de terroir

très prononcé et une sorte de réalisme tout américain, mélez enfin ce que la poésie a de plus idéal à ce que la science a de plus net et de plus tranchant, et vous aurez les principaux éléments de génie personnel de l'auteur de tant de livres populaires aux Etats-Unis, *l'Autocrate à déjeuner, le Professeur à déjeuner, Elsie Venner, L'Ange gardien, Courants et contre-courants.*" Quoted in McGee, p. 169.

28. "Cet étroit berceau de la civilisation et de génie américain, ce petit point sur la littoral de l'Atlantique qui est comme l'âme de la nation." Cited in John T. Morse, Jr., *Life and Letters of Oliver Wendell Holmes.*

29. "Voici une nouveauté curieuse, un Rabelais américain. Imaginez ce que serait le prodigieux Pantagruel, si notre curé de Meudon avait jeté des teintes élégiaques, transparentes et nacrées sur le canevas de sa vigoureuse ironie, et rehaussé de métaphysique panthéiste l'invention de ses arabesques. Imaginez Daphnis et Chloé ou Paul et Virginie dansant au sein des nuages, avec Aristote et Spinoza escortés de Gargantua et Garganelle, je ne sais quelle gavotte fantastique. OEuvre inouïe, digne d'un Rabelais sans gaieté, d'un Cervantes sans grace, d'un Voltaire sans goût, — *Mardi ou le Voyage là-bas* n'en est pas moins un des plus singuliers livres qui aient paru depuis long-temps sur la face du globe. On pourrait accumuler à ce propos toutes les épithètes que Mme de Sévigné affectionnait: — livre extraordinaire et vulgaire, original et incohérent, sensé et insensé, mal écrit et mêlé de pages éclatantes, farci de faits intéressans et de rabâchage, d'enseignemens profonds et d'épigrammes médiocres. Vous diriez le rêve d'un mousse qui a mal fait ses études, qui s'est enivré de haschich, et que le vent balance au sommet d'un mât pendant une nuit chaude des tropiques." Philarète Chasles, "Voyages réels et fantastiques," pp. 541-542.

30. "Il y a une idée juste au fond de ces récits amusans qui semblent humoristiques et de fantaisie; c'est le germe de civilisation que contiennent les coutumes les plus barbares et que M. Melville en dégage avec un mélange d'ironie et de sentiment pittoresque qui fait le charme de son livre." Chasles, "Voyages réels," p. 560.

31. "De ces préfaces il ressort clairement, — ses livres le confirment d'ailleurs, — que Hawthorne appartient à la classe de *humoristes,* des *humoristes* comme Sterne et Lamb." Cited in McGee, p. 84.

32. Interestingly, Chasles himself was called "a humorist in the purest sense of the term" by the *Illustrated London News,* April 14, 1860. The anonymous English critic was using the term precisely as Chasles used it — a fitting tribute to the French critic and one that would have warmed his crusty heart. Quoted in Chasles, *The Legacy of Philarète Chasles,* 1: xxvi.

33. Samuel L. Clemens, *Mark Twain in Eruption* (New York: Grosset & Dunlap, 1940), p. 202. See James C. Austin, *Artemus Ward,* p. 118.

34. W. T. Bandy, "New Light on Baudelaire and Poe," pp. 65-69.

35. Charles Pierre Baudelaire, *Baudelaire on Poe,* p. 68.

36. Baudelaire, pp. 124, 123-124, 132, 142.

37. Cited in Patrick Francis Quinn, *The French Face of Edgar Poe,* p. 48.

38. "S'amuse à créer des canards (s'il est permis d'employer ce mot vulgaire) auxquels son art subtil donne une vraisemblance saisissante." Cited in Léon Lemonnier, *Edgar Poe,* p. 143.

39. Lemonnier, pp. 108-111, 141-147, 153.

40. *The Life and Works of Edgar Allan Poe,* pp. 410, 510, 536.

41. *Edgar Poe, choix de contes,* pp. 19ff, 88. See also Asselineau's introduction to Poe's *Les Aventures d'Arthur Gordon Pym.*

42. Recent studies of humor in our "serious" American writers show that French interest in the subject is greater than ever. See Roger Asselineau, "Walt Whitman's Humor," and Maurice Gonnaud, "The Humane Seer: Humor and Its Avatars in Emerson." Jean Normand, *Nathaniel Hawthorne: esquisse d'une analyse de la création* (Paris: Presses Universitaires de France, 1964, published in English in Cleveland by the Press of Case Western Reserve Univ., 1970) emphasizes the dark side of Hawthorne but sees the "protean joker" and the self-deprecating storyteller as the obverse of that side.

CHAPTER SIX

1. "Lorsque M. Ampère, au retour de sa *Promenade en Amérique,* déclairait que la littérature des Etats-Unis n'était, à proprement parler, ni américaine ni démocratique, il ne tenait pas compte des humoristes. Les yeus fixés sur les écrivains de premier mérite, Prescott et Bryant, Emerson et Longfellow, Hawthorne et Washington Irving, dont les talens divers procèdent certainement des littératures européennes, et que la littérature anglaise en particulier pourrait revendiquer, bien qu'ils se soient inspirés de l'histoire et

des moeurs de leur patrie, l'éminent voyageur ne consentait pas à mettre au rang des écrivains ceux qui travaillent à l'amusement des masses. De ce groupe dédaigné devaient cependant surgir les poètes et les prosateurs absolument américains qu'il cherchait ailleurs sans les trouver." Blanc, Marie-Thérèse (Th. Bentzon), "Les Humoristes américains," p. 837.

2. "Il faut dire que certaines pages des *Eye-Openers,* des *Screamers,* etc., dont la grande réputation nous étonne, n'ont tout leur piquant que pour ceux qui connaissent à fond les abus qu'elles attaquent." Blanc, "Les Humoristes américains," p. 321.

3. See James C. Austin, *Artemus Ward,* pp. 119-120. All these errors were frequently made by Americans too.

4. "Un mélange agréable de bon sens, de gaîté honnête, de raillerie juste et fine, relevé par la dose voulue de sel *yankee,* voilà tout le talent de Josh Billings, et ce talent n'est pas à dédaigner. Au-dessus de lui, au-dessus d'Artemus Ward, il faut placer cependant Hans Breitmann, ou, pour le nommer par son vrai nom, M. Charles Leland." "Quand on considère le nombre incalculable des Allemands que l'émigration a jetés aux Etats-Unis, quand on songe que dans la plupart des villes et villages il n'est presque pas de boulangerie, d'épicerie, de confiserie ou de brasserie qui ne soit tenue par un des leurs, on ne s'étonne plus des germanismes qui continuent à se glisser tous les jours dans la langue anglaise telle qu'on la parle en Amérique. Ces hordes étrangères ont commencé ainsi une conquête qui va sans cesse grandissant sous des apparences pacifiques." Blanc, "Les Humoristes américains," pp. 855-856.

5. "Il y a dans l'esprit américain un penchant à la grosse gaîté, à la gaminerie, qui révèle que sous certains rapports ce grand peuple est encore un peuple enfant. Pour obtenir sa faveur, celle de l'ouest surtout, il faut savoir sacrifier aux pantalonnades; les orateurs politiques, les prédicateurs même sont obligés de tenir compte de ce goût dominant. . . . Si nous présentons à des lecteurs plus difficiles que les oracles du Pfaffs-Club des débauches d'esprit que l'on ose à peine nommer littéraires, c'est plutôt pour leur donner la mesure du goût d'un peuple qui se croit très supérieur aux vieux Européens que pour les faire assister au triste spectacle d'un homme de talent qui gaspille en bouffonneries de brillantes facultés." A footnote identifies "Pfaffs-Club" as "Club littéraire de New York." Blanc, "Les Humoristes américains," pp. 852-853.

6. "Quant à la finesse d'Artemus Ward, elle semble difficile à saisir; ce style bariolé de couleurs violentes, sillonné de métaphores inouïes, est autrement saugrenu que celui de Mark Twain. . . . Mark Twain est grave à côté d'Artemus." Henry Gauthier-Villars, *Mark Twain,* pp. 92, 108-110.

7. "De ce mélange de nationalités et d'éléments disparates modifiés par le contact, par le climat, par l'organisation sociale et les institutions politiques, est née une littérature particulière, un genre d'esprit qui n'est ni l'humour anglais, ni l'esprit français, ni le *Gemüth* allemand, qui ne rappelle pas plus Dickens et Thackeray que Henri Heine, About ou Dumas, qui est essentiellement américain." "Ceux qui sont originaires des Etats du Sud, on ne retrouve pas, en effet, cette amertume, cet *ensauvagement* qu'a si bien constaté Th. Bentzon. Leur gaieté plus franche est aussi plus naïve; leur rire est plus contagieux; sous le chaud soleil de la Géorgie et de la Virginie, la plante a porté des fleurs et des fruits autres que sous l'âpre climat du Maine ou des montagnes Rocheuses." "La Littérature comique aux Etats-Unis," pp. 695-696.

8. Julia Collier Harris, *The Life and Letters of Joel Chandler Harris,* p. 85. See the same author's "Uncle Remus at Home and Abroad," p. 85.

9. "On se rangerait volontiers de l'avis de Charles Dickens, qui, peu de mois avant sa mort, saluait avec une noble émotion l'avènement d'un rival . . . par sobriété, le talent rare de condenser en un petit nombre de pages le vif intérêt de l'action et l'analyse profonde des caractères, Bret Harte se rapprocherait plutôt d'un autre modèle exquis, Mérimée." "Son principal mérite consiste dans une étonnante vigueur de conception, dans un mélange de rudesse, d'ironie, et de sensibilité auquel rien ne saurait être comparé enfin dans l'étrangeté saisissante de sujets évidemment vus et vécus; il ne sait ni developper une thèse morale, ni conduire un dialogue, ni peindre avec finesse les minuties de la vie mondaine." Cited in Sidney-Lamont McGee, *La Littérature américaine,* pp. 147, 150.

10. "Nous n'avons pas eu connaissance des chiffres respectifs des tirages, mais il apparaît certain que Whitman ou Lafcadio Hearn, s'ils ont suscité en France des interprétations beaucoup plus attachantes et plus neuves que Mark Twain, s'ils ont eu plus que lui des points de contact avec nos lettres contemporaines, n'ont jamais rencontré ce succès presque populaire. Nous gagerions que, même aujourd'hui, ce nom est l'un des plus connus des lettres américaines, familier à plus d'un qui ne saurait rien d'Emerson ni de Longfellow." *Les Lettres américaines,* p. 77.

11. *The Literary Reputation of Mark Twain,* p. 16.

12. "On ne lit guère Mark Twain en France, on ne l'a jamais beaucoup lu." Maurice Le Breton, "Un Centenaire: Mark Twain," p. 401.

13. "Il n'a ses condées franches, il n'est absolument lui-même avec les instincts énergiques qui le portent aux difficultés et à l'aventure, avec ses explosions de gaîté vaillante, au milieu des circonstances les plus terribles, que dans ce *far-west,* où, le rire aux lèvres, il se fraie un rude chemin parmi les bandits et les Indiens, les déserts et les neiges, maniant tantôt le revolver, tantôt les outils du mineur, pour saisir enfin, après avoir brandi la pioche et secoué la *battée,* la plume du journaliste d'une main non moins vigoureuse. Les villes telles que Virginia-City conviennent à son tempérament de pionnier mille fois mieux que nos capitales européennes féodales et gothiques, reines déchues parfois et qui s'enveloppent dans leur deuil d'une silencieuse majesté que les initiés seuls savent comprendre." Blanc, "Les Humoristes américains," p. 332.

14. "Ce qui est intraduisible surtout, c'est ce qui fait le principal mérite de ces bigarrures, le style original et mordant, le tour *idiomatique,* le mélange bizarre et souvent pittoresque de néologie, de patois et d'argot qu'on appelle le *slang.* L'anglais reste la langue mère, fondamentale, mais c'est une nourrice vieillie dont les mamelles se tarissent souvent; elle ne peut exprimer que la civilisation européenne, et se trouve à court devant la surabondance d'idées, d'inventions, de découvertes, dont s'enorgueillit la jeune Amérique." "Les audaces d'un Bret Harte, les témérités plus grossières d'un Mark Twain nous étonnent encore; mais bientôt nous serons accoutumés à une langue américaine dont la verdeur savoureuse n'est pas à dédaigner, en attendant les qualités plus délicates et plus relevées que le temps lui apportera sans doute." Blanc, "Les Humoristes américains," p. 335.

15. Blanc, "L'Age doré en Amérique," pp. 319-343.

16. "Les préoccupations psychologiques, l'analyse des passions qui sont communes à l'humanité tout entière prendront la place de cette peinture, assez rude parfois, expressive toujours, des moeurs locales que le génie d'un Bret Harte sais rendre saisissante, qui devient gaie d'une gaîté tout exotique d'enfant à demi barbare, et spirituelle pourtant, sous la plume facile d'un Mark Twain, qui, avec Cable enfin, revêt une si étrange couleur de mélancolie passionnée . . . ils ont exploité la veine qui a fait leur célébrité jusqu'à ne rien laisser pour quiconque voudrait les suivre." Cited in McGee, p. 162.

17. "Il est évident que ce comique à gros grains n'a rien de commun avec le sel attique. Si l'on me pressait bien fort, j'avouerais même que pour mon compte je ne trouve qu'un médiocre charme à ce genre d'humour. L'humour, ce produit spécial de l'imagination anglo-saxonne, ne m'attire et ne m'enchante que lorsqu'il est habilement mélangé de poésie et de réalité, de rires et de larmes, comme chez Dickens, chez Holmes ou chez Bret Harte. Cette rude et vulgaire ironie de Mark Twain me fait toujours un peu l'effet de ces grosses plaisanteries campagnardes qui consistent en coups de poing et en bourrades, appliqués 'pour rire' dans le dos ou dans les côtes du patient. . . . Hélas! c'est le sort des sociétés démocratiques, en général, que cet envahissement du domaine littéraire par les oeuvres violentes et aux couleurs crues, où l'art de la composition, la pureté de la langue, la délicatesse des sentiments, la science du goût et des nuances ne sont plus comptés pour rien. Nous pouvons nous en apercevoir déjà chez nous où, sous prétexte de naturalisme, certains romanciers ont substitué à l'analyse psychologique la description minutieuse des appétits et des passions purement bestiales de l'animal humain. . . . Le grand art est mort!" Theuriet, cited in Gauthier-Villars, pp. 101-102.

18. "Quelques critiques s'imaginèrent que la vogue des humoristes n'était que le résultat d'un engouement passage, la crurent agonisante et en profitèrent pour lui détacher une ruade dédaigneuse; d'autres sont d'une jalousie plus clairvoyante, et combattent avec acharnement le succès de cette jeune école qui ose se déclarer indépendante. Ils comptent ses taches, soulignent ses défaillances, notent ses imperfections, et, âprement heureux de voir s'aligner en une longue colonne les erreurs qu'ils ont relevées avec une minutie méchante, ils s'écrient, avec une joie bien chauvine:

Ah! qu'on est fier d'être Français,
En regardant cette colonne!

Disons-le sans insister: notre époque était, d'ailleurs, moins que toute autre, apte à la compréhension de cette littérature sans-gêne; en effet, quels sont les écrivains à la mode? Des stylistes raffinés tyrans des mots et des syllabes, qui, composant une phrase avec des recherches minutieuses de mosaïstes, d'après les procédés de Théophile Gautier, de Flaubert ou de Goncourt, s'appliquent à être entortillés, alambiqués, précieux, et n'ont souci du naturel que pour le chasser au galop; il est trop évident que, pour eux, les productions américaines devaient être lettre close. En revanche, je n'ai pas cru que nous dussions, comme eux, faire fi de la gaieté, de la spontanéité, de ce que j'appellerai la *bonne santé littéraire,* qui s'epanouit si librement dans l'oeuvre de Mark Twain. Laissons les critiques modernes, ces fins renards, trouver ces qualités bonnes pour les goujats, et tâchons plutôt de les acquérir; faisons nos réserves, mais ne nous ingénions pas à chercher des brins de fumier dans les perles d'Ennius." "Que voulait-il, Mark Twain? Simplement inspirer quelques notions (pas trop subtiles) du juste et du bien à des gens qui n'étaient pas autrement disposés à les recevoir; or, ce n'est pas un mystère, notre pauvre nature humaine est ainsi faite qu'elle bâille volontiers au sermon et répète:

Une morale nue apporte de l'ennui;

il fallait donc envelopper cette morale d'un conte joyeux qui la fît passer avec lui: tel fut le rôle de Mark Twain." Gauthier-Villars, pp. 57, 93-94.

19. Samuel L. Clemens, *Mark Twain in Eruption* (New York: Grosset & Dunlap, 1922), p. 202. Written in 1906.

20. "Le jour où la race américaine s'est sentie assez forte pour secouer la tutelle anglaise, il lui restait encore beaucoup à faire pour consommer son indépendance; le drapeau britannique ne flottait plus sur le territoire de l'Union, mais l'influence commerciale et morale de la mère patrie n'en demeurait pas moins intacte dans la colonie, devenue nation." "Le représentant le plus complet et le plus remarquable de la littérature nationale aux Etats-Unis, est M. Clemens, plus connu sous le pseudonyme de 'Mark Twain' dont il s'est servi pour signer ses principaux ouvrages." *Etudes irlando-américaines,* pp. 7, 9.

21. "Le résultat de leurs efforts fut en échec presque complet." "Une ténacité remarquable à n'en rien changer." "On trouva sa plaisanterie macabre, son esprit brutal, son tempérament plein de sécheresse. Ses exagérations voulues furent prises pour des symptômes d'aliénation mentale." "On peut dire qu'au fond de tout lecteur français il y a un académicien qui sommeille; or, le talent de Mark Twain n'a rien de commun avec le genre académique." "En un mot, il a eu le très grand tort de ne pas toujours prendre au sérieux la nation la plus spirituelle du monde." "Mark Twain n'est pas uniquement un amuseur incorrigible et perpétuel. Il y a en lui une nature à part, une originalité vraiment savoureuse, des talents et des qualités. C'est un observateur sagace et pénétrant, qui voit bien et raconte juste; un voyageur infatigable, qui, tantôt fait défiler devant nous des pays étranges et inconnus, et tantôt apporte dans nos contrées un peu rebattues un élément de nouveauté et d'imprévu. Ses descriptions sont presque toujours interessantes et pleines d'exactitude, ses jugements marqués au coin du bon sens et libres de toute influence banale, de toute entrave conventionnelle. Le poncif n'entre pour rien dans cette nature indépendante et fougueuse, dont tous les ressorts sont neufs. Quand il lui arrive, plus souvent qu'on ne croirait, de traiter sérieusement un sujet, ses renseignemens sont nets et précis, puisés aux meilleures sources, et d'une authenticité irréprochable. Mais, alors même qu'il y introduit cette pointe de fantaisie drôlatique dont il a coutume et à laquelle il ne renonce guère complètement, l'intérêt de son récit reste toujours sa première préoccupation et ne tend jamais à disparaîte derrière une plaisanterie vide et sans but." "Les Caravanes d'un humoriste," pp. 880-882.

22. "L'humour est une 'spécialité' de MM. Courteline, Jules Renard, Alphonse Allais, Capus, Georges Auriol, Tristan Bernard, Pierre Veber, Willy et Grosclaude; ils en ont le monopole, comme l'Etat a celui de la fabrication des allumettes, et les raffineurs celui de l'industrie sucrière. C'est dire qu'ils n'ont pu prendre à l'humour américain que ses procédés extérieurs et ses moyens mécaniques. Ils sont restés eux-mêmes; mais ils ont contracté des habitudes d'insistance dans la plaisanterie, de lourdeur et de lenteur, quelque chose de gêné, de gauche et de mal à l'aise, ainsi qu'il arrive quand nous endossons des vêtemens qui ne sont pas faits pour nous. Goûter parfaitement l'oeuvre de Marck [*sic*] Twain est une joie à laquelle doivent renoncer ceux qui ne posèdent pas à merveille la langue anglaise, ou qui même n'ont pas dans les veines un peu de sang anglais." "Nos humoristes," pp. 924, 932, 933. For Daudet's debt to Twain see Franklin R. Rogers, "Mark Twain and Daudet: *A Tramp Abroad* and *Tartarin sur les Alpes,*" pp. 254-263.

23. "Mark Twain est Américain exclusivement, agressivement." "L'Américain est foncièrement sérieux. Les facéties souvent démesurées de l'humoriste sont pour ses nerfs trop intensivement tendus une sorte de réactif, de détente." "L'humour est peut-être le seul genre de fiction dont leur fantaisie soit capable." "Le meilleur de l'humour de Mark Twain c'est, encore plus que ses facéties, les physionomies qu'il prête aux hommes et aux choses. A les regarder à travers son esprit (l'humour n'est-il point avant tout un point de vue?) on les aperçoit tantôt complètement défigurés comme dans les miroirs concaves ou

convexes où les badauds se regardent à la foire—tantôt, au contraire, discrètement et spirituellement altérés et légèrement exagérés. En les soutenant avec complaisance à plus ou moins de distance de la réalité, l'humoriste transforme hommes et faits en types, en allégories qui ne laissent rien à envier à ceux que créèrent les classiques de la caricature et du burlesque." "Les histoires humoristiques de Mark Twain affirment l'ideal américain, comme les 'speeches' de Roosevelt et les conférences de William James. Au point de vue artistique, Mark Twain est, après Dickens, un des plus grands caricaturistes des lettres anglaises. Ainsi que l'auteur de Gargantua et celui de Don Quichotte, il a plus d'une fois donné à la satire la forme d'une épopée. Petitesses et grandeurs, limitations et étendue, la démocratie américaine est tout entière dans ses histoires. Mark Twain en est l'Homère, plus sérieux qu'on ne pensait, sous son travesti d'humoriste." "L'Envers d'un humoriste," pp. 432, 438, 439, 444.

24. "Mark Twain," pp. 425-439.

25. "En lisant les vives analyses de M. Régis Michaud et ses citations heureusement choisies en voyant défiler les types cocasses et vivants de cette oeuvre considérable, peut-être ce lecteur français, que nous avons entendu plus d'une fois déclarer Mark Twain inintelligible pour lui, reviendra-t-il sur son impression première, et se mettra-t-il lui-même en garde contre le péché de philistinisme, jamais plus grave que lorsqu'il est commis envers l'humour." "Mark Twain et l'humour américain," p. 185.

26. "C'est un peuple enfant, jeune, à peine sorti de la jeunesse." *L'Ame américaine,* p. 159.

27. "Humour anglais et humour américain," pp. 475-500.

28. "La plus grande partie de son oeuvre n'a pas été traduite: le grand public le connaît surtout chez nous par des extraits qui ne le montrent certes pas sous son meilleur jour. Quant aux critiques qui ont poussé plus loin la curiosité, ils l'ont en général traité sans indulgence et avec une nuance très marquée de dédain: son humour a paru trop gros pour avoir droit à une place dans la littérature qui se respecte, ses tableaux de la vie américaine ont été jugés trop crus par une critique timorée qui depuis en a vu bien d'autres. Mark Twain n'a pas soulevé, en France, l'intérêt qui s'est attaché à des écrivains plus respectueux des conventions, un Fenimore Cooper ou un Bret Harte. Son originalité et sa sincérité mêmes lui ont nui: nous lui avons préféré des talents plus conformes à notre idéal, des peintres plus romantiques de l'Amérique des pionniers et des prospecteurs, nous n'avons pas su voir sous l'humoriste un peu débraillé l'observateur le plus perspicace de la société du Middle West et le plus américain des écrivains de son temps." Le Breton, "Un Centenaire: Mark Twain," p. 401.

29. "Le ton de dénigrement, épicé de grosses plaisanteries, à propos des musées de peinture d'Italie, des palais et des cathédrales de France et d'Angleterre, qui amusa les fermiers de la vallée du Mississippi, ne nous semble pas heureux." *La Littérature américaine,* p. 104.

30. "Il a le rire énorme et bruyant de celui qui n'attend rien du monde qui veut à tout prix faire rire les autres pour se faire rire soi-même." *Mark Twain,* p. 258.

31. "M. James n'écrit pas pour le gros public, qui veut qu'on lui serve des émotions toutes prêtes et qu'à la fin du volume tout soit pour le mieux dans le meilleur des mondes possible, grâce au mariage de M. X. et de Mlle. ***." ". . . Traits d'esprit qui ne font que de discrets emprunts à l'*humour* tel qu'on l'entend en Amérique." "Analyser ce genre d'ouvrage si merveilleusement conforme au génie de M. James serait bien difficile, tout le charme, subtil comme la brillante poussière sur l'aile d'un papillon, étant dans le ton original et familier des lettres, la vivacité des conversations, l'amusante opposition des jugemens portés sur une même chose ou une même personne par un pédant de Goettingue, un Parisien entreprenant, des Américaines avides de tout acheter et de tout apprendre, des Anglaises scandalisées, etc. . . . L'auteur s'incarne dans chacun de ses personnages, prend tour à tour leurs préjugés, leurs passions, leurs ridicules, avec une souplesse et une habileté prodigieuses." Blanc, "Les Nouveaux romanciers américains," pp. 124, 131. In the Foreword to a recent collection of James's stories, *The Marriages and Other Stories* (New York: New American Library, 1961), Eleanor M. Tilton emphasized James's humor and the lack of recognition of it by American critics.

32. Léon Edel, "A Note on the Translations of Henry James in France," pp. 539-540. M. R. Garnier, *Henry James et la France,* pp. 215-216.

CHAPTER SEVEN

1. A. K., "First Chair of American Literature in France," p. 77. See also the *Dictionary of American Biography* on Barrett Wendell.

2. Delbert L. Gibson, "French Impressions of American Character and Culture," p. ii.

3. "Ainsi cette immense nation, qui a civilisé un monde de l'Ocean Atlantique à l'Ocean Pacifique, paraît n'avoir jamais eu le temps de donner à son esprit le bien-être qu'elle offrait à son corps. La littérature et les arts n'y ont pas de vie autonome." Gibson, p. 199.

4. "A l'heure où les Etats-Unis se placent délibérément à la tête des nations et des peuples qui sont l'histoire en marche vers l'avenir, l'impuissance de la littérature américaine, son caractère subordonné et mercantile, ses formes d'industrialisme démocratique, son acceptation servile de la loi du nombre, son âpre désir de plaire à tout prix et sa hâte à se plier aux moindres caprices d'une clientèle énorme et médiocre, toutes ces abdications, toutes ces défaites, toutes ces capitulations sont des signes dont on aurait tort de ne point s'inquiéter.

Plus nettement tranchés, plus accusés et par là plus visibles outre-mer, ces caractères, avec tous les degrés et toutes les nuances qu'on voudra, ne sont-ils pas la marque de l'état actuel—de plus en plus actuel de la *Civilisation Universelle*?

Sous cette appellation pompeuse, quelle tristesse et quel néant!" "Tocqueville et la littérature américaine," p. 261.

5. Gibson, pp. 4a-4b.

6. "Elle prend pas encore l'Amérique très au sérieux." "En matière de littérature comme de civilisation, c'est l'Amérique qui a les yeux tournés vers l'Europe. Cinq ans plus tard, les rôles seront renversés." *L'Interpretation française de la littérature américaine,* pp. 13, 14.

7. "American Literature through French Eyes," p. 86.

8. *L'Humour américain,* translated from *Essays and Literary Studies* (London, 1916).

9. "L'Américain est grave et sérieux de sa nature. Les facéties souvent démesurées de l'humoriste sont pour ses nerfs tendus à l'excès une gymnastique salutaire, une détente. . . . Si énormes qu'elles soient, avec leur fracas inattendu, elles correspondent au besoin qu'il a d'être surexcité. Ce qu'il y a, dans l'humour de Mark Twain, de violent et de démesuré, est fait à souhait pour le satisfaire." "Il s'agit, à la faveur d'un contraste, d'attirer l'attention sur tel ou tel point d'importance. . . . Introduire dans une description, un portrait, un récit, un élément qui fasse violence et tort à une autre et nous rejette vers un troisième point de vue qui est celui de l'humoriste, tel est le but de ces strategèmes." "Sa vie durant, Mark Twain connut de véritables triomphes dans le conte humoristique, dont une foule de récitants continuent la tradition outre-mer. Il y a là un genre éminemment national, une littérature populaire au vrai sens du mot, un riche folklore exploité par toute une lignée d'humoristes qui va d'Artémus Ward jusqu'à ce prince des pince-sans-rire américains d'aujourd'hui, le très moderne M. Dooley." Régis Michaud, *Mystiques et réalistes,* pp. 149, 151, 153, 155; 149-150, fn. 2.

10. "Il spiritualise quelquefois la matière; il matérialise souvent l'esprit. D'une façon générale, c'est la plaisanterie d'un homme qui se donne l'air de ne pas saisir la portée psychologique ou morale des faits qu'il rapporte." "A ce don d'observation objective, l'humoriste semble joindre une maîtrise particulière de soi. . . . Toute passion est permise à l'humoriste, mais toute expression directe d'une passion lui est interdite. Il joue, statue vivante, à imiter la matière impassible. Comme la plaisanterie anglaise, la verve américaine est robuste, mais d'une saveur souvent moins amère. . . . Jeunesse de l'âme américaine, sans doute, mais aussi, semble-t-il, sursaut de détente d'une énergie trop constamment en action. Au pays de la vie intense, le besoin de détente peut devenir plus impérieux qu'ailleurs." "L'Humour anglo-saxon," pp. 925, 934, 935-36, 939.

11. Elizabeth Sprigge, *Gertrude Stein: Her Life and Work,* pp. 125, 135, 156, 157, 158, 165.

12. "Dans cette universelle confusion, elle est restée intelligente; elle a gardé le sens de la poésie et même celui de l'humour." *Etudes américaines,* p. 16. For a compendious view of the life centered about the publishers of English-language books in Paris around the twenties, see Hugh Ford, *Published in Paris.*

13. Mark Schorer, *Sinclair Lewis,* pp. 319-320.

14. "Avec un art consommé qui tient ici à une sensibilité merveilleusement 'prenante' et dont on a peu d'exemples dans la fiction depuis Balzac et Dickens, Lewis a su recueillir et mettre en valeur les accessoires d'un portrait qui vit comme Grandet, M. Micawber, Tartarin ou Don Quichotte." Régis Michaud, "Le Roman américain," p. 192.

15. "Dans une société égalitaire l'originalité est impossible. . . . L'acuité avec la-

quelle les héros de Sinclair Lewis ont conscience de leurs misères est motif d'indulgence et d'espoir. Spéculons avec optimisme sur l'avenir littéraire d'un pays où s'écrivent *Main Street* et *Babbitt.*" Michaud, "Le Roman américain," pp. 194-195.

16. "Cent millions d'Américains vivent de la vie unanime. L'immense démocratie veut prospérer et se défendre. Elle s'impose des disciplines, des lois, des 'standards'. C'est son droit, son devoir, mais un danger la guette. Sacrifiés à l'impérialisme commercial, cent millions d'individus vont-ils se laisser enrégimenter sans crier gare? L'église, l'école, l'état, la presse et la tyrannie de l'opinion procèdent à un nivellement sans précédent dans l'histoire du monde. Cent millions d'êtres différents sont rendus semblables sous le poids du rouleau compresseur le plus formidable qu'on ait jamais connu. Mais il y a des résistances. L'individualisme est cher à l'Anglo-Saxon. Il y a toujours aux Etats-Unis des apôrtes de la 'self-reliance', de la pleine maîtrise de soi. Malaise, protestations, enquêtes, dénonciations, marquent la fin de l'époque dite de 'la vie intense'. Les nouvelles générations s'insurgent contre le caporalisme moral en vigueur. Et voici que la verve d'un satiriste génial vient à leur rescousse." Régis Michaud, *Panorama de la littérature américaine,* p. 175.

17. "Je n'ai jamais pu lire ses romans sans ennui, je dois l'avouer. Ils sont si longs, si lents, si vrais (si exagérément vrais, pourrait-on dire)." *Civilisation américaine,* p. 245.

18. "Les portraits et les caricatures de l'homme moyen abondaient depuis trente ou quarante ans dans le roman américain. Vers le début du nouveau siècle, le moment semblait venu d'en essayer la synthèse et c'est Sinclair Lewis qui s'en est chargé. Mark Twain lui avait préparé les voies en caricaturiste génial, mais ses portraits étaient des charges. Sinclair Lewis satiriste serre de plus près réel." Michaud, *Panorama,* p. 174.

19. "C'est un humoriste. Aucun des naturalistes de la période précédente ne l'avait été. Et c'est peut-être ce qui distingue le plus Lewis d'un Dreiser, d'un Norris ou d'un Crane. Il a retrouvé et fait passer dans son oeuvre l'humour de Mark Twain, l'humour de la 'frontière' américaine, l'humour perdu par les naturalistes tristes. . . . Ce genre d'humour, on le voit, n'est pas nécessairement mordant ou léger. Il peut être féroce, mais la plupart du temps, c'est l'humour 'bonhomme' du Middle-West." *Les Ecrivains américains,* pp. 68-69.

20. See Gibson, pp. 203-204. Charles Cestre and B. Gagnot, eds., *Anthologie de la littérature américaine.* Maurice Dekobra, ed., *Le Rire dans le brouillard.*

21. Micheline Flak, "Léon Bazalgette, découvreur de la littérature américaine," pp. 184-185 and *passim.* See also Léon Bazalgette, *Henry Thoreau: Sauvage* (Paris: Rieder, 1924), trans. Van Wyck Brooks as *Henry Thoreau: Bachelor of Nature.*

22. *Life among the Surrealists,* pp. 123-125. Gibson, p. 211. But see Georges Duhamel, *America: The Menace,* pp. 23-41: "American movies are not art but a part of the encroaching bourgeois culture that America foreshadows."

23. Jean Simon, "French Studies in American Literature and Civilization," p. 177. Harry Levin, "France-Amérique: The Transatlantic Refraction," p. 87.

24. Thelma M. Smith and Ward L. Miner, *Transatlantic Migration,* pp. 135, 136. Richard Beale Davis, "American Literature in the World Today," p. 279. Percy G. Adams, "The Franco-American Faulkner," p. 7. Maurice Coindreau's recent book on Faulkner, *The Time of William Faulkner,* characterized *The Reivers* as Faulkner's "final stroke": "a burst of laughter, a piece of buffoonery . . . culminating the cycle of his work." But Coindreau failed to stress the increasing comic spirit in Faulkner's novels that led to this culmination.

25. Smith and Miner, pp. 105, 106, 112.

26. Cited in Smith and Miner, p. 146.

27. Cited in Stewart H. Benedict, "Gallic Light on Erskine Caldwell," p. 391.

28. Smith and Miner, pp. 149, 151.

29. Benedict, p. 397.

30. Justin O'Brien, "American Books and French Readers," p. 481 — also the source for the rest of the paragraph.

31. *Etats-Unis 39: Journal d'un voyage en Amérique,* p. 151.

CHAPTER EIGHT

1. Thelma M. Smith and Ward L. Miner, *Transatlantic Migration,* pp. 20-30. See also William S. Hall, "Selling American Books in Europe: Part III," pp. 721-725; and Howard C. Rice, "Seeing Ourselves as the French See Us," pp. 432-441.

2. "French and American Pessimism," p. 268.

3. Smith and Miner, p. 20. See also Jean-Paul Sartre, "American Novelists in French Eyes," pp. 114-118.

4. André Maurois, *Etats-Unis 39: Journal d'un voyage en Amérique,* p. 69; *Etudes américaines;* "Ce qu'on lit aux Etats-Unis," p. 7; "Ecrivains américains," pp. 10-11. See also Maurice Coindreau, *Memoires d'un traducteur.*

5. "American Literature through French Eyes," pp. 432-433, 434.

6. See Harry R. Garvin, "Camus and the American Novel," pp. 194-204.

7. Simone de Beauvoir, "An American Renaissance in France," p. 7. The quotation from Simon is cited in Smith and Miner, p. 19.

8. "Si la lecture des Faulkner, Hemingway, Steinbeck et autres apporte un choc insolite, tel que certains ont pu dire qu'on ne pouvait à notre époque prétendre écrire d'une façon valable sans s'y référer, cela tien à diverses raisons plus ou moins sujettes à caution, un certain snobisme, entre autres." In Jean Desternes, ed., "Que pensez-vous de la littérature américaine?" (January 23), p. 2.

9. "Il faut la suffisance des nouveaux patriotes pour penser qu'on vient encore chercher chez nous des façons de vivre et de penser. Notre littérature actuelle, il faut le dire sans plaisir mais sincèrement, a cessé d'intéresser le monde. C'est la littérature américaine qu'on lui préfère. C'est celle-ci désormais, et pour un laps de temps que nous ne pouvons pas prévoir, qui exprime le plus complètement et avec le plus de force 'les problèmes moraux, sociaux et metaphysiques de notre époque.' " "Que pensez-vous de la littérature américaine?" p. 116.

10. "Qui parle de Dreiser (qui fut le vrai pionnier du roman américain) ou d'Upton Sinclair ou de Sinclair Lewis; qui parle de Whitman? On fait des articles éperdus sur K. Patchen (le Miller de la poésie), mais on a proprement enterré Carl Sandburg. En fait, il ne s'agit ni plus ni moins que d'un systématique assassinat littéraire." "Il y a deux littératures américaines," p. 3. See also the same author's preface to Samuel Clemens, *Les Aventures d'Huckleberry Finn.*

11. Neil D. Isaacs, "Faulkner with a Vengeance: 'The Grass is Greener,' " pp. 427-433. Desternes, *passim.* Richard Beale Davis, "American Literature in the World Today," pp. 277-278.

12. "Il y a sans doute des décalages de réputation, mais ce ne sont point des bouleversements, et en fait notre grand public est beaucoup mieux informé des choses littéraires américaines qu'il ne l'est des anglaises. Alors que pour l'Angleterre les guides font défaut, ici ils abondent. Alfred Kazin, John Brown, Claude-Edmonde Magny, Michel Mohrt, Cyrille Arnavon, Jean Simon, Maurice Coindreau, pour ne citer que quelques-uns des meilleurs commentateurs récents, tant indigènes que français, ont dégagé pour nous les perspectives du roman américain, tracé les voies d'approche, analysé et défini les tendances des générations, éclairé notre progression jusque parmi les plus jeunes de nos contemporains. Si bien que malgré les inévitables différences d'optique et de réaction, il n'est pas tellement facile de se tromper." Raymond Las Vergnas, "Dix ans de traductions. 2: L'Amérique," p. 6.

13. "Europe's Faith in American Fiction," p. 52.

14. Percy G. Adams, "American Literature in the Universities of France," pp. 175-184. Charles Angoff, "American Literature in Europe and Israel," pp. 388-391. *American Studies News,* December 1966, p. 4.

15. From a mimeographed newsletter of the AFEA. There is some reaction against this enthusiasm. Speaking of American literary scholarship, which the French academicians are emulating, Cyrille Arnavon wrote: "La monographie dite critique a été utilisée pour tout de figures ou de questions d'un intérêt souvent minime qu'avec la poussée démographique et la multiplication de diplômes, on se demande non sans inquiétude chez certains maîtres de littérature américaine vers quelles recherches on pourra bien orienter les futures impétrants au doctorat en philosophie! Les bibliographies donnent déjà le vertige." "L'Ecrivain en face de l'américanisme," p. 11. See also Haakon Chevalier, "A bas l'américanisme, vive l'Amérique," pp. 237-240.

16. "Du moins avons-nous donné les titres de celles de leurs oeuvres que des Français cultivés auraient plaisir ou profit à lire." Charles Cestre, "Avant-propos," *La Littérature américaine.*

17. "L'humour n'est pas le réalisme, mais souvent il l'accompagne ou le favorise. Sous le travesti de la plaisanterie se cachent l'observation et le bon sens. Le remous de drôlerie est le bouillonnement de la franchise, de la satire clairvoyante, de l'intention moralisatrice, à base de vérité. Le comique anglo-saxon, en Amérique, comme en Angleterre, relève généralement de l'humour dans l'acception précise du mot, c'est-à-dire du risible exprimé sur un ton d'apparente gravité; le choc qui fait éclater le rire est renforcé par la contradiction entre le fond, imprégné d'exagération, d'absurdité, de cocasserie, de grotesque, et la forme, habilement maintenue dans un faux-semblant de sérieux, de

raison, de logique, de précision technique. Les gens de l'Ouest pratiquaient volontiers cette gaîté de pince-sans-rire, comme délassement, le soir, autour de verres de whisky. Ils furent les premiers à applaudir les humoristes professionnels, dont la réputation reflua des rives du Mississippi vers l'Est et devint nationale." Ibid., p. 102.

18. "Si l'on a pu dire de Franklin qu'il fut le premier Américain civilisé, d'Irving on peut dire qu'il fut le premier Américain uniquement homme de lettres. D'ailleurs est-ce là sa seule véritable originalité." "Ses thèmes ne sont pas nouveaux, mais elle y apporte toujours une vivacité, un esprit de satire et un humour qui les rendent originaux malgré tout." "C'est en fait une caricature de littérature noire, toutes ses caractéristiques y étant portées à l'excès." "Steinbeck a même tendance à croire que les mauvais garçons tout particulièrement ont de la bonté, comme il le montre dans ses très amusants *Tortilla Flat* (1935), et *Cannery Row* (1945), sortes de recueils de contes fantastiques pour grandes personnes, du plus délicieux humour." *La Littérature américaine,* pp. 10, 72, 117, 119.

19. "L'humour a toujours été et sera de nouveau, dès les années 1840, en pays anglo-saxon (comme chez Thackeray), ennemi de l'effusion passionnée. Le jour où l'intensité lyrique s'épuise faute de sincérité, il y aura nécessairement des esprits prompts à rire du ridicule qui s'attache aux attitudes inspirées ou grandiloquentes. En Amérique, on l'a vu, les poses romantiques, byroniennes en particulier, ne s'étaient jamais vraiment répandues parce qu'elles heurtaient les convictions égalitaires de la démocratie militante. Cet esprit de simplicité s'accordera au contraire à la tonalité des humoristes qui procèdent plus ou moins directement des couches populaires. L'humour qui, en un sens, est négation de la triste réalité—et partant évasion—peut cependant, en introduisant une matière quotidienne et vulgaire dans les lettres, ouvrir la voie au réalisme. Chez les conteurs et les romanciers, l'humour et l'inventaire de tendance réaliste sont fréquemment concomitants.

Il ne faut pas chercher à définir trop étroitement l'humour américain. Le contraste par lequel on l'oppose à la variété anglaise est souvent artificiel. On peut dire cependant que les bouffons tonitruants de la 'frontière' outrepassent souvent, dans une farce énorme, les limites qu'une pudeur très britannique, celle de l'émotion, assignait à l'effet humoristique." Cyrille Arnavon, *Histoire littéraire des Etats-Unis,* p. 215. See Hans Galinsky, "Literary Criticism in Literary History," pp. 31-40.

20. "Un clivage profond entre deux variétés de littérature, l'une noble, sérieuse, conforme à des canons depuis longtemps définis, l'autre populaire, vive, exubérante, mais contrevenant à toutes les règles, se moquant des bienséances et désordonnée jusqu'à la confusion." Jean Béranger and Maurice Gonnaud, *La Littérature américaine jusqu'en 1865,* p. 117.

21. "Dans la littérature moderne américaine, on trouve peu de vrais humoristes. Il semble que la période difficile d'après guerre et les années de dépression aient surtout développé chez les jeunes écrivains le sens de la critique mordante ou de l'ironie incisive. Sinclair Lewis a flétri avec dureté les travers des parvenus et des matérialistes. Dos Passos a pris parti, avec passion, dans les luttes sociales et politiques. Quant aux fantaisistes, les parodies burlesques d'Erskine, les contes et les sketches de Thurber laissent transparaître un amer pessimisme. Ils n'ont point la grâce désinvolté d'un Saroyan, ni la verve imaginative d'un Christopher Morley qui, dans ses contes, nous fait pénétrer dans un domaine enchanté où la poésie et l'humour se confondent et transportent le lecteur dans une sphère d'utopie et parfois de féerique illusion." *Voix d'Amérique: études sur la littérature américaine d'aujourd'hui,* p. 155. Mention should perhaps be made of Claude Magny's critical interpretation of the twentieth-century American novel, *L'Age du roman américain* (Paris: Seuil, 1948), although it had nothing to add to our study of humor.

22. "Car un dialogue humain vraiment 'nature' est souvent lassant de banalité. Je sais bien qu'Hemingway le remplit de son expérience d'aventurier plantureux et humoriste: l'autre guerre sur le front italien, le Paris des années 20, les chasses en Afrique, tout un monde de boxeurs, de jockeys, de marin,—et je réserve l'Espagne. La technique, bien possédée, de tous les métiers que font ses personnages, de tous les sports qu'ils pratiquent, nourrit leurs propos d'une substance savoureuse. L'ironie de l'auteur, et sa franchise désinvolte, mettent plaisamment en place cette moisson de vérités humaines non raffinées. Oui, tel est bien le tumulte de la vie, mais qui fait beaucoup de bruit inutile, surtout quand les parleurs sont saoûls, comme dans certains romans d'Hemingway presque d'un bout à l'autre. Et le dialogue des hommes prend au contraire sa valeur, non plus quand il fait scintiller leurs vérités extérieures mais quand il relève, serait-ce d'un mot qui passe, la vérité essentielle de l'homme, la clef unique de la farce, du drame et du diorama." *Littérature du vingtième siècle,* 3: 248.

23. "Ce qui peut-être a fait la fortune de Lewis satiriste, c'est son sens de l'humour. Les livres de Frank Norris, de Stephen Crane, étaient tristes. Les romans de Dreiser sont dépourvus d'humour au point que la lecture en est pénible. Lewis, lui, semble avoir retrouvé la tradition de Mark Twain. Et il faut savoir combien cet humour facile, bon enfant, sans portée le plus souvent, est typiquement américain pour comprendre son succès. Pas un orateur, dans une cérémonie ou un banquet officiel, ne croira déroger à la solennité en glissant dans son discours une anecdote qui provoque le rire. Lewis, lui, s'en donne à coeur joie. La plaisanterie est constante sous sa plume. L'humour est dans les situations, dans la gaucherie des gestes, dans la bouffonnerie des titres ou des extraits de presse donnés pour réels, dans les propos des moindres personnages, ou des plus graves. Et toute l'oeuvre du romancier s'en trouve allégée; elle amuse, elle entraîne. Ce qui l'indigne le plus parvient à peine à effacer son sourire. C'est sans doute le secret de son succès." *Le Roman américain au XXe siècle,* p. 83. See also pages 13, 14, 36, 39, 82-84, 91, 104, 108, 127, 157, 160-161, 174-178, 179.

24. "C'est essentiellement un humoriste et peut-être le plus dynamique des poètes humoristiques américains. . . . Ajoutons que Nash, véritable jongleur, a utilisé toutes les techniques possibles et imaginables pour donner cours à son humour qui va l'acidulé à la fantaisie la plus debridée." *Europe,* February-March 1959, p. 142.

25. Pierre Brodin, *Présences contemporaines:* Bellow, "un arrière-fond d'humour et d'ironie," p. 39. Capote, "un humour de grande classe," p. 47. Malamud, see footnote 6, p. 94. O'Connor, "l'humour . . . et même la tendresse," p. 132. Powers, "la qualité prédominante . . . n'est pas la satire, mais plutôt l'humour," p. 145. Roth, "un don incontestable du comique," p. 155. Salinger, "un certain don d'humour, de satire . . . et d'ironie," p. 165.

26. Brodin: "L'humour et l'ironie, déjà fort apparents dans les poèmes et les contes, éclatent joyeusement dans *Rabbit Run,*" p. 197. "Etroitement lié à la triple notion de cocasse, d'absurde et d'insanité, cet humour ne rejette pas le jeu de mots, le *pun,* le *slogan* grotesques *(If it's the Optic White, it's the Right White),* et utilise largement la *joke* exprimée dans les *blues,* qui reconcilient la violence et la dignité humaine à travers l'ironie," pp. 56-57.

27. "Leurs héros sont des 'innocents' qui se sentent coupables (ou des 'coupables' qui se sentent innocents), des hommes libres qui sont aussi des esclaves, des *victimes-rebelles* comme Prométhée, comme Oedipe, comme Don Quichotte, comme tant d'autres représentants des grands mythes de la littérature et de l'art, des martyrs, des anarchistes, des clowns, des rêveurs qui rêvent d'immortalité dans un monde délimité par la souffrance et la mort. Ce sont des héros de l'*absurde,* mais de l'absurde envisagé avec *ironie* plutôt qu'avec rancoeur. Ils vivent dans un état de tension ou d'aliénation vis-à-vis de la société. Ce sont des 'étrangers', un peu comme celui de Camus, mais avec, derrière eux, toute une tradition d'*innocence* spécifiquement américaine, — l'innocence d'un pays neuf qui a rejeté, ou cru rejeter, les péchés du Vieux-Monde et s'étonne toujours et se scandalise de les voir renaître sur une terre vierge." Ibid., pp. 15-16.

28. *Les Ecrivains américains d'aujourd'hui:* "Les écrivains du possible sont à la fois plus et moins originaux que tous ceux qui ont été présentés jusqu'ici. Conscients des diverse 'attitudes' — qu'ils ont parfois incarnées au cours de leur carrière littéraire — ils en tentent une suprême synthèse où la dominante est cette fois le sentiment que l'homme est un être, sinon libre, du moins capable d'un certain nombre de choix," p. 88. "Cette exploration implique, chez le personnage, certaines qualités dont les plus importantes sont la lucidité — indispensable pour se diriger; l'amour — qui mène à l'autre; le goût de la liberté — qui incite à la découverte; une certaine forme de passivité — qui encourage la résistance à l'absurde; et un sens de l'humour — qui permet de s'en tirer avec une certaine désinvolture," p. 91. "Les distinctions traditionelles entre le comique, le tragique, le satirique, le lyrique s'estompent encore davantage," p. 92.

29. "Le rire jaune et l'humour noir finissent par être aussi monotones, aussi gratuits que l'optimisme en rose de certain littérature féminine." *Panorama de la littérature contemporaine aux Etats-Unis,* p. 262. Bibliographical details of the other books mentioned in this paragraph are included in the bibliography.

30. Maurice Le Breton, ed., *The Student's Anthology of American Literature.*

31. Pierre Deflaux et al., eds., *American Trails: An Anthology of Representative Writers,* 1: 3.

32. André Breton, ed., *Anthologie de l'humour noir.*

33. Michel Chrestien and Jacques Sternberg, eds., *Un Siècle d'humour anglo-américain.*

34. Jacques Sternberg et al., eds., *Les Chefs d'oeuvre du sourire.*

35. "Un esprit volontiers neurasthénique que rien ne peut consoler." In Ambrose Bierce, *Le Dictionnaire du diable* (Paris: Nouvel Office d'Edition, 1964), p. 14.

36. "Un des humoristes les plus vigilants, les plus virulents, que les Etats-Unis aient jamais connus." In Robert Benchley, *Benchley* (Paris: Julliard, 1963), p. i.

37. "Il n'existait pas en France de collection consacrée à l'humour—tout au moins à celui qui contient cruauté, froideur, poésie—et que l'on appelle humour anglais—aux yeux des amateurs le seul, le pur, le vrai.

La collection *Humour Secret* a pour but de donner à cet humour-là les lettres de noblesse qu'il n'a pas encore acquises en France. C'est qu'il existe dans le monde entier mais plus particulièrement aux Etats-Unis et en Angleterre, un certain nombre d'écrivains de grande valeur dont l'humour virulent est généralement inconnu hors de leurs frontières. C'est donc un domaine pratiquement inexploré que la collection se propose de prospecter. Elle défendra un certain humour qui n'est peut-être rien d'autre qu'un certain sourire et certainement pas le fou rire." *Benchley,* book jacket.

38. "Et quand enfin on fera le point sur l'apport littéraire de ce siècle, quand on cherchera à savoir quels sont les auteurs qui ont le mieux décrit ce XXe siècle, ceux qui l'ont ressenti avec le plus d'acuité, il n'est pas interdit de penser que ces humoristes auront bien plus d'importance que tous les subtils analystes dont la littérature fait une si ample consommation. Alors seulement, ils prendront leur revanche." In James Thurber, *Thurber* (Paris: Julliard, 1964), p. 18.

CHAPTER NINE

1. On maps France looks like a hexagon. It has been a convenient reminder for generations of schoolchildren. The word is now widely used. Robert Beauvais, a TV producer, showed in *L'Hexagonal,* a humorous book about the French language, that French is now colonized by technocracy.

2. In *Elle,* a counterpart of *Vogue.*

3. See Edgar Morin, *Les Stars* (Paris: Seuil, 1972): "Ainsi l'evolution de Chaplin nous démontre quasi exemplairement que le bouc émissaire purificateur de la *slapstick comedy* porte en lui les germes d'un héros qui se sacrifie, disons même d'un dieu qui meurt et sauve. . . . Le héros comique est donc, lui aussi, héros qui se charge du mal pour purifier autrui. Il détient virtuellement un pouvoir mythique et sacré. On ne l'aime pas seulement parce qu'il nous fait rire. Il nous fait rire pour qu'on l'aime."

4. In *Clefs pour l'Amérique,* written after World War II, Claude Roy also made it clear that the American was pressed to conform like a new tenant in a condominium.

5. "Dans toute l'histoire, la mort et la folie dansent un ballet sans cesse recommencé. Au reste, on n'observe pas seulement les stratégies de la folie; surviennent aussi des actes fous. . . . Ainsi raisonnements, règlements, prétentions et conduites, rigoureusement enchaînés, se répondent au sein d'une situation organisant la mécanique implacable et indéfinie de l'absurde, en la présence immanente de la mort." Paul Racamier, "Entre humour et folie," pp. 655-668.

6. Mark Twain said that a Frenchman's house is where another man's wife lives.

Bibliography

Adams, Percy G. "American Literature in the Universities of France." In *Studies in Honor of Hodges and Thaler,* edited by Richard Beale Davis, pp. 175-184. Knoxville: The Univ. of Tennessee Press, 1961.

______. "The Franco-American Faulkner." *Tennessee Studies in Literature* 5 (1960):1-11.

Aldridge, Alfred O. "The Debut of American Letters in France." *French American Review* 3 (1950):1-23.

______. *Franklin and His French Contemporaries.* New York: New York Univ. Press, 1957.

Ampère, Jean Jacques. *Promenade en Amérique.* Paris: Michel Lévy Frères, 1855.

Angellier, Auguste. *Robert Burns.* Paris: Hachette, 1893.

Angoff, Charles. "American Literature in Europe and Israel." *College English* 26 (1965):388-391.

Ansermoz-Dubois, Félix. *L'Interpretation français de la littérature américaine de l'entre-deux-guerres (1919–1939).* Lausanne: Imprimerie la Concorde, 1944.

Arnavon, Cyrille. "L'Ecrivain en face de l'américanisme." *Europe,* February-March 1959, pp. 4-17.

______. *Histoire littéraire des Etats-Unis.* Paris: Hachette, 1953.

______. *Les Lettres américaines devant la critique française (1887–1917).* Paris: Société d'Edition les Belles Lettres, 1951.

Asselineau, Roger. "Introduction," *Les Aventures d'Arthur Gordon Pym,* by Edgar Allan Poe, translated by Charles Baudelaire. Paris: Aubier Mantaign, 1973.

______. *The Literary Reputation of Mark Twain from 1910 to 1950.* Paris: Didier, 1954.

______. "Walt Whitman's Humor." *American Transcendental Quarterly,* Spring 1974, pp. 86-91.

Asselineau, Roger, ed. *Edgar Poe: choix de contes.* Paris: Aubier, 1958.

Asselineau, Roger, and Copans, Simon. "American Studies in France: The New Face of a Tradition," *American Studies* 12 (1974): 3-11.

Austin, James C. "American Humor in France." *Papers on Language and Literature* 5, Supplement (Summer 1969): 100-102.

______. *Artemus Ward.* New York: Twayne, 1964.

Baldensperger, Fernand. "Les Définitions de l'humour." *Etudes d'histoire littéraire,* vol. 1, pp. 176-222. Paris: Hachette, 1907.

Bandy, W. T. "New Light on Baudelaire and Poe." *Yale French Studies,* Autumn 1952, pp. 65-69.

Batault, Georges. "Tocqueville et la littérature américaine." *Mercure de France* 135 (September 16, 1919):248-261.

Baudelaire, Charles Pierre. *Baudelaire on Poe,* translated and edited by Lois and Francis E. Hyslop, Jr. State College, Pennsylvania: Bald Eagle Press, 1952.

______. *The Essence of Laughter and Other Essays, Journals, and Letters,* edited by Peter Quennell. New York: Meridian Books, 1956.

______. *Selected Critical Studies of Baudelaire,* edited by D. Parmée. Cambridge: The University Press, 1949.

Bazalgette, Léon. *Henry Thoreau: Bachelor of Nature,* translated by Van Wyck Brooks. New York: Harcourt, Brace, 1924.

Beauvoir, Simone de. "An American Renaissance in France." *New York Times Book Review,* June 22, 1947, pp. 7, 29.

Benedict, Stewart H. "Gallic Light on Erskine Caldwell." *South Atlantic Quarterly* 60 (1961):390-397.

Béranger, Jean. *Nathaniel Ward (ca. 1578-1652).* Bordeaux: Sobodi, 1969.

______. "Voices of Humor in Nathaniel Ward," *Studies in American Humor* 2 (October 1975), 96-104.

Béranger, Jean, and Gonnaud, Maurice. *La Littérature américaine jusqu'en 1865.* Paris: Armand Colin, 1974.

Bergson, Henri. "Laughter." In *Comedy,* edited by Wylie Sypher, pp. 61-190. Garden City, New York: Doubleday, 1956.

Bibliothèque Nationale. *Benjamin Franklin et la France.* Paris: Bibliothèque Nationale, 1956.

Bier, Jesse. *The Rise and Fall of American Humor.* New York: Holt, Rinehart and Winston, 1968.

Binsse, Harry Lorin, and Trounstine, John J. "Europe Looks at Sinclair Lewis." *The Bookman* 72 (January 1931): 453-457.

Blanc, Marie-Thérèse (Bentzon, Th.). "L'Age doré en Amérique." *Revue des deux mondes,* March 15, 1875, pp. 319-343.

______. *Choses et gens d'Amérique.* Paris: Calmann Lévy, 1898.

______. "Les Humoristes américains." *Revue des deux mondes,* July 15, 1872, pp. 313-355, and August 15, 1872, pp. 837-862.

______. *Littérature et moeurs etrangères.* Paris: C. Lévy, 1882.

______. "Les Nouveaux Romanciers américains: Henry James." *Revue des deux mondes,* May 1, 1883, pp. 120-164.

Bonaparte, Marie. *The Life and Works of Edgar Allan Poe,* translated by John Rodker. London: Imago, 1949.

Bond, D. F. et al. "Anglo-French and Franco-American Studies: A Current Bibliography." *Romantic Review* 29 (1938), 39 (1948).

Bosc, R. "Mark Twain et l'humour américain." *Revue de synthèse historique,* vol. 29, pp. 181-187. Paris: Leopold Cerf, 1919.

Breton, André, ed. *Anthologie de l'humour noir.* Paris: Sagittaire, 1940.

Brion, Marcel. "Le Contrepoint poétique de Gertrude Stein." *Echanges* 3 (June 1930):122-128.

Brodin, Pierre. *Les Ecrivains américains de l'entre-deux-guerres.* Paris: Horizons de France, 1946.

______. *Présences contemporaines: écrivains américains d'aujourd'hui.* Paris: Nouvelles éds. Debresse, 1964.

Brown, John L. *Panorama de la littérature contemporaine aux Etats-Unis.* Paris: Gallimard, 1971.

Bush, Robert. "Grace King and Mark Twain." *American Literature* 44 (March 1972):31-51.

Cabau, Jacques. *La Prairie perdue: histoire du roman américain.* Paris: Seuil, 1966.

Cahen, Jacques Fernand. *La Littérature américaine.* Paris: Presses Universitaires (Collection que sais-je?), 1950.

Cambiaire, Célestin Pierre. *The Influence of Edgar Allan Poe in France.* New York: G. E. Stechert, 1927.

Cargill, Oscar. Review of *Les Lettres américaines devant la critique française: 1887-1917* by Cyrille Arnavon. *Modern Language Notes* 49 (January 1954):72-73.

Cazamian, Louis. *The Development of English Humor.* Durham, North Carolina: Duke Univ. Press, 1952.

______. "L'Humour de New York." *Essais en deux langues,* pp. 149-161. Paris: Henri Didier, 1938.

______. "Humour et amour." *Essais en deux langues,* pp. 141-147. Paris: Henri Didier, 1938.

______. "Le Mécanisme de l'humour." *Etudes de psychologie littéraire,* pp. 97-160. Paris: Payot, 1913.

Cestre, Charles. "American Literature through French Eyes." *Yale Review* 10 (October 1920):85-98.

______. *La Littérature américaine.* Paris: A. Colin, 1945.

______. Review of *Josh Billings,* by Cyril Clemens. *Revue anglo-américaine* 10 (1933):561.

Cestre, Charles, and Gagnot, B., eds. *Anthologie de la littérature américaine.* Paris: Delagrave, 1926.

Charpentier, John. "Humour anglais et humour américain. A propos du centenaire de Mark Twain." *Mercure de France* 264 (December 15, 1935):475-500.

Chartier, Emile [Alain]. *Propos sur le bonheur.* Paris: Gallimard, 1928.

Chasles, Philarète. "Des tendances littéraires en Angleterre et en Amérique." *Revue des deux mondes,* April 15, 1844, pp. 497-545.

______. *The Legacy of Philarète Chasles,* edited by A. Levin. Chapel Hill: Univ. of North Carolina Press, 1957.

______. "Littérature pseudo-populaire en Angleterre et en Amérique." *Revue des deux mondes,* September 15, 1847, pp. 1106-1115.

______. "Scenes de la vie privée dans l'Amérique du Nord." *Revue des deux mondes,* April 15, 1841, pp. 306-325.

______. "Voyages réels et fantastique d'Hermann Melville." *Revue des deux mondes,* May 15, 1849, pp. 541-570.

Chevalier, Haakon. "A bas l'américanisme, vive l'Amérique." *Europe,* February-March 1959, pp. 237-240.

Chinard, Gilbert. *L'Amérique d'Abraham Lincoln et la France.* Washington: Institut français de Washington, 1945.

______. *Apothéose de Benjamin Franklin.* Paris: Librairie Orientale et Américaine, 1955.

______. "Random Notes on Two Bagatelles." *Proceedings of the American Philosophical Society* 103 (December 1959):727-760.

Chrestien, Michel, and Sternberg, Jacques, eds. *Un Siècle d'humour anglo-américain,* preface by André Maurois. Paris: Les Productions de Paris, 1962.

Coindreau, Maurice Edgar. *Aperçus de littérature américaine.* Paris: Gallimard, 1946.

______. *Memoires d'un traducteur.* Paris: Gallimard, 1974.

______. *The Time of William Faulkner: A French View of Modern American Fiction,* edited by George M. Reeves. Columbia: Univ. of South Carolina Press, 1971.

Copans, Simon, Professor, Institut d'Etudes Américaines, Paris. Unpublished research on the French image of America in the last half of the nineteenth century (1974).

Davis, Richard Beale. "American Literature in the World Today." In *American Studies in Transition,* edited by Marshall W. Fishwick, pp. 268-297. Philadelphia: Univ. of Pennsylvania Press, 1964.

Deak, Etienne. *Dictionnaire d'américanismes contenant les principaux termes américains.* Paris: Dauphin, 1957.

Debouzy, Marianne. *La Genèse de l'esprit de révolte dans le roman américain, 1875-1915.* Paris: Minard, 1968.

Debusscher, Gilbert. *Edward Albee: Tradition and Renewal,* translated by Anne D. Williams. Brussels: American Studies Center, 1967.

Deflaux, Pierre; Martin, Jean-Pierre; Royot, Daniel; and Guiguet, Jean, eds. *American Trails: An Anthology of Representative Writers.* Paris: Armand Colin, 1970.

Dekobra, Maurice, ed. *Le Rire dans le brouillard.* Paris: Flammarion, 1927.

Delattre, Floris. "La Naissance de l'humour dans la vieille Angleterre." *Revue anglo-américaine,* April 1927, pp. 289-307.

______. "Sur une théorie nouvelle de l'humour," *Revue anglo-américaine,* August 1931, pp. 534-538.

Desternes, Jean, ed. "Que pensez-vous de la littérature américaine?" *Combat,* January 3, 4, 5-6, 7, 8, 17, 21, 23, 26-27, 28; February 2-3, 6, 7, 13, 1947, p. 2.

Diderot, Denis. "Paradoxe sur le comédien." *Diderot: Oeuvres,* pp. 1033-1088. Paris: Gallimard, 1951.

Digeon, A. Review of *Le Rire dans le brouillard* by Maurice Dekobra. *Revue anglo-américaine,* October 1923, pp. 86-88.

Dommergues, Pierre. *Les Ecrivains américains d'aujourd'hui.* Paris: Presses universitaires de France, 1965.

Dommergues, Pierre, ed. *Les U.S.A. à la recherche de leur identité: rencontres avec 40 écrivains américains.* Paris: Grasset, 1967.

Doumic, René. "Nos Humoristes." *Revue des deux mondes,* October 15, 1899, pp. 924-935.

Duhamel, Georges. *America: The Menace,* translated by Charles Miner Thompson. Boston: Houghton Mifflin, 1931.

Dulck, Jean et al. *Humour anglais.* In *Bulletin du centre d'études de littérature générale de Bordeaux,* fasc. 7, Séance du 13 Février, 1959.

Dumont, Léon. *Des causes du rire.* Paris: Auguste Durand, 1862.

Echeverria, Durand. "Antoine Jay and the United States." *American Quarterly* 4 (1952):235-252.

______. *Mirage in the West: A History of the French Image of American Society to 1815.* New York: Octagon Books, 1966.

______. " 'The Sale of the Hessians.' Was Benjamin Franklin the Author?" *Proceedings of the American Philosophical Society* 98 (1954):427-431.

Edel, Léon. "A Note on the Translations of Henry James in France." *Revue anglo-américaine* 7 (August 1930):539-540.

Epuy, Michel, ed. *Anthologie des humoristes anglais et américains.* Paris: C. Delagrave, 1910.

Escarpit, Robert. *L'Humour.* Paris: Presses Universitaires de France, 1963.

Les Etats-Unis à travers les livres. Paris: Services Américains d'Information, 1952.

Europe, February-March, 1959.

Fabre, Lucien. *Le Rire et les rieurs.* Paris: Gallimard, 1929.

Faÿ, Bernard. *Bibliographie critique des ouvrages français relatifs aux Etats-Unis (1770-1800).* Paris: E. Champion, 1925.

______. *Civilisation américaine.* Paris: Sagittaire, 1939.

______. *Franklin, The Apostle of Modern Times.* Boston: Little, Brown, 1929.

Feinberg, Leonard. "Sinclair Lewis as a Satirist." Ph.D. dissertation, Univ. of Illinois, 1946.

Flak, Micheline. "Léon Bazalgette, découvreur de la littérature américaine." *Europe,* No. 483-484 (1969), pp. 180-187.

Fonteney, Antoine. "Littérature américaine: Washington Irving—'The Alhambra.' " *Revue des deux mondes* 6 (1832):515-549.

Ford, Hugh. *Published in Paris.* New York: Macmillan, 1975.

Forgue, Guy Jean. *H. L. Mencken: l'homme, l'oeuvre, l'influence.* Paris: Minard, 1967.

Forgues, Eugène. "Les Caravanes d'un humoriste: Mark Twain." *Revue des deux mondes,* February 15, 1886, pp. 879-918.

Forgues, Eugène-D. "La Fantaisie aux Etats-Unis." *Revue des deux mondes,* July 15, 1860, pp. 410-435.

"French Opinions of American Authors." *United States Literary Gazette* 1 (June 15, 1824):76.

Freud, Sigmund. "Humour." *The Standard Edition of the Complete Psychological Works of Sigmund Freud,* vol. 21, pp. 160-166. London: Hogarth, 1961.

______. *Jokes and Their Relation to the Unconscious,* translated by James Strachey. New York: W. W. Norton, 1960.

Galinsky, Hans. "Literary Criticism in Literary History: A Comparative View of the 'Uses of the Past' in Recent American and European Histories of American Literature." *Comparative Literature Studies* 1 (1964):31-40.

Garnier, M. R. *Henry James et la France.* Paris: Champion, 1927.

Garvin, Harry R. "Camus and the American Novel." *Comparative Literature* 8 (1956):194-204.

Gauthier-Villars, Henry (Willy). *Mark Twain.* Paris: Gauthier-Villars, 1884.

Gibson, Delbert L. "French Impressions of American Character and Culture: The United States as Seen in the Leading French Literary Periodicals from 1900 to 1930. An Analysis with Annotated Bibliography." Ph.D. dissertation, Univ. of Wisconsin, 1938.

Gonnaud, Maurice. "The Humane Seer: Humor and Its Avatars in Emerson." *American Transcendental Quarterly,* Spring 1974, pp. 79-85.

______. *Individu et société dans l'oeuvre de Ralph Waldo Emerson: essai de biographie spirituelle.* Paris: Didier, 1964.

Guérard, Albert. "French and American Pessimism." *Harper's Magazine,* September 1945, pp. 267-272.

Hall, William S. "Selling American Books in Europe: Part III." *Publishers' Weekly,* August 23, 1947, pp. 721-725.

Harris, Julia Collier. *The Life and Letters of Joel Chandler Harris.* Boston: Houghton Mifflin, 1918.

______. "Uncle Remus at Home and Abroad." *The Southern Literary Messenger* 2 (1940):84-86.

Harzic, Jean. *Faulkner: présence littéraire.* Paris: Bordas, 1973.

Hellman, George Sidney. *Washington Irving, Esquire.* New York: Knopf, 1925.

Hornstein, Simon. *Mark Twain.* Paris: Renée Lacoste, 1950.

Isaacs, Neil D. "Faulkner with a Vengeance: 'The Grass Is Greener.'" *South Atlantic Quarterly* 60 (1961):427-433.

Jeune, A.-L. "L'Humour anglo-saxon." *Correspondant* 271 (June 10, 1918):925-940.

Josephson, Matthew. *Life among the Surrealists.* New York: Holt, Rinehart and Winston, 1962.

Jouvenel, Renaud de. "Autour de numéro." *Europe,* February-March 1959, pp. 17-24.

Jusserand, Jean Jules. *A Literary History of the English People.* New York: G. P. Putnam, 1906-1909.

K., A. "First Chair of American Literature in France." *American Notes and Queries* 1 (August 1941):77.

Kanapa, Jean. "Il y a deux littératures américaines." *Les Lettres français,* February 5, 1948, p. 3.

______. "Preface" to *Les Aventures d'Huckleberry Finn* by Samuel Clemens, translated by Suzanne Nétillard. Paris: Editions d'Hier et d'Aujourd'hui, 1948.

Kruh, Reine. "Un Siècle de magazines californiens, 1850-1950." Ph.D. dissertation, Univ. de Paris, 1962.

Laffay, Albert. *Anatomie de l'humour et du nonsense.* Paris: Masson, 1970.

Lanson, Gustave. *Manuel bibliographique de la littérature française moderne.* Paris: Hachette, 1925.

Las Vergnas, Raymond. "Dix Ans de traductions. 2: L'Amérique." *Nouvelles littéraires,* December 19, 1957, p. 6.

______. *Thackeray l'homme, le penseur, le romancier.* Paris: Champion, 1932.

Lautrec, Gabriel de. "Mark Twain." *Mercure de France,* June 1, 1910, pp. 425-439.

Lautrec, Gabriel de, ed. *Contes choisis, par Mark Twain.* Paris: Mercure de France, 1900.

Leacock, Stephen. *L'Humour américain.* Paris: 1918.

Le Breton, Maurice. "Un Centenaire: Mark Twain." *Revue anglo-américaine* 12 (June 1935):401-418.

Le Breton, Maurice, ed. *The Student's Anthology of American Literature.* Lyon: IAC, 1955.

Lemonnier, Léon. *Edgar Poe et la critique française de 1845 à 1875.* Paris: Presses Universitaires de France, 1928.

______. *Mark Twain: L'homme et son oeuvre.* Paris: Arthème Fayard, 1946.

Levin, Harry. "France-Amérique: The Transatlantic Refraction." *Comparative Literature Studies* 1 (1964):87-92.

______. "Some European Views of Contemporary American Literature: Its Relation to Ideas." In *The American Writer and the European Tradition,* edited by Margaret Denny, pp. 168-184. New York: McGraw-Hill, 1950.

"La Littérature américaine traduite en français." *Le Navire d'argent* 1 (December 1925, January 1926):350-355, 477-486.

Lopez, Claude-Anne. *Mon cher papa: Franklin and the Ladies of Paris.* New Haven: Yale Univ. Press, 1966.

Lynes, Carlos, Jr. "The 'Nouvelle Revue Française' and American Literature, 1909-1940." *French Review* 19 (1946):159-167.

MacClintock, Lander. "Sainte-Beuve and America." *PMLA* 60 (1945): 427-436.

MacDonald, Edgar Edgeworth. *Les Sources étrangères du roman epique de James Branch Cabell.* Ph.D. dissertation, Univ. of Paris, 1957.

McGee, Sidney-Lamont. *La Littérature américaine dans la "Revue des deux mondes" (1831-1900).* Dissertation, Univ. of Montpellier, 1927.

Mantz, Harold Elmer. *French Criticism of American Literature before 1850.* New York: Columbia Univ. Press, 1917.

Maurois, André. "Ce qu'on lit aux Etats-Unis." *Les Nouvelles littéraires,* August 1, 1946, pp. 1, 7.

______. "Ecrivains américains." *Revue de Paris,* April 1947, pp. 9-24.

______. *Etats-Unis 39: journal d'un voyage en Amérique.* Paris: Les Editions de France, 1939.

______. Etudes américaines. New York: Editions de la maison française, 1945.

Mayer, Tony. *L'Humour anglais.* Paris: Julliard, 1961.

Mayoux, Jean-Jacques. "L'Humour anglais" (Review of *The Development of English Humor* by Louis Cazamian). *Critique* 8 (December 1952): 1011-1026.

Michaud, Régis. "L'Ame américaine." *Revue universelle* 36 (March 1, 1929):536-548.

______. "L'Envers d'un humoriste: Mark Twain." *Revue du mois* 9 (April 10, 1910):430-444.

———. *Mystiques et réalistes anglo-saxons, d'Emerson à Bernard Shaw.* Paris: A. Colin, 1918.

———. *Panorama de la littérature américaine.* Paris: Kra, 1929.

———. "Le Roman américain: 'Babbitt,' par Sinclair Lewis." *Revue de France,* June 1, 1923, pp. 191-195.

Miller, Perry. "Europe's Faith in American Fiction." *Atlantic,* December 1951, pp. 52-56.

Mohrt, Michel. *Le Nouveau Roman américain.* Paris: Gallimard, 1955.

Montégut, Emile. "Du Génie de la race anglo-saxonne et de ses destinées." *Revue des deux mondes,* September 15, 1851, pp. 1027-1045.

———. "Un Humoriste anglo-américain: Halliburton." *Revue des deux mondes,* February 15, 1850, pp. 731-748.

Morin, Violette. "L'Histoire drôle." *Communication,* 1968, pp. 102-119; 1976, pp. 102-114.

Morris, George D. *Fenimore Cooper et Edgar Poe d'après la critique française du XIXe siècle.* Paris: Larose, 1912.

———. "French Criticism of Poe." *South Atlantic Quarterly* 14 (1915):324-329.

———. *Washington Irving's Fiction in the Light of French Criticism.* Indiana University Studies, vol. 3, May 1916.

Morse, John T., Jr. *Life and Letters of Oliver Wendell Holmes.* Boston: Houghton, Mifflin, 1896.

Nadeau, Maurice. "Que pensez-vous de la littérature américaine?" *La Revue internationale* 3 (1947):113-116.

Normand, Jean. *Nathaniel Hawthorne: An Approach to an Analysis of Artistic Creation.* Cleveland: Press of Case Western Reserve Univ., 1970.

O'Brien, Justin. "American Books and French Readers." *College English* 1 (1940):480-487.

Peckham, H. Houston. "Is American Literature Read and Respected in Europe?" *South Atlantic Quarterly* 13 (October 1914):382-388.

Peterson, M. S., "Joaquin Miller." *Revue anglo-américaine* 8 (December 1930):114-121.

Peyre, Henri. "American Literature through French Eyes." *Virginia Quarterly Review* 23 (1947):421-438.

Phillips, E. Margaret. *Ph. Chasles, critique et historien de la littérature anglaise.* Paris: E. Droz, 1933.

Poli, Bernard. *Mark Twain, écrivain de l'ouest.* Paris: Presses universitaires de France, 1965.

Poli, Bernard; Le Vot, André; Fabre, Geneviève; and Fabre, Michel. *Francis Scott Fitzgerald.* Paris: Armand Colin, 1969.

Quinn, Patrick Francis. *The French Face of Edgar Poe.* Carbondale: Southern Illinois Univ. Press, 1957.

Racamier, Paul. "Entre humour et folie," *Revue française de psychanalyse* 37 (July 1973), 655-668.

Radiguet, L. Lionel. *Etudes irlando-américaines.* Paris: C. Marpon et E. Flammarion, 1885.

Rémond, René. *Les Etats-Unis devant l'opinion française, 1815–1852.* Paris: Armand Colin, 1962.

Remords, Georges. "Les Lettres américaines devant la critique universitaire française." *Bulletin de la faculté des lettres de Strasbourg* 35 (1956):160-177, 205-220.

Rice, Howard C. "Seeing Ourselves as the French See Us." *French Review* 21 (May 1948):432-441.

Richepin, Jean. *L'Ame américaine.* Paris: Flammarion, 1920.

Rogers, Franklin R. "Mark Twain and Daudet: *A Tramp Abroad* and *Tartarin sur les Alpes.*" *Comparative Literature* 16 (Summer 1964):254-263.

Rousseaux, André. *Littérature du vingtième siècle.* Paris: Albin Michel, 1949.

Royot, Daniel. "Aspects of the American Picaresque in *Little Big Man.*" In *Les Américanistes.* New York: Kennikat Press, 1977.

______. "Eléments phonologiques du dialecte noir dans 'Huckleberry Finn.'" *Les Langues modernes* 1 (1972):79-83.

Royot, Daniel, ed. *Revue française d'etudes américaines,* No. 3 (October 1977). Special edition on American humor.

Sainte-Beuve, Charles-Augustin. "Franklin." *Causeries du lundi,* vol. 7. Paris: Garnier frères, n.d.

Saporta, Marc. *Histoire du roman américain.* Paris: Seghers, 1970.

Sartre, Jean-Paul. "American Novelists in French Eyes." *Atlantic,* August 1946, pp. 114-118.

Schorer, Mark. *Sinclair Lewis.* New York: McGraw-Hill, 1961.

Silhol, Robert. *Les Tyrants tragiques.* Paris: Presses universitaires de France, 1969.

Simon, Jean. "French Studies in American Literature and Civilization." *American Literature* 6 (May 1934):176-190.

______. *Le Roman américain au XXe siècle.* Paris: Boivin, 1950.

Smith, Anne W. "Criticism of American Life and Letters in the *Revue encyclopédique.*" Ph.D. dissertation, Northwestern University, 1943.

Smith, Thelma M., and Miner, Ward L. *Transatlantic Migration: The Contemporary American Novel in France.* Durham, North Carolina: Duke Univ. Press, 1955.

Sprigge, Elizabeth. *Gertrude Stein: Her Life and Work.* New York: Harper, 1957.

Sternberg, Jacques. "Avant-Propos" to *Benchley* by Robert Benchley, translated by Paulette Vielhomme. Paris: Julliard, 1963.

______. "Preface" to *Thurber* by James Thurber, translated by Christiane Potesta and Claude Dalla Torre. Paris: Julliard, 1964.

______. "Presentation" to *Le Dictionnaire du diable* by Ambrose Bierce, translated by Jacques Papy. Paris: Nouvel Office d'Edition, 1964.

Sternberg, Jacques; Bergier, Jacques; and Grall, Alex, eds. *Les Chefs d'oeuvre du sourire.* Paris: Planète, 1964.

Taine, Hippolyte. *Notes on England,* translated by Edward Hyams. Fair Lawn, New Jersey: Essential Books, 1958.

Tocqueville, Alexis de. *Democracy in America,* edited by Richard D. Heffner; translated by Henry Reeve and Francis Bowen. New York: New American Library, 1956.

Tournier, Jacques. "M. E. Coindreau découvre la littérature américaine." *La Table ronde,* September 1948, 1547-1550.

Vail, Eugène A. *De la littérature et des hommes de lettres des Etats-Unis d'Amérique.* Paris: Charles Gosselin, 1841.

Varigny, Charles de. "La Littérature comique aux Etats-Unis." *Revue bleue,* April 16, 1887, pp. 695-701.

Vaucher-Zananiri, Nelly. *Voix d'Amerique: études sur la littérature américaine d'aujourd'hui.* Cairo: R. Schindler, 1945.

Villard, Léonie. *La France et les Etats-Unis: échanges et rencontres (1524-1800).* Lyon: IAC, 1952.

______. "La Vie américaine d'après le conte et la nouvelle." *Mercure de France,* December 1, 1923, pp. 289-331.

Wagner, Jean. *Runyonese: The Mind and Craft of Damon Runyon.* London: Stechert-Hafner, 1966.

Weber, Carl J. "New England through French Eyes Fifty Years Ago." *New England Quarterly* 20 (1947):385-396.

Weisz, Pierre. "James Thurber." Ph.D. dissertation, University of Paris, 1965.

Williams, Stanley T. "The First Version of the Writings of Washington Irving in Spanish." *Modern Philology,* November 1930, pp. 185–201.

———. *The Life of Washington Irving.* New York: Oxford Univ. Press, 1935.

Wilson, Mark K., "Mr. Clemens and Madame Blanc: Mark Twain's First French Critic." *American Literature* 45 (January 1974):537–556.

Withington, Robert. "Brother Jonathan." *College English* 6 (1945):200–206.

Index